CONTRARIAN
INVESTMENT
STRATEGY

Also by David Dreman

PSYCHOLOGY AND THE STOCK MARKET

CONTRARIAN INVESTMENT STRATEGY

The Psychology of
Stock Market Success

David Dreman

RANDOM HOUSE New York

Copyright © 1979 by David Dreman

All rights reserved under International and Pan-American Copyright Conventions. Published in the United States by Random House, Inc., New York and simultaneously in Canada by Random House of Canada Limited, Toronto.

Library of Congress Cataloging in Publication Data
Dreman, David N.
  Contrarian investment strategy.
  Includes index.
  1. Speculation. 2. Stocks. 3. Investments.
I. Title.
HG6041.D66   332.6'78   78–21820
ISBN 0–394–42390–9

Manufactured in the United States of America
98765432
FIRST EDITION

Grateful acknowledgment is made to the following for permission to reprint previously published material:

AMACOM: Chart reprinted by permission of AMACOM, from *Psychology and the Stock Market,* by David Dreman. Copyright © 1977 by AMACOM, a division of American Management Association, p. 154. All rights reserved.

The American Finance Association: Table adapted from *Journal of Finance,* June 1977, p. 866.

Arlington House, Inc.: Graph from *Panics and Crashes,* by Harry D. Schultz, reprinted by permission of Arlington House, Inc.

Ernest Benn, Ltd., and MacMillan Publishing Company: Quotations from *The Crowd,* by Gustave LeBon, reprinted by permission of Ernest Benn, Ltd., and MacMillan Publishing Company.

Decision Research: Graph, "Average Changes in Confidence and Accuracy with Increasing Amounts of Information," reprinted by permission of Decision Research, Inc.

Dow Jones & Company, Inc.: Graph, "Annualized Rates of Return," reprinted by permission of the *Wall Street Journal.* Copyright © Dow Jones & Company, Inc., 1977. All rights reserved.

Drexel, Burnham, Lambert, Inc.: Graph, "Average Price Increase per Year, 1948–1964," reprinted by permission of Drexel, Burnham, Lambert, Inc.

Financial Analysts Journal: Tables, "Annual Earnings Related to Mean Prices" and "Lower P/E Relative to Market and Industry," reprinted by permission of *Financial Analysts Journal.*

Financial Management: Tables adapted from R. Malcolm Richards, James J. Benjamin, and Robert W. Strawser, "An Examination of the Accuracy of Earnings Forecasts," *Financial Management*, Fall 1977, p. 82.

Forbes Magazine: Graph, "A 700-Year Consumer Price Index," reprinted by permission of *Forbes Magazine*, November 15, 1976, issue.

Fortune Magazine: Table, "Returns on Total Corporate Capital," reprinted by permission of Fortune Art Department/Gabor Kiss, *Fortune,* November 1977.

For Rowena

ACKNOWLEDGMENTS

In the preparation of the manuscript, I have been very fortunate to have had the advice and criticism of a number of talented people. In particular, I'd like to acknowledge the help I received from the following:

Professor Edward Conolley, a psychologist at USC, and Professor Fred Renwick of the Graduate School of Business Administration at New York University read the manuscript and made many excellent suggestions, as well as directing my attention to important academic studies relevant to the topic. I'm also grateful to Dr. Paul Slovic of Decision Research, Inc., for introducing me to recent work in cognitive psychology, which I think is important to understanding investor behavior.

On the Street side, I owe a considerable debt to Michael Clowes, Louis Conhaim, Theodore H. Halligan, and Sim Trotter, all of whom combed through the manuscript and recommended constructive changes. I'd also like to thank Rauscher Pierce Refsnes, and in particular Jim Bayless, president, and Steve Denning, executive vice-president, for their help in initiating a fairly extensive computer study described herein. Jane Ruefli carried out a part of the programming, and Kirit Patel, a Ph.D. in computer sciences, proved invaluable in extending and modifying the findings. Susan Osberg, Nan Miller, Margery Adams, and Lyn Dominguez provided excellent research assistance as well as making many good suggestions.

My relationship with Random House has been a pleasant one. I particularly appreciate the hours that Jason Epstein gave to the manuscript and his major contributions, on both the concept and the editorial levels. Grant Ujifusa also put in a great deal of time and effort seeing this project through. Carolyn Lumsden did an excellent job of copy editing, putting in far more than the required effort to do so.

Finally, I'd like to thank the numerous investment organizations and firms—brokerage, advisory, and consulting—that allowed me to use charts, tables, and other materials which I consider important to the text. Needless to say, the caveat that any errors found are the writer's sole responsibility applies here.

—David Dreman
New York
June 1979

CONTENTS

LIST OF TABLES

PART I

CURRENT INVESTMENT PRACTICE

CHAPTER ONE

Surviving in a New Investment World

Sometimes making money has appeared simple. On June 19, 1815, for example, the Rothschilds learned via carrier pigeon that the French had been crushed the previous evening at Waterloo many hours before the news reached London by more customary means. When the market opened that morning, Rothschild agents buzzed the news of a major British defeat, and Nathan Rothschild himself began to sell, which triggered a large break. Near the low point, other inconnu family agents began to buy heavily, not long before the expected arrival of the more conventional couriers. The market that day closed considerably higher than it opened, further adding to the family coffers.

Such exciting coups are the stuff of investor dreams and indeed have occurred in one manner or another for many of the legendary names associated with the world of finance—the Morgans, Rockefellers, Astors, Harrimans, and Kennedys. But for the average investor, making money or even protecting existing capital has never been easy, and in the last decade and a half the task has seemed to become almost impossible.

This book is an attempt to show you why this has happened and what you as an individual trying to survive and even prosper can do in an investment world gone topsy-turvy . . .

● ● ●

In late 1977 a seat on the New York Stock Exchange traded for $35,000, some $20,000 less than what a taxi medallion cost on the same day. Over the previous eight years, the Big Apple's tough, shrewd, and talkative cabdrivers had seen the worth of their medallions double. During the same period its tough, shrewd, and not so untalkative brokers had watched a seat on the New York Stock Exchange decline some 94 percent.

So hapless had the market become by the beginning of 1977 that an organization called Bull and Bear, Inc., set up two new mutual funds with opposite purposes: a bull fund for people believing the market would go up and a bear fund for investors who believed stocks would go down. Both lost money! That year, the bull fund declined 15 percent and the bear fund 9 percent.

And since then, although seats have again leaped ahead of taxi medallions, things have generally seemed to get worse. In mid-1979, the market's most widely followed index, the Dow-Jones Industrial Average, was 18 percent below its price of fourteen years earlier, and in constant dollars under the level it was at in 1951, or for that matter, the end of 1929.

The result is not surprising—individuals have exited en masse from the marketplace. Brokers too have suffered. Scores of member firms, some dating back a century or more, have gone out of business or been forced to merge. To date, over fifty thousand jobs have disappeared on Wall Street since the beginning of the decade. Harvard Business School graduates, those supposed savants of where opportunity lies, now shun the Street like the plague.

Events have proven equally depressing for many people who have avoided the stock market entirely. Because of escalating inflation, individuals who can afford little risk now see the rapid erosion of what have traditionally been safe investments—savings bank deposits, bonds, and so on. Investors have never faced the hyperinflation of the present era. The rise in prices in absolute terms in the past four decades is larger than it had been in the previous six hundred years—and the rate is accelerating.

This new inflation and its roots seem mystifying even to the experts. Never before have so many interlocking forces kindled inflationary fires—OPEC raising the price of oil 50 percent in the first half of 1979 and a staggering tenfold since 1972, with further increases an almost certainty; a cabal of junior OPECs ranging from diamonds to uranium to coffee, all trying to trigger large price hikes and sometimes succeeding; agricultural and industrial prices, stable for almost two decades, more than doubling since 1970, with the probability of continued increases ahead; workers in the free world and particularly in this country demanding and receiving large wage boosts, which not only offset inflation but often increase their purchasing power in real terms; and businessmen responding to this new environment with "anticipatory price boosts" to offset continually rising prices. All these factors initiate price rises or at least react to those of the others, creating a baffling and seemingly irreversible spiral.*

As the *Wall Street Journal*'s weekly front-page economic review put it in boldface type on September 11, 1978: "The [government] policy-makers depict themselves as victims of changing economic circumstances that neither they nor their colleagues in academia and industry fully understand. They insist, moreover, that the economic profession hasn't provided them with new tools and the old ones are inadequate."

Economists, like generals fighting a previous war, continue to apply various traditional fiscal and monetary poultices to these problems, remedies that have been working as effectively as bleeding did for the eighteenth-century physician. For a decade we have had repeated "stagflation," and more recently "slumpflation,"† accompanied by the weakening dollar abroad and ebbing confidence at home.

As if this was not enough, the investor is faced with a tax structure that becomes increasingly regressive as the rate of inflation soars. If inflation continued at the 9 percent rate of 1978, an investor in a 25 percent tax bracket—the typical bracket of widows and orphans (see table 1, page 6)—would require a 12 percent investment return just to sustain purchasing power, while a businessman in a 50 percent tax bracket would require an 18 percent return. Even if he chose a good tax-exempt bond presently yielding 6½ percent, he would still lose 2½ percent of his purchasing power a year.‡

As the table shows, if inflation persists at a 10 percent level or higher, certainly not impossible, the returns required become fright-

---

*Chapter 12 will look at these problems in greater detail. The Carter energy proposals, introduced as this work went to press, would appear, if anything, to increase the inflationary problems connected with rising energy costs if passed.

†A word coined by Nobel Laureate Milton Friedman.

‡Probably more, because out-of-state tax-exempts are subject to state and municipal taxes, where they exist.

Table I
RETURNS REQUIRED TO MAINTAIN PURCHASING POWER OF CAPITAL

INFLATION RATE	25%	30%	35%	TAX BRACKET 40%	45%	50%	55%
5%	6.7	7.1	7.7	8.8	9.1	10.0	11.1
6%	8.0	8.6	9.2	10.0	10.9	12.0	13.3
7%	9.3	10.0	10.8	11.7	12.7	14.0	15.6
8%	10.7	11.4	12.3	13.3	14.5	16.0	18.5
9%	12.0	12.9	13.8	15.0	16.4	18.0	20.0
10%	13.3	14.3	15.4	16.7	18.2	20.0	22.2
11%	14.7	15.7	16.9	18.3	20.0	22.0	24.4
12%	16.0	17.1	18.5	20.0	21.8	24.0	26.6

ening—at an 11 percent rate, a taxpayer in the top bracket must earn 24.4 percent simply to stay even. To give you a bench mark, only a handful of the most profitable businesses in the United States provide returns even approaching this level on a continuing basis.

We might have been amused by the 2½ percent interest the English received on their government bonds in the nineteenth century. But 2½ percent was a reasonable rate of return in a period of price stability that by and large lasted close to a hundred years. If the present inflation continues at an 8 percent rate, an individual today in the 50 percent tax bracket purchasing a ten-year government 9 percent bond will have only 66 percent of his original capital left (including interest) in constant dollars when the bond matures. It's as if the bonds defaulted and paid 66 cents on the dollar—worse than the performance of most corporate bonds during the Great Depression. In terms of purchasing power, the Englishmen of the last century, even with their low coupons, would have had twice the purchasing power of this modern investor a decade later.

So it is clear that the customary investment vehicles of people in retirement and others who need to be conservative have broken down. A Cleveland investment firm, McDonald and Company, summed it up well: "Individuals along virtually the entire income spectrum are forced into a position where the purchasing power of their savings is constantly being eroded if they hold conventional investment vehicles. In these circumstances, *a penny saved is a penny lost.*"

It is not surprising, then, with many of the traditional norms of prudent investment having vanished or become inoperative, that capital has darted from country to country and from investment to investment. In 1978 people lined up at housing developments in California, many paying large premiums for second and third homes, not to live in but as speculative vehicles. Prices, the buyers believed, could only go higher. I saw a near tar-paper shack on Malibu Beach with sixty feet of ocean frontage sell for $450,000, up from $200,000 a year earlier. Rural Illinois farmland was recently valued at triple the price relative to income it would have produced as IBM stock.

Speculative money also flows into diamonds, jewelry, and artwork. In the past decade Chinese ceramics have increased at a 19 percent annual rate, Art Deco at 16 percent, U.S. stamps at 15.4 percent, old master paintings at 13 percent, and nongold coins at 12 percent.

Faced with greater economic uncertainties, baffling inflation, and a disintegrating dollar, people today appear more willing to speculate on the past, as represented by precious stones, metals, or artwork, than in the future of our industrial economy.

Our institutions seem equally bewildered. Pension funds, the largest institutional investors, have reduced their equity exposure from 75 percent of their assets at the end of 1972 to a little more than 50 percent at year-end 1978. Even so, they are saddled with enormous cash flows and are uncertain as to what to do with them. Thus, near the end of 1978, almost $52 billion of institutional funds were held on the sidelines. Some institutional money seeks shelter in the higher-priced markets abroad in investments made even more costly by a dollar that has been in a free fall. With the failure of stocks and bonds to protect the investor in the last decade, many believe this has become a world, as one observer put it, "where gambling or speculation is not a vice, but a necessity."[1]

Yet it is in this environment that you must attempt to protect your capital and enhance it if you can. At first, the task may appear overwhelming. True, it is not easy to make money or keep it, but it never has been. Even in far more tranquil and prosperous periods, investors on the whole have not fared well in the marketplace. Although innumerable prophets have appeared with endless theories on how to get rich—indeed, the greater the failure, the more rapidly they seem to spawn—we will see that there are no widely followed methods that can be used with any assurance of success.

In good times and good markets, poor investment results are often masked. While the record of most investors may be lackluster, they generally still make some money or at least break even. In bad times, such as those today, the full extent of the failure is apparent.

Certainly a downbeat enough message up to this point, but I'm not out to play muckraker or Chicken Little, nor to offer another wrinkle in the how-to-make-a-million genre. Rather, this book attempts to lay out a guide for the concerned investor aware of today's problems. By studying the breakdown of the market and its causes in more detail, I believe there is every chance for an upbeat ending, particularly for the individual investor. In fact, rarely have there been opportunities of the type that exist for the individual in the contemporary marketplace. But obviously, after what you've just read, these opportunities will require some explaining.

A Curious State

Even as Art Deco, real estate, jewelry, and Chinese ceramics have gone through the roof, the largest and strongest companies in corporate America have languished. Never before have they traded for as long a period at a 30 to 40 percent discount from the real value of their real estate, plant, and equipment. Prime companies such as Ford, Travelers, Aetna, and General Tire & Rubber are priced to provide 25 to 33 percent returns annually on their aftertax profits— equivalent to 50 to 66 percent before taxes. Such returns are normally reserved for only the riskiest and most unstable of ventures.

And company fundamentals have been improving steadily. Earnings and dividends, considered to be the prime influence on stock prices over time, have been increasing at a faster rate than inflation. Most corporations have been able to offset higher inflation by raising selling prices. And so, in spite of escalating costs, profits and dividends have been moving up in real terms. Through the last six years of accelerating inflation, earnings of the S&P 500* have

*The broadest based of the popular indices, accounting for about three quarters of the market value of companies listed on the New York Stock Exchange.

increased at an almost 12 percent annual rate, some 50 percent faster than the climb in prices. *In a word, our major corporations have fared far better against inflation than is generally realized.*

Thus, when we measure stocks by a number of the most crucial valuation criteria—book value, P/E ratio, rate of earnings, and dividend increase—we see the popular indices, such as the S&P 500, are at some of the lowest valuations in the postwar period,* a conclusion underscored by the wave of takeovers by both foreign and domestic companies. And as domestic money flows abroad, foreign investors, attracted by the political stability, the cheap dollar, and strong fundamentals of American markets, invest growing amounts of funds here.

If there appears to be underlying strength in our stocks, why, you might ask, is it not more widely realized—particularly by professional investors? And here we come to one of the most important considerations in contemporary markets.

Professional investors—managers of bank trust departments, insurance companies, mutual and pension funds, and others—control vast stores of capital: in all, an estimated 70 percent of the trading and almost 50 percent of the stock ownership on the New York Stock Exchange.

Yet this expert opinion—which many investors rely on—is very often wrong and not infrequently dramatically so. In fact, the errors are so great, people would do better in most instances selecting stocks by throwing darts at the stock pages, or perhaps even having their family dogs choose them by pawing the financial pages—a method tried recently by one frustrated Minneapolis advisor. Indeed, because professionals control so much of the trading and ownership of securities, they may have in no small measure been responsible for the desultory performance of stocks in recent years.

For these reasons I think it is important for us to consider briefly the record of the professionals.

---

*Again, a more detailed discussion of the fundamentals that I believe make the case for investing in U.S. stocks as strong as it has been in decades will be found on pages 238–246 in chapter 12.

To begin, let's look at investment advisory services—firms that sell their advice to the public on a subscription basis. The key service they provide is to tell you when to get in or out of the market.

Would you have profited by subscribing to such services? In a word, *no.* The accompanying chart (figure 1) was compiled from the recommendations made by approximately seventy-five of the nation's leading advisory services for the 1967–78 period. The chart indicates that there is an almost perfect correlation between the investment advice given and the future course of the market—unfortunately, almost perfectly wrong.

As markets reach their lows, large and increasing numbers of advisors become negative, and as they reach their peaks, the opposite occurs. As you can see, swings in opinion are invariably far wider than the movements of the market. At the time of the Tet offensive in Vietnam in early 1968, the market declined slightly over 5 percent, while the advisors swung from being 60 percent bullish to 85 percent negative at the bottom. In the next several months, the S&P rallied 11 percent; the advisors followed suit, turning 70 percent bullish at the intermediate top.

Figure 1.
How investment advisory sentiment trails the market.

Data from Standard & Poor's and Investment Intelligence Service.

The same pattern is repeated again and again. As the market reached a low in the spring of 1970, 62 percent of the advisors predicted that stocks would head down; at the 1972 high, 75 percent believed prices would continue to move up. At the bottom of the 1974 market, two thirds looked for lower prices—just before one of the sharpest rallies of the postwar period.

In fact, for a short time, coinciding almost perfectly with the market bottom, twenty advisors ran bearish ads in *Barron's,* the nation's largest financial weekly. How many bullish ads ran during the same period? The answer is none.

Moving on to mutual funds: the proper course for the funds is to be fully invested near market bottoms—having very low cash reserves at such times—after having snapped up bargains dumped on the market by panicky individual investors. Conversely, near market tops, they should be heavy sellers, accumulating large cash reserves by taking advantage of the speculative whims of an excited public. Again, exactly the opposite case prevails. The funds are heavy sellers at market bottoms and heavy buyers near market tops. Mutual funds were most bearish at the market bottoms of 1966, 1970, and 1974 (cash reserves rose to 9.7, 11.8, and 13.5 percent respectively) and were fully invested near the market tops of 1967 and 1972 (when these reserves dropped to 5.7 and 6.2 percent respectively).[2] The funds also appear to be poor judges of the market's direction.* Additional studies indicate that the record of other institutional investors is no better.[3]

But poor as the forecasting record has turned out to be, it is only one aspect in the evaluation of professional performance. By far the most important measure is how these organizations have performed managing their clients' money over time. Even if they missed the tops and bottoms, they could have done better than the market. How good, then, are their investment records?

A survey of the one hundred largest bank trust departments in the country for the one- and five-year periods ending in mid-1976 indicated that only 9 percent did as well as the market averages.[4] This sort of performance is not an aberration. A more recent study covered 141 pooled equity funds,† large banks, and insurance companies

---

*Ordinarily, common stock mutual funds keep about 7 percent of assets in cash or its equivalent and do not change these reserves markedly. The high and low figures presented are thus quite extreme.

†The funds of many clients are pooled or commingled. This provides a client with more intensive management and greater portfolio diversity than he would otherwise receive, while allowing the institution economies of scale.

—institutions that managed $140 billion at the time. The results are presented in table 2. In every holding period the averages outdistanced the pooled funds. In almost every time span 75 percent of the individual funds performed worse than the averages. Other broad studies of the performance of mutual funds, pension funds, and investment advisors came up with similar results. A. G. Becker, for example, measured the equity record of three thousand of the largest pension funds in the country for the 1962–75 period and found that 87 percent* underperformed the S&P 500.†[5] Updating the study to the end of 1978, it found that only 16 percent of a large sample matched or exceeded this index in the past decade.[6]

These findings and a substantial amount of corroborating evidence indicate a widespread failure of modern money management, in spite of the investment professionals' training, intelligence, and experience, as well as the best research money can buy. Rather than fulfilling the hopes of superior performance promised to their clients, the professionals have generally lagged behind the market averages. The most sophisticated generation of financial managers ever has demonstrated an incapacity to manage money effectively.

Some Basic Questions

Our brief tour of the new investment world brings to mind three critical, interrelated questions for which investors must attempt to find answers:

Table 2
ANNUALIZED RATES OF RETURN

	1969–76	1973–76	1975–76	1976
S&P 500	4.1%	1.6%	30.4%	23.8%
DJIA	5.0%	4.2%	33.5%	22.9%
Pooled funds median	2.1%	−1.2%	23.5%	19.0%

NOTE: Both the averages and the pooled funds median are adjusted for dividends.
SOURCE: Reprinted by permission of The Wall Street Journal, copyright © Dow Jones & Company, Inc., 1977. All rights reserved.

*Ninety percent in the ten years ending in 1977.
†When Becker began measuring the performance of institutional investors, it was not exactly greeted with accolades by the money managers. In fact, Becker's parent brokerage firm lost several million dollars in commissions from irate former clients as a result.

1. Why have professionals, regardless of their training and experience, done so poorly over the years?

2. Why, if stocks in fact do provide good relative values, has this been so little noted or acted upon?

3. How can the average investor take advantage of the unsettled environment both to protect and to increase his personal capital?

A Common-Sense Rule

Logic dictates that if one group, such as the experts, seems wrong time and again,* there must be other people who are right. Sometimes, of course, the winners are winners simply by chance—no different from betting on the jockey's colors at the race track. But others are consistent, and their consistency involves discipline and method. These investors must consciously be doing something quite different from the underperformers.

But what is it that causes this success or failure? Much of the answer appears to lie within the realm of investor psychology, one of the most used but least understood phrases on the investment scene today. All of us hear of how investor psychology has turned positive or negative on an industry or company or on the market as a whole. And many an experienced investor has pondered the extreme psychological variations that markets have displayed over time. The problem we face as investors is not that we aren't aware that psychology plays a part, but that we don't really know what this part is or how to invest once we've understood it. Certainly, there are a few men with brilliant intuitive reactions who can take advantage of market psychology, but most of us are not so gifted.

How, then, do we isolate and identify common investor behavioral patterns in order to use them in a workable investment framework? For a long time, this question could not be answered because the necessary diagnostic tools did not exist. It has only been through work done in recent years that some clear-cut patterns of behavior have been analyzed that show that people in groups often prove wrong, sometimes remarkably so.

As you continue reading, you'll see numerous examples of what happens when people act blindly in groups, ranging from policy

*We will come back to this topic in chapter 5.

making at the higher levels of government to medical diagnostics to crowd stampedes in the stock market. Over and over again, when the degree of consensus was the greatest—in whatever field of activity —the extent of the error was the most pronounced.

Drawing on recent findings in both cognitive psychology and financial statistics, we can see how powerful and very often destructive the tendency of people, even among experts, to follow current fashions and trends can be. In fact, the investment arena provides almost the perfect atmosphere for these fashions and trends to flourish. Though our prime emphasis will be placed on the stock market, the psychological principles apply to any form of investment from real estate to stamp collecting.

The fact that even market professionals succumb to the same mistakes repeatedly, training and experience notwithstanding, for a long time puzzled me. And to be honest, I became one of these lemmings on one or two occasions. The power of group action struck home. Why, I wondered, should so many of us who presumably know better not learn from experience?

Living through a number of these cycles, I became increasingly convinced that the investment methods in which we are all schooled are not sufficient by themselves to make us consistent winners. Without a grasp of systematic ways to protect ourselves against psychological overreactions, chances are that we will continue to make the same or very similar mistakes time and again.

This book will attempt to prove that some relatively new methods provide just such protection. These are based on contrarian principles—principles that normally result in going against the popular opinion of the day. This approach has worked for my clients and myself over the years—no small inducement to belief. But far more important, the assumptions underlying the method are well documented statistically and psychologically.

The work will try to show that if you want to make money, you must stubbornly cling to contrarian principles. When everyone is rushing in, whether it be to buy Art Deco, Chinese ceramics, or Krugerrands, and systematically deflating another investment, like the stock market today, history demonstrates that there is a chance and probably a good one to profit by going in the opposite direction. The same rule applies within the stock market itself among favored and unfavored stocks and industries.

The new findings explain why people in markets often behave

like crowds at a theater fire—all running toward the same exit, although many others are available. In one age it was tulip bulbs, in another blue-chip stocks, in others bonds or Art Nouveau—but at any moment most investors rush for the same door at once, and many get trampled.

You might ask if being a contrarian is enough by itself. Naturally, crowds and groups can be perfectly right a good part of the time. As an investor, can you really spot when they are wrong and take advantage of such situations?

Fortunately, the answer to both questions is yes. The pressures to which I have alluded lead to predictable patterns of investor behavior, so predictable that it is possible to derive successful investment strategies that will allow you to benefit from other people's mistakes. In fact, numerous statistical studies extending over a period of almost forty years pinpoint investor overreactions in a systematic enough manner so that the investor applying the principles consistently will have a good chance of outdoing the market.

One of the most recent surveys, covering all the stocks on the New York Stock Exchange and the major companies on the American Stock Exchange and over-the-counter markets from 1968 to 1977, showed certain of these strategies yielding annual returns of well over 10 percent,* and this at a time when the market returned only 4 percent.

The strategies are relatively simple and require little time on your part to learn and use effectively, although the research behind them, as you might well imagine, is quite complex.

No investment strategy should be followed blindly, and a good part of this work is devoted to understanding why the methods work. I believe such understanding is essential to their effective use. Informed opinion almost always advocates the popular course, so you must steel yourself to stand apart. To be a contrarian is to be an outsider—until you're proven right.

Napoleon once said that "in warfare, the psychological is to the material as three to one." The ratio appears to be at least as high in the stock market. Although no book can teach you how to "get rich," I believe this one can give you a markedly better chance of improving your investment performance. I'm convinced the individual investor

*See chapter 7.

today has an exceptional opportunity to beat both the market and the experts. All that is required is an open mind and the courage of your convictions. If you are a serious investor, I think our journey will prove rewarding.

CHAPTER TWO

Can You Read the Future?

Attempting to foretell the future has been a timeless, if questionable, preoccupation of man, in view of its usual rewards. Still, there are some areas where a knowledge of the future would prove invaluable —a not unimportant one being the accumulation of wealth.

Not surprisingly, then, countless schemes exist to predict the future in financial markets. I was introduced to an intriguing one when I was sixteen. A three-shopping-bag man wandered into my father's local brokerage firm, where I was visiting at the time, and offered me a chance at a financial coup. The shopping bags were large, and each bulged with long, narrow cylinders of tightly wrapped tracing paper. I could see, even at that age, that the man was not your typical brokerage-house type. He could have used a shave, a haircut and less worn clothes, but all this was unimportant as he explained to me that he had an unfailing system to make money and that the secret lay right there in his shopping bags.

Over the years, the man said, he had studied the relationship between commodity price movements and the concentric circles found inside tree trunks, from which he had developed a method of predicting future market movements. The shopping bags contained dozens of important tree trunk tracings, all full scale, that he would teach me to read—for only five dollars.

Five dollars was more than I could afford, so I declined. He then

17

offered me an abbreviated version—using tracings of smaller tree trunks—at half price. This method, good as it was, did not provide quite the same results as the use of the larger tracings. Again I declined, possibly forfeiting a chance of becoming a millionaire in my teens.

While we all know intuitively that such advice is valueless, it is anything but easy to judge the quality of the counsel with which the average investor is bombarded—particularly when many of the professional advisors are intelligent, claim outstanding records of success, and display detailed knowledge of their subject. Thus, I think it is important that before examining the methods I will propose, readers unfamiliar with current investment approaches look at them in some detail.

These methods represent the conventional wisdom of the trade, and most expert advice is based upon them. Just as the State Department candidate is required to have some political-science background (if not, as in the past, to have attended the "proper" schools), to pass certain exams, and to have read the prescribed books, so the professional investor must also qualify by studying securities techniques—first at college and later on the job. But as we shall see, when these methods are scrutinized closely, they do not help us very much, if at all.

Some of them remind me a little of the techniques used by the eccentric scientists who inhabited Laputa, the moving island in the sky visited by Gulliver. Initially, the scientists' reasoning seemed sensible, even precise, but a closer investigation proved it otherwise. Thus, measurements for a suit were taken with sextant and compass for greater accuracy, with results leaving much to be desired.

The methods we shall examine, some of which seem to provide valuations with an almost mathematical precision, simply don't work any better than did Laputa's compass and sextant. The simpler tape and pins prove far more effective for a real-world tailor, as should the less complicated investment approaches that will be provided later. But before I get ahead of myself, let's look more closely at conventional investment methods.

The Market's Hatfields and McCoys

Until a decade ago, there were two dominant stock market schools
—the technical and the fundamental. And, as is so often the case
with economic, political, and religious ideas, each school stood inal-
terably opposed to the other.

The fundamentalist school, which we will discuss at some
length in the next chapter, believes that markets are rational. All
stocks have inherent values that can be determined. To ascertain
these values, the investor must examine detailed information related
to the general economy, the industry, and the individual company,
and then apply time-tested evaluative formulas to find the appropriate price. The fundamentalist believes the market is often wrong in
its appraisal of a stock's worth. Using his rational criteria, he determines if the current market undervalues, overvalues, or fairly values
a given stock, and then makes his decisions to buy or sell accordingly.

The technical school, on the other hand, views such analysis as
a colossal waste of time because all fundamental information about
the security is already reflected in the price. Supply and demand in
the marketplace are the sole factors to study in predicting future
price movements. As John Magee, considered the dean of technical
analysts, writes, "The market price reflects . . . the hopes and fears
and guesses and moods, rational and irrational, of hundreds of potential buyers and sellers, as well as their needs and resources—in total,
factors which defy analysis and for which no statistics are obtainable,
but which are nevertheless all synthesized, weighed, and finely ex-
pressed in one precise figure [the price]."[1]

Joseph Granville, another leading technical analyst, says it
more sharply: "Technicians look ahead, fundamentalists look back-
wards. The true language of the market is technical. . . . The majority
of those involved in the market are bombarded with mis-timed fundamental data which nine times out of ten haven't a blessed thing
to do with where the price of the stock or the market is headed."[2]
So speak the McCoys.

To the technician the concept of intrinsic value has no meaning
in the marketplace. How can it? Memory would have to be extraordinarily short to forget that General Motors traded at above 80 in
1972 and at 28 in 1974, or that McDonald's dropped from 82 to 13
in the same period, although its fundamentals remained unchanged.

To the pragmatic technician, analysis of price and volume statistics is the key to understanding the direction of future price movements. "[The technician's] central thesis is 'the past is prologue,' " writes Vartanig G. Vartan, financial columnist of the *New York Times.* "They believe that analysis of past price and trading volume patterns —both for individual issues and the market in general—can provide clues to the future. . . . A pure chartist is almost monklike in dedication, believing the essential truth about the market is to be found in squiggles and figures on graph paper. He is unmoved by a plant explosion or a profit explosion."

Technicians think that both individual stocks and the general market move in discernible trends that continue until a clear signal is received of a change in course. Because stocks never proceed in a straight line but invariably retrace a portion of each advance or decline, the analyst must be able to filter the useful information about trends from a vast amount of market static.

A technician will usually favor one method but will use a number of others to confirm or reject his conclusions. In the following pages we will review some of the more common technical theories and methods.

Sunspots and Waves

Unfortunately, any brief overview of a subject as complex as technical analysis can merely outline some of the major landmarks, and then only with broad brushstrokes. The field is replete with interesting concepts applying not only to the stock market but to the analysis of economic activity itself.

A theory was proposed in 1875, naturally by an Englishman, that sunspots have a significant influence on economic activity. Economist William Stanley Jevons observed that sunspots normally occur in eleven-year cycles that correspond to changes in climatic conditions on earth, particularly to magnetic storms and increasing rainfall. Jevons compared the periods of sunspot activity with the fluctuations of commodity prices for a 150-year period beginning in fourteenth-century England. But his paper drew widespread criticism, and he eventually withdrew it, although he never really abandoned his notion.

The concept of powerful waves affecting market and economic

behavior has intrigued generations of investors. It also influenced the thinking of a brilliant Russian economist, Nikolai D. Kondratieff. At the age of twenty-five, he already held a high position in the provisional Kerensky government, and under Lenin he founded the Moscow Business Conditions Institute in 1920. Between 1920 and 1928, Kondratieff published a series of major books and papers. Using U.S., English, German, and French statistics, he concluded that the Western world had experienced two and a half long economic cycles since the end of the eighteenth century, each lasting approximately fifty years.

In his work Kondratieff noted that peaks in commodity prices approximated periods of major wars—in November 1814, August 1864, and May 1920—and that sharp drops had occurred thereafter. The third wave, which began in 1890–93, was in progress when he wrote his most important article, in 1925.[3] The Kondratieff wave correctly pretraced the declining business conditions commencing in 1929 and the strong upward path of business in the 1960s and early 1970s in the next cycle, as figure 2 shows.

Ominously, according to figure 2, the current crest has passed, and we are once again approaching the stage of acute crisis and panic. Given the nature of markets, numerous professionals put forward the Kondratieff analysis to justify their wide-scale liquidation of securities during the sharp break of 1973–74. But with the rising market that followed, Kondratieff's theory again fell into neglect on the Street. If the professor's ideas unsettle you as they did me when I first encountered them, you may be somewhat reassured

Figure 2.
Twentieth-century business cycles and crisis points
projected by the Kondratieff wave.

SOURCE: Harry D. Schultz, *Panics and Crashes* (New York: Pinnacle Books, 1975).

to know that each period of decline and panic was accompanied by massive price deflation, something that hardly seems likely at the moment.

Kondratieff was sharply attacked by orthodox Marxists for daring to postulate that the waves were self-correcting rather than indicating the eventual collapse of the capitalist system. In 1930, in one of the earlier Stalinist purges, he was incarcerated, and he died in prison on an unknown date. The influential *Soviet Encyclopedic* dismissed his work with the sentence "This theory is wrong and reactionary."

Another interesting wave theory has been proposed by an American, R. N. Elliot, also a student of cycles. Elliot studied the work of the early-thirteenth-century Italian Leonardo Fibonacci, who had concluded that for the design of the Great Pyramid at Giza the Egyptian architects used the following progression of numbers: 2–3–5–8–13–21–34–55–89. In this series, the ratio of successive numbers approximates 1.618, and the reciprocal is .62.

So-called Fibonacci series are frequently found in nature, which may account for how the architects of antiquity derived them. The number of branches on a tree increases each year in a Fibonacci series; the progression is also found in the rings on an elephant's tusks, the diameter of spirals on a seashell, the bumps on a pineapple, the leaves of a tree, and many other such developmental patterns.

Intrigued, Elliot began to apply Fibonacci numbers to the stock market, breaking market movements into waves composed of Fibonacci series. He divided each bearish component of the market cycle into two downswings and an upswing, and each bullish part into three upswings and a downswing. And, as with a snow crystal, the closer Elliot looked, the more intricate the patterns became. Each of the subcomponents could again be divided by the Fibonacci numbers of 3, 5, and 8, and these could in turn be divided by 13, 21, 34, and so on.[4] Not surprisingly, detecting the waves—some of which he named flats, inverted flats, and reverse inverted flats—has proven complex. Although the theory is fairly widely followed, Elliot's students often disagree about the proper interpretation of a given swing, sometimes for years after the fact.

It is ironic that one of the most important technical theories bears the name Dow, after Charles Dow, publisher of the *Wall Street Journal* and cofounder of the Dow-Jones empire, since Dow was at heart a fundamentalist. While he discovered and studied what he considered clear-cut patterns of market activity, Dow thought that stock prices were ultimately determined by earnings—a central tenet of the fundamental creed. Before his untimely death in 1902, he put forward his ideas about stock price movements in a number of editorials in the *Journal,* but he never published a full-fledged theory himself. William P. Hamilton, for several decades after assuming editorship of the *Journal* in 1908, synthesized and broadened Dow's premises to the extent that the current Dow theory is really Hamilton's rendition of the original.

The basis of the theory is that the Dow-Jones averages reflect all the fundamental facts and all the emotions and judgments of millions of market participants. The stock market is thus the best barometer of financial and business activity. Nothing is unknown to it except perhaps acts of God, and even these—as Hamilton wrote of the San Francisco earthquake of 1906—are quickly reflected in market movements. Dow observed that three movements occur within the marketplace at the same time. The most important, the primary trend, is a broad-based upward or downward swing usually lasting from one to several years. For Dow theorists, determining this trend is the master key to successful investing. Figure 3(a) graphs a primary uptrend and figure 3(b) a primary downtrend. In the uptrend, each new peak is above its predecessor, while on the downward leg, each new valley is below the previous one.

Figure 3(a).
Primary uptrend.

Figure 3(b).
Primary downtrend.

The investor, once he discerns that a bull market has actually started, should buy securities and continue to hold them until he receives a clear-cut sell signal. The more aggressive investor may attempt to trade on the intermediate moves, which normally last from one to several months. In figure 3(a), *AB* and *CD* are intermediate downtrends in a bull market, while *FG* and *HI* in figure 3(b) are intermediate upward reactions in a bear market. Normally, intermediate swings retrace one third to two thirds of the previous advance or decline. Finally, there are minor trends lasting from only hours to as long as several weeks.

Since the beginning, Dow theorists have discussed the phases of the market using the symbolism of tides, waves, and ripples. (In fact, there is some speculation that Dow conceived the basic elements of his theory because of his interest in the sea.) As long as the cap of each wave is higher than the previous cap and the trough is above the previous trough, it is safe to assume that the market tide is rising. With a falling tide, the order is reversed. While the theory's followers acknowledge that market behavior is not nearly as predictable as the tides, the principles remain the same.

Another important rule developed by Hamilton is that a primary trend in either industrials or rails has to be confirmed by the other average. If, for example, the industrial average signals the start of a new bull market by moving above the previous peak, this signal can't be considered reliable unless the rails give it too. Acting in tandem, the two averages filter out many of the false breakout signals one or the other may temporarily reflect.

Although the concepts are simple in principle, it has been difficult in practice to pinpoint the signals. Even expert Dow theorists have widely differing opinions of the primary trend at critical market junctures. Hamilton correctly predicted the market break in a famous editorial, "A Turn of the Tide," on October 25, 1929. Had his advice been followed, investors would have saved 260 points (86 percent) of the drop to the 1932 low. However, he first called the bear market turn in 1926, after which the industrial average almost tripled.

The technician's single most important tool is the chart. Through the recognition of dozens of different chart patterns, he believes he can pinpoint the all-important trends. The most common form of chart is the bar chart or vertical line chart, illustrated in figure 4. These are normally plotted on a daily basis, though weekly or monthly movements are tracked for longer-term perspective. The thin vertical lines in the upper part of the figure indicate the daily trading range, with the small horizontal tick across the line showing the closing price. The series of vertical lines at the bottom of the chart represent daily volume.

Trend lines are as important to the chartist as to the Dow theorist because of the paramount principle that a trend once started does not easily change course. The chartist can thus follow an established market direction until he receives some sign of a reversal. He draws trend lines to connect a series of reactions to a primary move. Figure 5(a) is an uptrend; the trend line connects the reaction lows at the bottom of the channel. Conversely, in figure 5(b), the trend line connects the reaction highs at the top of the channel, with the primary trend being down. Trend lines can also be curved to fit intermediate bottoms, as in figure 5(c), or intermediate tops, as in figure 5(d).

Figure 4.
Vertical line chart.

SOURCE: Mansfield.

A key task of the technician is to recognize a change in trend. Spotting one quickly allows him both to protect his current position and to benefit from the new market course. Technicians have identified a large number of patterns that they believe clearly indicate a reversal of direction either for the averages or for individual stocks.

One of the most important reversal patterns is the head and shoulders, shown in figure 6. This shape normally emerges after a spirited advance by a stock for a period of weeks, perhaps even months. In the classic pattern, the first peak (the left shoulder) is formed with rising volume on the way up and declining volume on the fallback. Shortly thereafter, a second advance begins on slightly less volume and forms the middle peak (the head). Usually, the nadir of the head is above that of the left shoulder. The pattern is completed by the formation of the right shoulder on low volume. If the right shoulder breaks through the neckline on the decline, the chartist reads a strong sell signal. By contrast, he considers a reverse head and shoulders pattern, such as that shown in figure 7, to be bullish.

There are numerous siblings in this family of formations, some of them with names sounding like sideshow attractions—aborted head and shoulders, deformed heads, multiple heads and shoulders, and two heads with one shoulder, to cite but a few.

Double tops and bottoms are other common patterns. In a double top, illustrated in figure 8, page 28, the left peak is ordinarily somewhat taller than the right. Volume usually runs fairly high on

Figure 5.
Some typical trend lines: (a) Uptrend line. (b) Downtrend line. (c) Up-curving trend line. (d) Down-curving trend line.

(a)   (b)   (c)   (d)

SOURCE: Harvey A. Krow, *Stock Market Behavior: A Technical Approach to Understanding Wall Street* (New York: Random House, 1969).

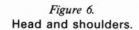
Figure 6.
Head and shoulders.

Figure 7.
Reverse head and shoulders.

the first peak, but drops significantly in the formation of the second —the last charge of the dying bull. The pattern is completed when, after the second top, the price falls below the level of the valley between the peaks. The bull is now officially dead and can be dragged out of the arena, as the braver bears begin to sell short.

The double bottom in figure 9, page 28, is the reverse of the double top and flags a lucrative buying opportunity. There are also such things as triple tops and bottoms. But few actually exist; according to experienced technicians, most sightings of these, like those of UFOs, turn out to be false.

There are many other reversal patterns, as is shown in figure 10, page 28. The nomenclature of the chartist is filled with such terms as "diamond wedges," "exhaustion gaps," "fan movements," and "flags flying at half mast." Though one author pointed out that the labels on the formations are unimportant except to improve an in-

Figure 8.
Double top.

Figure 9.
Double bottom.

Figure 10.
Other reversal patterns: (a) Saucer bottom. (b) Coil bottom.
(c) Spike top.

(a)   (b)   (c)

vestor's status as a name dropper, it is essential for the technician to be able to recognize the numerous possible patterns. Since each can give false signals, the technician's judgment and experience play powerful roles in shaping his decisions.

Other Technical Measures

It is not surprising, then, given the complexity of properly reading trends, that sophisticated technicians rely on numerous backup indicators to confirm favorite yardsticks. Support levels and resistance zones have long served this purpose. A support level indicates a valley a stock has climbed out of; a resistance zone is usually a previous peak. At a support level, sufficient demand is available to halt a further decline in price, at least for a time. A resistance zone, on the other hand, prevents further upward movement; enough stock is placed on the market at that price to halt temporarily and perhaps to stop a stock's climb altogether.

The reasoning behind both concepts is primarily psychological.

A buyer has purchased stock at a previous top—say, 20—made on high volume, and unhappily watched it decline to 16. If the stock again approaches 20, he and many others who bought it at that price will try to sell. Their supply of stock will provide resistance against further upward movement.

On the other hand, a support level forms under a stock when it approaches a previous area of heavy trading. People shrewd enough to sell at 20 in the last instance may want to repurchase the stock when it drops back to 16, particularly if this was an area of large turnover earlier. Other buyers who missed the rise to 20 might also go in at this point, helping put a floor under the stock.

Relative strength is another tool popular among contemporary technicians. Stocks are bought that are performing better than the market, while those that are performing worse are weeded out. Alternatively, price-volume systems are used with relative strength or as independent indicators. Stocks moving up on high volume are considered to be in a strong uptrend, with the converse also applying. Finally, filter techniques are used when a stock appears to be reversing a trend. If other indicators show that an advance is ending and a stock declines a further 10 percent, it may be sold; or if the indicators show that an advance is beginning and the stock rises 10 percent, it may be purchased. The amount of the movement—the filter—will be determined by the technician in conjunction with his other tools.

Although the technician's information has multiplied almost exponentially with the advent of the computer, the basic problem remains. To quote Joseph Granville again, while the "indicators may be crystal clear in definition and theory, they often break down and render false signals."[5] In practice, perfectly symmetrical formations are extremely rare. Frequently, as I have indicated, patterns are so complex that even leading chartists may disagree about their interpretation. And the level of static surrounding the actual market movements is often so intense that the numerous indicators can flash red, yellow, and green all at the same time.

"There is nothing wrong with the charts, only the chartists"— so an old Wall Street saying goes. Maybe so, but as we can see, there is little doubt that an extremely high degree of interpretive capability is required of anybody willing to undertake the task.

To compound the problem, many wolves disguised in technician's clothing await the tyro. A friend of mine, an office manager with one of the brokerage giants, recalls how the firm's own commodity technicians would have dozens of managed accounts buy wheat or soybeans once they believed they had spotted definite breakouts. Because the firm followed the prudent principle of "cutting your losses and letting profits ride," a stop-loss order* was placed for each account 3 or 4 cents under the market in the commodity, protecting that customer. Wheat would be bought at $3.08, for example, with a stop-loss placed at $3.04. Accordingly, if the new trend proved false, the client would sell at only a small loss.

This was fine in theory. In practice, the wolves were also astute technicians and could determine the levels of the stop-loss orders set by the firms. By selling short, they forced the price down to this point (in our case, $3.04), triggering a rash of sell orders, all at market.† The resultant unloading invariably dropped the price enough for the wolves to buy back at a profit. After being ravaged by this pack a number of times, the firm's technicians adopted more circumspect stop-loss procedures.

The Technician's Moment of Truth

Technical analysis is widespread on Wall Street, and the daily market commentaries in most newspapers are liberally sprinkled with its jargon. While fundamental research has a greater overall following, many a fundamentalist sneaks "a peek at the charts" before making a final buy or sell decision. Thus, there was considerable consternation among the many believers in the technical school when, in the past two decades, academic research began to demonstrate that no trends, tides, or waves could be shown to actually exist. Technical analysis, the academic findings strongly intimated, had no basis in fact.

To the technician, indeed to most financial readers, such findings seemed implausible. We can all see at a glance that stock charts show clearly discernible patterns. The professors, however, provided some extremely convincing evidence that seeing does not always warrant believing.

The first findings that price movements were random—that they displayed no predictable pattern of movement—emerged at the

*The stock is sold automatically when it falls to a predetermined price.
†To be sold at whatever price can be received; if there are few buyers, the decline can be significant.

turn of the century. Louis Bachelier, a brilliant French mathematics student, presented such evidence in his doctoral dissertation, written under the supervision of the internationally famous mathematician Jules Henri Poincaré.[6] Bachelier's work, which dealt with commodity prices and government bonds, concluded that past price movements could not be used to predict future changes. This work lay dormant for sixty years, until financial researchers rediscovered it in 1960.

About the same time other academicians had embarked on the same course. One early study showed that randomly chosen series of numbers, when plotted on a chart, closely resembled actual patterns of stock price action.[7] Another found that stock price fluctuations were remarkably similar to Brownian motion, the random movements of microscopic particles suspended in fluids.[8]

A good many researchers tested the proposition that stocks move in discernible trends. Important work was conducted by Arnold Moore in 1964,[9] Clive Granger and Oskar Morgenstern in 1963,[10] and Eugene Fama in 1965.[11] Granger and Morgenstern used the advanced new statistical technique of spectral analysis. Their data base included seven hundred weeks of price information for various industries in the 1939–61 period as well as the Standard & Poor's and Dow-Jones indices between 1915 and 1961. Eugene Fama analyzed the price movements of thirty stocks in the Dow-Jones averages for intervals of one to fourteen days over a five-year period.

All the studies demonstrated that future price movements cannot be predicted from past changes. Without exception, the findings indicated randomness in price—day to day, week to week, even month to month. A new hypothesis, called random walk by its proponents, grew out of the work.

The random walk hypothesis states that past price and volume statistics do not contain any information by themselves that will allow the investor to obtain results superior to those he would achieve by simply buying and holding securities. The theory thus maintains that technical analysis is valueless as a forecasting method. No matter how convinced the technician is about the market's or the stock's next move, he has no more chance of being right than he would have by tossing a coin. Statisticians tell us that when a true coin is tossed, even if it comes up heads a dozen times in a row, there is still a fifty-fifty chance that it will come up tails on the next throw. Or, in market terms, if a stock closes higher for a dozen days in a row, the next day the stock has a fifty-fifty chance of closing down. An overwhelming body of statistical research has now been developed refuting the central thesis of the technical school: that markets display major trends that can be readily identified.*

The Computer Dreadnought

If you have met technicians, you know that most are tough and grizzled veterans who have been through many a market campaign. They are not about to be told by a bunch of computer-worshiping Ph.D.'s, some barely approaching thirty, that they are obsolete.

The technicians could fall back on a second line of defense, and they did. Although the new research indicated overall randomness, they said, there could be useful directions in price changes within a given period, such as week to week or month to month, which would appear clear only when selected data, such as reversal patterns, were used.

The technicians challenged the academics to test their systems directly rather than by merely studying overall price movements. This proved to be a mistake. By the beginning of the 1970s, computerized research had become very stylish in academe. The technicians were met by a wave of peach-fuzzed youths armed with spanking-new computers. The trustworthy technical tools were systematically dissected by the academics and just as systematically relegated to the scrap heap.

A number of earlier tests were conducted on various filter systems, ranging in size from 1 to 50 percent.[12] After deducting commissions, none of the systems worked successfully.

Spurred on by their success, the academics approached the untouchable itself—the formidable Dow theory. Under merciless computer examination, peaks, valleys, support, and resistance levels all melted away. Price action proved random after both buy and sell signals. Even the double and triple peaks and valleys—the Maginot Line of the theory—gave no clearer signals.

Price-volume systems held up no better.[13] The size of neither price nor volume changes appeared to influence the direction of

*This is only the first stage of the random walk hypothesis. A more comprehensive form with far broader implications to the investor will be presented in the next chapter.

future price movements. Stocks moving up on high volume were just as likely to decline in the next trading period, and stocks going down in heavy trading might as likely reverse course. Relative strength met the same fate. All in all, the findings were enough to make many a chartist want to slink into the East River.

Nothing remained. One ambitious project analyzed 540 stocks trading on the New York Stock Exchange over a five-year period. In a most unsportsmanlike gesture, the academics programmed their computer to recognize thirty-two of the most commonly used patterns—including head and shoulders formations, and double and triple tops and bottoms—and to act on the information as a chartist would. The computer would sell, for example, if the right shoulder broke through the neckline of a head and shoulders formation, or buy if the market pushed higher through a triple top. When the results were measured, no correlation was found between the buy and sell signals and subsequent price movements.[14]

The computer *Wunderkind* had won again. Tests had shown conclusively that the technician's charting techniques did not result in superior returns.

The evidence supporting the random walk hypothesis is voluminous and still expanding. Although some research has indicated that a number of marginally profitable trading rules do work, they all involve substantial brokerage charges. Once these are deducted, the trader will have lost all his expected profits, sometimes more.

Every technician I know claims that his particular system works, of course. And he will say that in the end, it is his judgment that is important in determining which of the dozens of available tools to use and what emphasis to put on each. To examine this assertion, an infinite number of tests would have to be devised. But in the previous chapter, we saw the caliber of practitioners' judgments at crucial market turning points, as well as the overall record of professional performance—not particularly supportive of their claims. To the best of my knowledge, nothing has been forthcoming from the technicians, either in theory or in practice, that disputes the academic evidence.

To me, the case made for random walk is convincing to this point. Still, it was strange how, near the bottom of the 1974 market, as prices cascaded four or five points a day, I was jolted momentarily when a leading technician said the Dow would drop another two hundred points—though I was convinced that a sharp recovery was imminent. Perhaps there is a part in all of us reserved for the faith healer, the Ouija board, or the technician. It was also interesting to see how, when the market had rallied three hundred points, this prominent oracle managed to retain his aura with the financial press. (He was looking for another three-hundred-point advance this time.)

Curiously, despite the fact that the major tenets of technical analysis have been continuously refuted for a period of almost two decades, chartists continue to flourish, boasting of their successes and forgetting their equally numerous bad calls as though their doctrines had never been challenged. In fact, their importance and their status have been increasing on Wall Street in recent years. And this gives us a first key to a pattern we will find repeated in the chapters ahead. Theories in the end rest far less squarely on facts than on the willingness of their followers to believe that they work. Facts that seem to support the theory are pressed forward, while other damaging information often slips by.

Einstein said it all succinctly decades ago: "The theory shapes the observations."

CHAPTER THREE

Fundamental Analysis— The Slippery Rock

In the last chapter we looked at the case made by the technical analyst and found it wanting. Neither his charts nor his numerous other indicators prove to have any value when subjected to statistical measurement. Some academic researchers have cheerfully suggested that the technician broaden his indicators to include the signs of the zodiac or tea-leaf reading, which, the professors say, are at least as scientific.

Now let's examine fundamental analysis, the method practiced by the great preponderance of bank trust departments, pension funds, mutual funds, and investment advisors, as well as by most brokers. As we have already seen, this school states that the value of a company can be determined through a rigorous analysis of its sales, earnings, dividend prospects, financial strength, competitive position, and other related measures. To arrive at the proper worth of a stock, the analyst synthesizes and weighs all relevant information, often supporting his work with actual visits to senior company management.

The fundamentalist believes that stock prices will often diverge sharply from intrinsic value. His methods allow him to search out worth, buying solid companies that are underpriced and selling those overvalued. The market, he thinks, must eventually recognize the error of its ways and correct them.

To use a simple but appropriate analogy: value for the fundamentalist is like an anchor to which a boat is moored by a long line. Like the boat, price moves respond to the prevailing market winds. Often it is blown far in one direction, only shortly thereafter to be tossed as far in the opposite. Knowing where the anchor lies allows the investor to profit from the various gusts.

The fundamentalist does not claim to know exactly where the anchor rests; even the best analysis can only find its approximate location. But the anchor nevertheless is there, and because it is, the skillful practitioner can benefit from the prevailing market winds time and again.

Fundamental theory is considered to be far more sophisticated than its technical sibling because the former draws on the advanced techniques of accounting, business, and economics. Not unexpectedly, then, it has always been the currency of the investment establishment. All the same, as we shall see, it is a currency that has depreciated steadily in recent years.

The Intrinsic Value Theory

Research has demonstrated that earnings and dividends are the most important determinants of stock prices over time. The core of fundamental analysis is thus the development of techniques that will estimate these factors accurately. One of the most exacting methods of establishing a stock's value, called the intrinsic value theory, was introduced in the late 1930s by John Burr Williams.[1] According to the rational economic school that Williams represents, the investor values a stock in terms of what he expects to receive from it over time. Williams holds that the price of a stock is worth the present value of its anticipated dividends. He believes that if earnings could be projected and from them the dividends, one could derive a precise estimate of worth.

To do this, he used a method known as discounting. A payment received a year from now is worth less than one received today, since you could invest the current payment and have it with interest twelve months hence. Likewise, a payment two years from now is worth less by the interest for this time span, and so on. Discounting the stream of dividends by the appropriate rate of return, the analyst arrives at the current value of a stock.* All very neat and precise, but not very representative of how investors value stock—at least on this planet.

Williams's work was extended by Nicholas Molodovsky, the late editor of the *Financial Analysts Journal.* Molodovsky recognized that security analysts are more comfortable estimating earnings and then projecting the proportion paid out in dividends. The Molodovsky formula is found below.†

Lest you think that this is the last word on the subject, more complex equations have been developed to adjust for changes in the rate of earnings growth during different time periods. One formula solves for four separate growth rates for the company and a final rate of residual growth once the company matures.‡

---

*Williams's calculations begin with the following formula, which requires only some knowledge of high school algebra to understand:

$$\frac{D_1}{1 + R}$$

In this formula, D_1 is the dividend in the first year, and R is the rate of return the investor wants in order to buy the stock. This return includes not only interest, normally the going rate on good long-term bonds, but also an added sum to compensate for the greater riskiness of the equity investment. The formula to derive the present value *(V)* of all dividends is written as follows, with $D_2/(1+R)^2$ the current value of the second year's dividends, and so on to the last dividend, n years out:

$$V = \frac{D_1}{1+R} + \frac{D_2}{(1+R)^2} + \frac{D_3}{(1+R)^3} + \cdots + \frac{D_n}{(1+R)^n}$$

In this example, if D is \$2.00, R is 10 percent, and dividends increase 11 percent a year for the first three years, the present value of these dividends would be calculated as follows:

$$\frac{\$2.00}{1+.10} + \frac{\$2.22}{(1+.10)^2} + \frac{\$2.46}{(1+.10)^3} + \$1.82 + \$1.83 + \$1.85 = \$5.50$$

To get the current worth of the stock, one would discount this stream over the company's expected life.

†The Molodovsky formula is:

$$V = \frac{E_1P}{1 + R} + \frac{E_2P}{(1 + R)^2} + \frac{E_3P}{(1 + R)^3} + \cdots + \frac{E_nP}{(1 + R)^n}$$

Where E is the earnings, P is the percentage paid out in dividends, and R is the rate of return in each year.

‡Intrinsic value $= \dfrac{e_0(1 + g_1)p}{1 + r} + \dfrac{e_0(1 + g_1)^2p}{(1 + r)^2} + \cdots + \dfrac{e_0(1 + g_1)^{n_1}p}{(1 + r)^{n_1}} +$

$\dfrac{e_0(1 + g_1)^{n_1}(1 + g_2)p}{(1 + r)^{n_1+1}} + \cdots + \dfrac{e_0(1 + g_1)^{n_1}(1 + g_2)^{n_2}p}{(1 + r)^{n_1+n_2}} +$

$\dfrac{e_0(1 + g_1)^{n_1}(1 + g_2)^{n_2}(1 + g_3)p}{(1 + r)^{n_1+n_2+1}} + \cdots + \dfrac{e_0(1 + g_1)^{n_1}(1 + g_2)^{n_2}(1 + g_3)^{n_3}p}{(1 + r)^{n_1+n_2+n_3}} +$

$\dfrac{e_0(1 + g_1)^{n_1}(1 + g_2)^{n_2}(1 + g_3)^{n_3}(1 + g_4)p}{(1 + r)^{n_1+n_2+n_3+1}} + \cdots$

Before you close this book, deciding it's not for you, let me say that I am demonstrating the formulas only to show what hasn't worked, *not* what has. As we shall see, this dose of castor oil not only won't help you, but may prove positively harmful to your investment health.

There is nothing wrong with the formulas themselves. In fact, if we could see into the future with perfect clarity, they would be very useful. And for those of us who find algebra distasteful, I am sure that given our current nurturing of graduate students, we could find any number willing to do the calculations for us at the going minimum wage.

No, the real problem is that forecasting the future has always proved perilous. Just how perilous even one year ahead will be seen later. Yet the models call for projections ten to twenty years out or more, not only for earnings but also for the growth rate of dividends and the discount rate. These estimates, as chapters 5 and 7 will detail, are implanted in quicksand. While the formulas appear "scientific," thanks to their mathematical complexity, a dangerous false precision is built into them, which the theorists, concentrating on the elegance of the equations, often seem to forget.

In his book, *Investments: New Analytic Techniques,* [2] Professor Williamson clearly demonstrates the problem in his valuation procedure for IBM. Using a formula similar to the last of the three just given, he initially forecast an earnings increase of 16 percent for ten years and 2 percent thereafter, and applied a 7 percent discount rate and a 40 percent dividend payout ratio. These figures gave him a value of $173, about half the then-current market price (1968). Extending the 16 percent growth rate to twenty years, he got a value of $433, well above the market price. When he changed the discount rate to 10 percent, the value dropped to $206, again well under the market. Modifications resulted in other major price variations.

As intricate and impressive as a valuation formula may appear, it is only the frame housing the forecasting engine. If you do not have an engine that can reliably and continuously predict the complex variables of earnings, dividend payout, and rate of return, the frame

$$+ \frac{e_0(1 + g_1)^{n_1}(1 + g_2)^{n_2}(1 + g_3)^{n_3}(1 + g_4)^{n_4}p}{(1 + r)^{n_1 + n_2 + n_3 + n_4}} +$$

$$\frac{e_0(1 + g_1)^{n_1}(1 + g_2)^{n_2}(1 + g_3)^{n_3}(1 + g_4)^{n_4}(1 + g_5)p}{(r - g_5)(1 + r)^{n_1 + n_2 + n_3 + n_4}} .$$

is of no practical use. More likely it is dangerous. As Williamson's example illustrated, investors can crank any numbers into the equation that their current mood dictates and wind up with the price they want.

Sketches have been found in a notebook of Leonardo da Vinci's for an aircraft that aeronautical engineers believe might well have been airworthy. Not having a workable engine, Leonardo did not proceed further—an example perhaps lost on some of the present-day model builders.

The Bible of Wall Street

Although fundamental analysis has had its share of abstract theoreticians, it also has had some eminently practical ones. Next, we'll look briefly at some of the major tenets of security analysis, first to become more familiar with its principles and then to explore various problems that may preclude their successful implementation. The background here is important to the investment strategy that will be evolved in Part III.

The most systematic work in the field is the 778-page epic *Security Analysis,* by Benjamin Graham and David Dodd, first published in 1934 and revised three times subsequently.[3] This book has been called the bible of fundamental practitioners, and for decades Graham has been regarded as the leading prophet.

In the 1920s, relying on his own valuation techniques, Graham became a highly successful portfolio manager—so much so that he attracted the eye of Bernard Baruch, who offered him the chance to become his junior partner. Graham declined, having made $600,000 the previous year on his own. However, the year was 1929, and Graham's clients suffered in the Crash like everybody else. But he managed to keep them solvent, and over the next several decades he consistently compiled a creditable investment record.

Benjamin Graham was a classical scholar, fluent in Greek, Latin, German, and Spanish. But his first love was investment theory, and he devoted more than forty years to teaching it, first at Columbia and later at UCLA. One of his early students was a young academic, David Dodd, who eventually became his coauthor.[4]

Graham's investment techniques stress the preservation of capital. Investors are advised to keep between 25 and 75 percent of their capital (depending on their personal circumstances) in high-grade bonds, bank accounts, and other assets that were riskless in his time. The remainder can be invested in well-diversified portfolios of ten to thirty stocks. Each company selected has to be large, prominent, and conservatively financed, with a long record of continuous dividend payments. Stocks should always be bought by applying stringent valuation formulas, which normally eliminate new issues, concept stocks,* and growth stocks. In *Security Analysis* rigorous investment procedures are laid out to determine intrinsic value. Because of the difficulty of pinpointing real worth precisely, Graham always insisted on an "adequate" margin of safety as a protective cushion in his calculations. His rules were so stern that some fund managers only half-jokingly spoke of him as the reincarnation of an eighteenth-century Yankee businessman—there wasn't an ounce of speculation in him.

Assessing Earning Power

The principal method of appraising stocks according to Graham and Dodd is through the determination of earning power. The investor should measure the record of a company over an extensive period, usually seven to ten years, to gauge its basic profitability. Using its financial record and supporting data, he should meticulously analyze its earnings and dividend trends, financial strength, debt structure, depreciation reserves, bank lines of credit, backlogs, capital spending plans, and other relevant information. Qualitative factors such as the growth prospects of the company, the strength of its management, its position in its industry, and product development should also be assessed. After thorough analysis, he will be in a position to work out conservative projections of future earning power.

Graham and Dodd devote a full section to accounting, some 175 pages in all. It is essential that the analyst understand numerous accounting conventions that can significantly overstate or understate earnings. To get as accurate a picture as possible of the actual operat-

---

*Stocks in a company that may or may not have a financial record but definitely has a "good story to tell" that promises an outstanding future.

ing profit, adjustments must be made for each accounting item that will distort earnings.*

The authors' preoccupation with accounting principles is not simply an obsession. "Creative" accounting has always been an exceptional tool in the hands of the adroit corporate manipulator. In the go-go market of 1967–68, two computer leasing firms, Data Processing & Financial General and Levin-Townsend, both traded at 40 times earnings, almost triple the average ratio of the S&P 500, thanks to their rapidly growing earnings, produced solely by clever accounting. When more conservative reporting policies were adopted, their earnings disappeared entirely, and both dropped 90 percent from their highs. And University Computing, a Dallas-based computer service company of the era, topped even this, trading as high as 118 times accounting-manufactured earnings before plummeting 98 percent.

Graham and Dodd recommended that security analysts use a fairly extensive list of financial ratios to measure a company's performance. One of the more important ones is the return on equity —the aftertax profit divided by net worth.† Another is pretax return on sales.‡ While there are, of course, variations from industry to industry, the higher and more stable these ratios, the better regarded the firm. The two ratios will range from 10 or 12 percent for the average company to as high as 20 or even 30 percent for the more spectacular growth stocks.

A number of important ratios deal with financial strength. The current ratio§ is one of the most commonly followed. For most companies, a current ratio of 2 to 1 or better is considered sound, although this too will vary from industry to industry.

Other ratios will be used to determine how capable a company is of meeting its debts, since in bad times a high debt structure can lead to default and possible bankruptcy. A commonly used rule of thumb for industrial concerns is that common shares should represent at least 50 percent of the capital structure, which is the combined value of its common stock, preferred stock, and bonds.

*For example, a one-time gain from the sale of a plant or land must be excluded from that year's operating income.

†The value of all common stock and retained earnings. This ratio calculates the owners' (common stock holders) capital in the business.

‡Income before taxes as a percentage of sales.

§The ratio of current assets to current liabilities. This ratio determines how able the company is to pay its near-term debts—those due in a year or less.

After satisfying himself as to the accounting, financial strength, and profitability of a business, the analyst, Graham and Dodd advise, should project trends ahead for seven to ten years. To do so, averages should be taken of past sales and earnings figures, with conservative projections into the future made from these. The emphasis is placed on the past record of earnings and whether it can continue rather than on whether the company can expand rapidly.

Security Analysis lays out four essential components of common stock evaluation, repeatedly cautioning the practitioner to tie the first three firmly into the record of the past:

1. Expected future earnings
2. Expected future dividends
3. A method for valuing expected earnings
4. The asset value

Once average future earnings are estimated, an evaluative measure is used to establish what the price should be. The price/earnings (or P/E) ratio is the yardstick investors most commonly use to determine price. It is simply the current price divided by earnings per share. If a stock is trading at 10, earned $1.00 last year, and is expected to earn $1.25 this year, it is said to be trading at a price/earnings ratio of 10 on the latest full year's earnings and at 8 on the anticipated earnings for the current year. The higher the P/E ratio, the more favorable the company's prospects are believed to be, while the lower the multiple the more lackluster its anticipated future.

A cardinal conviction of Graham and Dodd's is that investors tend to overreact to near-term prospects—to overprice companies for which these are favorable and underprice those for which they are poorer. The formulas establish multipliers that are designed to keep the disparity between P/E's for companies with differing outlooks on a tight leash, as all too often the forecasts have proven wrong. In the 1955 edition of *The Intelligent Investor,* *[5] for example, the spread between stocks with better and poorer outlooks was 8 to 20. Companies with average prospects were given a multiplier of 12. Although the P/E ratios have changed with changing market conditions over the years, the same principle has always been maintained.

*Benjamin Graham's book written for individual investors.

Security Analysis provides a second method of evaluating stocks— that of ferreting out companies trading at a significant discount to their book or net asset value.* Again, to adopt this approach, the student must be steeped in the intricacies of accounting. Graham and Dodd were fascinated by the fact that the net asset or book value is often the most important factor in determining the worth of a private company, but that once the firm becomes public, the market shifts its focus dramatically, concentrating almost exclusively on earnings instead. Various formulas are provided for the investor to take advantage of companies selling under book.

In recent years, the basic methods of security analysis have been extended by other theorists to include computer techniques and various forms of economic forecasting. One approach relying on the computer is called probabilistic forecasting. The analyst's uncertainties about variables in his estimates can be quantified into probabilities. For example, if the price of lead is essential in calculating a mining company's earnings, the practitioner can make a number of calculations of demand under varying sets of industry conditions for this commodity, and assign probabilities that each price will occur. From this data, both a range of earnings estimates and the likelihood that each will occur can be projected.

Conditional forecasts allow the analyst to tie his estimates into those of the economist. Taking the economist's model of GNP, capital spending, disposable income, level of interest rates, and other inputs, the analyst forecasts sales and earnings at different levels of economic activity. Using the computer, projections are made of how a company should fare at various stages of the industry and general economic cycles. Such advanced techniques allow the analyst to delineate his individual company projections more sharply.[6]

Although all fundamental analysis is derived from the same tree, one branch, the growth school, has dominated it for considerable periods. This branch perplexed Graham and Dodd. As they write in *Security Analysis,* "We are haunted as it were by the spectre of growth stocks—by the question of how best to deal with them in the context of our own basic principles." Let's face this specter next.

*The value of the common stock after deducting all liabilities and preferred shares. Usually this is calculated per common share by dividing the total by the number of shares outstanding.

Had someone put $10,000 into Haloid-Xerox in 1960, the year the first plain paper copier, the 914, was introduced, the investment would have been worth $16.5 million a decade later. McDonald's earnings increased several thousand times in the 1961–66 period, and then, more demurely, quadrupled again by 1971, the year of its eight billionth hamburger. Anyone astute enough to buy McDonald's stock in 1965, when it went public, would have made fortyfold his money in the next seven years. An investor who plunked $2,750 into Thomas J. Watson's Computing and Tabulating Company in 1914 would have had over $20 million in IBM stock by the beginning of this decade. It is hardly surprising, then, with our industry based as it is in science and invention and their by-products of rapid expansion and sudden change, that the growth school has so often ruled fundamental analysis.

American history is full of stories of investors who seized dynamic new opportunities and made fortunes. In 1910 a leading banker, unable to control his laughter, walked out of a meeting after an auto manufacturer told him that the industry would someday produce half a million cars. By 1929 almost six million were streaming off the assembly lines. At the turn of the century, someone believing in the growth of mass merchandising and buying Sears would have made eleven thousand times his money by 1950. And so it goes.

The tradition of Xerox, McDonald's, General Motors, and Sears is deeply rooted American. Participating in new, potentially vast enterprises produces an exciting sense of communion with the Edisons, Watsons, Carnegies, and Fords, and more important, a chance to reap spectacular gains by our foresight. In an age when the opportunities for the individual entrepreneurs are progressively diminished by the large, impersonal corporations, it is a vision hard not to follow.

The growth analyst sharply hones his analytical tools to attempt to pinpoint those companies that can expect rapid and stable expansion. Like his more conservative Graham and Dodd counterparts, he takes the past record as his starting point, but his emphasis lies on the future. Companies are sought out that he believes will continue to have superior profit margins and earn above-average returns on equity. A growth company should be far less affected by economic uncertainties and should produce rising earnings through both inflationary and recessionary conditions, when many firms falter.

Growth stock analysis must accurately spotlight future trends: how well a new line of computers will do for Digital Equipment, how many SX-70 cameras Polaroid will sell, how big a market exists for a new drug of Upjohn's. Extensive analysis goes into determining product growth, market share, development of competition, maintenance of profit margins, and dozens of other important factors affecting growth rates. Growth stocks have traditionally traded at lofty multiples—often two, three, four, or even more times the P/E ratios of their more pedestrian compeers—which makes an error in projections fatal.

A growth company is believed to have a remarkable degree of control over its destiny. It normally has a solidly entrenched position in a large and rapidly expanding market. Sometimes its muscle comes from patent protection, as with the large ethical drug companies (or in the recent past with Xerox and Polaroid); sometimes from a superb and hard-to-duplicate marketing force, as in the case of Avon ("which never had a *product,*" as one money manager remarked with grudging admiration, "that couldn't be duplicated in a garage"); and sometimes from an imaginative adaptation of production and marketing techniques long standard in manufacturing to a service industry, as is true of McDonald's.

Growth companies have excellent managements, some with the vision to create entirely new markets. Xerox's management foresaw the importance of dry copying and correctly predicted that its revenues would grow from $30 million in 1960 to $1 billion ten years later. On the other hand, Sperry Rand, the original developer of the computer, estimated a total market of less than half a dozen or so data processors and was left in the dust by IBM.

The growth stock analyst must thoroughly analyze the factors contributing to growth. Can the company continue to control both its costs and its sales prices? What prohibits destructive competition from entering the marketplace? How labor-intensive is it? (Normally, a growth company is not.) Are its raw materials abundant and a small part of the overall selling price? (A change in the price of steel will affect Chrysler much more than a higher transistor price will IBM.)

Growth stocks are often self-financing—that is, their profitability is high and stable enough to pay for a good part if not all of the plant and equipment required for rapid expansion. A fast-growing company that can generate the bulk of the funds it needs internally is of course far more desirable than one that must rely heavily on outside borrowing or on the sale of common stock, which would dilute the present shareholders' equity. The higher the return on capital, the more likely the firm will finance its own growth.

As in the case of more basic fundamental analysis, the tenets of growth stock investing are varied and extensive. But once again, unfortunately, a system that appears eminently sensible in theory has proved exceptionally refractory in practice.

Why Don't They Work?

To judge from the record presented in chapter 1, fundamental research has had no greater success than technical analysis. However, the whys are considerably more bewildering because the fundamental school seems to build on much more solid underpinnings.

Graham and Dodd, always skeptical of growth techniques, have given some good reasons why this branch of analysis may not work. The first lies in the nature of the analysis itself. While conceding value analysis is always difficult, they believe that a forecast based on the clearly measurable earnings power of the past is more secure than one built on growth trends extrapolated into the future. Such projections, they repeatedly warn, are fraught with danger. Earnings forecasts even for prime growth companies can be very chancy. Then, too, for every real growth stock there are many that appear to be but are not.*

The second problem with growth investing is that even if the analysis proves accurate, there is still the question of what multiple should be used to evaluate earnings. The record of the Kidder Peabody Top 50 in figure 11 illustrates as much. The Top 50 are the fifty favorite stocks on the New York Stock Exchange as determined by their P/E ratios.† A comparison of this index with the Standard & Poor's 500 from 1973 to the spring of 1977 is enlightening: the P/E's

*For details, see chapter 8.
†In computing the table, Kidder excludes companies with nominal earnings.

of the Top 50 dropped 50 percent—from ratios averaging more than 3 times the S&P to 1.5 times.* Investors had simply changed their minds about what to pay for the prime growth stocks. The evaluation problem, then, appears to be just as difficult as the forecasting problem. High P/E's can be subject to drastic revisions as market moods change.

Now let's turn to a more troublesome question: If the scenario described in the first chapter is accurate, why have the proponents of even the more basic Graham and Dodd model not fared better? First, despite Graham's admonitions, one of his most important rules has been downgraded or disregarded entirely in practice. Standard security analysis has increasingly emphasized correctly estimating near-term company conditions, such as sales and earnings, while continually downplaying other important fundamental factors.† Thus, forecasting, with the same inherent dangers indicated previously, also plays an overly important role in more basic fundamental analysis as it is practiced today. Perhaps this is the reason Graham once said he might be one of the most read and most forgotten men on Wall Street.

Second, although certain issues may appear to be substantially undervalued, there is no guarantee that the market will recognize this to be so. If it doesn't see this as the case, the stocks may continue to trade at low prices for many years to come.

Figure 11.
Relative price/earnings ratios of the Kidder Peabody Top 50.

SOURCE: The "Top 50" is a monthly publication of Kidder, Peabody & Co., Incorporated.

*The stocks in the Top 50 change every month; the original Top 50 from 1972 have declined even more.
†Among such other criteria, price/earnings ratios, book value, yield, and financial strength.

A third reason was given by one of Graham's most successful followers, Warren Buffett, who accumulated some $75 million in the 1960s and then proved canny enough to get out near the market top and stay out. Buffett said that his success came from a consistent application of fundamentals that "others cavalierly disregarded."[7]

But were many of these fundamentals in fact "cavalierly disregarded"? Or were there instead very important problems with the methods that led to their abandonment, most often involuntarily, by their adherents? Part II will examine this important question—central to the poor professional record—in some detail.

Meanwhile, let's look at another device born of mixed fundamental and technical lineage—market timing.

Market Timing—Myth or Reality?

A fascinating aspect of markets is how ideas that have fallen into wide disrepute can be periodically recycled, repackaged, and reintroduced as entirely new products. A good example is the current resurrection of market timing. The essence of the theory, as the name implies, is to time purchases and sales according to the phase of the market.

If this could actually be done, the rewards would be high. In the past decade, catching the major swings would have more than tripled the results of simply buying and holding the S&P 500 over the period.

One professional, defending the resurgence of the theory, wrote that "1973 was a bad year for those who doubted the value of market timing." He then goes on to give the following incisive advice: "In general, the strategy should be to buy and hold good long-term stocks when they are going up, and let someone else hold them when they are going down." More simply stated, buy low and sell high—a principle not unknown to Mesopotamian merchants some five millennia earlier. Investment placebo or not, the advice is currently well heeded.

Market timing has become extremely popular among professional money managers and their clients. A study by Leuthold Associates, a special consultant to the Minneapolis-based brokerage house of Piper, Jaffray and Hopwood, found that 168 firms managing

$88 billion (42 percent of all pension fund assets) claimed to "make some use of market timing."[8] And a number of the major banks, including Morgan Guaranty, Manufacturers Hanover, Irving Trust, and Crocker National, have indicated that they will use the procedure.

Their consistent underperformance of the market averages in recent years has led some institutions to the path after a great deal of soul-searching. Others have set their feet on the road less hesitantly. In the words of one candid money manager: "Sure, we're telling our clients we're prepared to use market timing. What the hell else can we tell them after 1973–74?"[9]

As noted, market timing is, in practice, a hybrid of fundamental and technical ingredients, blending business analysis and technical projections. Market timers watch such economic conditions as the trend and level of interest rates, the degree and direction of business activity, corporate profits, and industrial production. If, for example, inflation is decelerating, interest rates have peaked and are edging down, and employment is beginning to pick up after a decline, economic factors are considered very favorable. And if simultaneously technical patterns are encouraging, a buy signal has been given—one with pennants flying and bands marching, at that. On the other hand, if interest rates are ominously moving higher, business is declining, and corporate profitability and employment are beginning to slip, while technical patterns look menacing, we know it is time to sell. What could be simpler?

Unfortunately, in the real world, market movements give dozens of signals, all madly flashing buy, sell, and hold at once. To further complicate the situation, institutions as a group watch the same leading technicians (Robert Farrel, Charles O'Hay, Edson Gould, Elliot Janeway, and a handful of others) and the same indicators as well as each other. Thus, the major money managers are all likely to react to the same information at about the same time. Since they currently control a large percentage of all stock trading, market timing, if it is widely practiced, may create a self-fulfilling prophecy serving to accentuate market swings.

Various academic and institutional studies of market timing have indicated the failure of the method. William Sharpe, a leading academic researcher, found that a money manager who wishes to market-time profitably must be right three times out of four after commissions and advisory costs,[10] something our chart in chapter 1 shows has not happened. Another major study, by Merrill Lynch, found that "the great majority of funds lose money as a result of their timing efforts, and when the effects of commission costs are included, virtually everyone loses money."

Once again, as we saw in the last chapter, the evolution and acceptance of widely popular investment theory seems to have little to do with the underlying realities.

A Purposeful Random Walk

If fundamentalists are perplexed about why results aren't better, the academics certainly are not. Starting in the past decade, they progressively began to shift their research firepower from the technical to the fundamental front. Extensive studies were made of the performance of large groups of mutual funds, the great majority of which subscribe to security analysis. Evidence began to mount that the funds did no better than the market. Michael Jensen, for example, measured the record of 155 mutual funds between 1945 and 1964, adjusting for the fact that some were more and others less risky than the market as a whole,* and found that only 43 of 115 funds outperformed it after commissions.[11]

In 1970 Friend, Blume, and Crockett of the Wharton School completed the most comprehensive study of mutual funds yet made.[12] They measured 136 funds between January 1, 1960, and June 30, 1968, and found that the funds showed an average return of 10.7 percent annually. During the same time span, shares on the New York Stock Exchange averaged 12.4 percent annually.† The study was then extended to cover the year ending July 1969. For this period, the average fund decreased 3.8 percent, compared with a

*Techniques have been developed by financial academics to measure the volatility of a single stock or a portfolio against the market (normally an index like the S&P 500) over a period of time. From these correlations, predictions of future movements relative to the market can be made. Such past correlations are claimed to have useful predictive value. Beta is a commonly used measure of volatility. The market is considered to have a Beta coefficient of 1. Stocks or portfolios with a higher coefficient are more volatile than the market, while those with a lower one are less so. Thus, a portfolio with a Beta coefficient of 2 should move, on the average, about twice as far as the market in either direction, while one with a coefficient of 0.5 should show about half the movement of the market. Some adjustment for the relative riskiness of different portfolios or stocks is necessary in order realistically to measure them against either the market averages or one another over any period of time.

†Value-weighting for the number of shares of each company outstanding (which gave far more emphasis to the changes of the larger companies), the increase was 9.9 percent.

decrease of 3.3 percent for the value-weighted average of the Big Board stocks. Hardly comforting to those fund managers who present the picture of superior performance.

Academic analysis proved to be as unsparing of the fundamental practitioner's sensibilities as it had been of the technician's. Friend, Blume, and Crockett also established that if the degree of risk remains unchanged, there is no correlation between a fund's performance record in one period and its performance in another, dispatching the myth of the hot money manager. Funds in the top 10 percent in one period might be in the bottom 10 percent the next, or vice versa.

Other widely prevailing beliefs were treated as harshly. No link was found between portfolio turnover and subsequent performance. Rapid turnover does not improve results, but in fact seems to damage them slightly. And the idea that high sales charges are justified cannot be sustained. Any relationship between performance and commission charges (front-end loads,* as they are commonly called) appears to be mildly negative. No-load funds and funds with low sales charges perform marginally better. Finally, if the risk factor is held constant, there is little difference in the results of funds of various sizes. In sum, the report firmly concluded that no evidence exists that mutual funds can outperform the market.

To explain discoveries such as these, academic investigators proposed a revolutionary new hypothesis. Called at first the stronger form of the random walk theory, it has come to be known as the efficient-market hypothesis. It holds basically that competition between sophisticated and knowledgeable investors keeps stock prices about where they should be. This happens because all facts determining stock prices are analyzed by thousands of interested investors. Incoming information, such as a change in a company's earnings outlook or a dividend cut, is quickly digested and immediately reflected in the stock price. Like it or not, competition by so many investors, all seeking hidden values, makes stock prices reflect the best estimates of their real worth. Prices may not always be right, but they are unbiased, so if they are wrong, they are just as likely to be too high as too low.

Because the market is efficient, the theorists continue, investors

---

*Those funds charging a commission ranging as high as 8¾ percent of principal on purchase. No-loads do not charge a front-end commission.

should expect to receive only a fair return commensurate with the risk of purchasing a particular stock. Securities or portfolios with greater risk should normally provide larger rewards over time.

Since meaningful new information affecting the overall market and individual companies enters the marketplace unpredictably, prices react in a random manner. This is the real reason that charting and technical analysis do not work. Nobody knows what new inputs will enter the marketplace, whether they will be positive or negative or whether they will have a general impact or affect only a single company or industry.

According to the efficient-market hypothesis, it is most unlikely that any investor or his advisor will outrun the pack over time, regardless of method. The competition is just too keen. In fact, money managers who trade a good deal, trying to stay in front, will probably perform worse because of the high cost of commissions. As we have seen, the track record of professionals appears to confirm as much. Because the market is highly efficient, the theory goes on, the investor's best strategy is to buy and hold a portfolio bearing the degree of risk he desires.

The efficient-market hypothesis has much wider implications than the original random walk theory, which said only that investors would not benefit from technical analysis. The new argument effectively tears the very heart out of fundamental research—the detection of overvalued and undervalued issues. For if enough buyers and sellers have correctly evaluated and acted upon new information, such stocks will be very rare indeed.*

The theorists also admit that markets may not always be efficient for the stocks of smaller companies or for obscure convertibles or warrant issues, and that some extremely gifted individuals may divine major developments from public information. But these possibilities are considered extremely rare—financial albinos. For most publicly traded companies, the markets are believed to be highly efficient. Which means we cannot outsmart them.

Although they might wish to shoot one another on sight, the efficient-market adherents and the chartists share the same essential premise. James Lorie and Richard Brealey, stating the academic

---

*Here the efficient-market theorists acknowledge a paradox. Since it is fundamental analysis that is largely responsible for keeping markets efficient, if enough practitioners believed the efficient-market hypothesis and stopped their analytic efforts, markets might well become inefficient.

view, have written, "A startling idea—current prices reflect what is knowable."[13] Actually, what is startling is the similarity to Charles Dow's statement: "The market as a whole represents a serious, well-considered effort on the part of far-sighted and informed men to adjust prices to values such as exist or which are expected to exist in the not too remote future."[14] Or William Peter Hamilton's remark: "It cannot too often be said that the stock market reflects all everybody knows about the business of the country."[15] Once again the same basic thought leads to widely divergent market paths.

And Still More Tests!

The extensive measurements of the performance of mutual funds and other classes of money managed professionally provided support for the efficient-market hypothesis. Another line of testing has been formulated to determine how quickly the market adjusts to new information, since a major proposition of the theory is that it does so almost instantaneously, so investors normally cannot benefit.

One important study explored the market's understanding of stock splits. In effect, when a stock is split, there is no free lunch—the shareholder still has the same proportionate ownership as before. If markets are efficient, enough knowing investors would sell the stock that has split if prices were run up by more naive traders. This proved to be the case. Tests confirmed that stock prices after a split maintain about the same long-term relationship to market movements as before.[16]

Another study, measuring the earnings of 261 large corporations between 1946 and 1966, concluded that only 10 to 15 percent of the data in the earnings reports had not been anticipated by the reporting month, indicating the market's wide awareness of information.[17] Other tests came up with similar results, all demonstrating that the market quickly adjusts to new inputs.

The strongest form of the efficient-market hypothesis claims that no information, including that known by corporate insiders or by specialists trading the company's stock (who have confidential material about unexecuted orders on their "books"), could outperform the market. In the few studies done to date, some evidence has surfaced that both insiders[18] and specialists[19] display an ability to beat the market. However, these exceptions to the concept of perfectly efficient markets are considered inconsequential.

In the space of the last few dozen pages, we have seen the academic dismantlement of the two most important market theories of our day and their replacement, at least intellectually, by a third. The new theory has swept like a brush fire, first through the universities and then progressively through the SEC, legislators, the financial press, individual and corporate investors, and finally among professionals themselves. On the assumption that it is impossible to outdo the market, index funds have been formed that attempt only to mirror the results of the averages—a fitting tribute to the power of an idea conceived less than two decades earlier. At the same time, sad, for in accepting the new way, the money manager acknowledges that his prime raison d'être—to earn superior returns for his client —is beyond reach.

But it's not time to throw in the towel yet. Although the efficient-market hypothesis seems to unravel some of the investment knots we have seen, it fails to untie many others. How, for instance, could professional investors not merely equal the market in recent years, but in fact do worse? How could the bulk of professional opinion prove so consistently and dramatically wrong at crucial market turning points? Or how, if investors are so unfailingly rational, could periods of euphoria and panic occur so often through market history?

None of these phenomena are possible, according to the theory. One nonacademic observer noted that Disney fell 86 percent between 1972 and 1974, with its P/E ratio declining from 64 to 21, though earnings and profit margins improved throughout this period. "When was the market efficient?" he asked. "When it took Disney up to 119⅛, or when it put it back to 16⅝?" Obviously, perfectly efficient markets should not exhibit such behavior.

Thus, before accepting the academic theory that ours is the best of all possible financial worlds—that our advanced analytical methods result in highly efficient markets—let's move back to the questions posed a few pages earlier. Are there flaws, and perhaps very serious ones, in the analytical methods themselves that lead to consistent investment error? We will find the answers in the next section.

PART II

UNDERSTANDING YOUR PSYCHOLOGICAL ODDS

CHAPTER FOUR

The Strange World of Reality

London during the first days of 1524 was a city awaiting its doom. Crowds of anxious people of every social stratum gathered to listen to the numerous astrologers and fortune-tellers along bustling thoroughfares. All said the same thing: on February 1 the Thames would suddenly rise from its banks, engulf the entire city, and sweep away ten thousand homes. The vision was described in terrifying detail to increasingly larger throngs.

It had started the preceding June, when a few soothsayers began to bandy about the prophecy, which quickly permeated their ranks. Month after month the warnings were repeated with total assurance, and as time passed, they became accepted by most of the population, even though the Thames had always been the most docile of rivers.

At first, only a handful of families began to leave the city, but as the time grew near, people left in ever-increasing numbers. Long streams of laborers on foot, trailed by their wives and children, tramped the muddy roads to higher ground, fifteen or twenty miles away. They were joined by their more prosperous neighbors, whose horse-drawn carts were piled high with possessions. Nobles and clergy followed suit, fleeing to safe country estates. By the middle of January over twenty thousand people had departed. London was rapidly becoming a ghost town.

Electing to stay, the prior of Saint Bartholomew's built a tower-like structure on Harrow-on-the-Hill and provisioned it for two months. He also acquired several boats manned by expert rowers—just in case.

When the ill-fated day arrived, some braver souls stayed behind to watch. The soothsayers had predicted that the river would rise slowly, allowing those fleet enough to escape. The hour finally came and, to the consternation of the watchers, nothing happened. The tide quietly ebbed and flowed, and ebbed and flowed as it always had. An awareness slowly spread over the good people that they had been had. Still, to be safe, most stayed up that night and continued their watch.

The next morning, with the Thames continuing to flow peacefully within its banks, the crowd, joined by the returning evacuees, was boiling with fury. Many shouted to throw the pack of soothsayers into the river.

Fortunately, the prophets were prepared. In a clever maneuver —seemingly not lost on present-day chartists—they said they had scrupulously rechecked their calculations the previous night and found a minute error. London was most certainly doomed, the stars were, as always, undeniably right. But, because of the minor oversight, the great flood would occur in 1624, not 1524. The good townspeople could go home—at least for a while.[1]

This story, whose many variations have been replayed through history, has a great deal more to do with financial markets than you might at first think. In the last two chapters, we examined the most popular tools of present-day investors and found them wanting. Some might be dismissed almost on sight. Others, particularly thorough fundamental methods, such as those outlined by Graham and Dodd, seem far more logical. But although the tools appear to be practical, they rest on a bed of psychological quicksand. Without understanding how investors form opinions and the psychology that affects their decision making, people's odds are considerably reduced in the marketplace.

A good place to start examining what goes wrong with established investment methods is to observe how groups or crowds affect our ability to exercise independent judgment, even in areas where we think we can be totally objective. In this chapter, we will look at crowd behavior and how it can influence us as investors.

It is important to recognize that people in groups tend to be continually swept by one idea or trend after another. Sometimes, as

in the London of 1524, they have no supporting facts and still participate in crowd action that to an impartial observer borders on the
insane. On each occasion most people justify and often enthusiasti-
cally back the new thinking. While we can always look back and
shake our heads at group folly in the past, it is far harder to remain
unaffected by these influences in our own time.

The American Civil Liberties Union considered itself very brave
indeed to defend the right to demonstrate of a handful of Nazis in
1978, a group who—though thoroughly repugnant—represented no
real threat at the time. But at the height of McCarthyism during the
early 1950s, the ACLU was swept along like most people and refused
to defend suspected Communists. And while we may laugh at the
absurd carryings-on of the seventeenth-century Dutchmen who frantically sold their gold, jewelry, crops, and houses to buy tulip bulbs,
investors made remarkably similar decisions in the 1960s and 1970s
—only this time in stock rather than tulip markets.

To survive in the marketplace, it is essential to avoid being
carried away by the current mood of the crowd. The investor must
find some means of being able to withstand the tide—a task anything
but simple. It is necessary first to understand exactly how these
crowd influences affect investment decisions and why they are so
powerful. Armed with this knowledge, you can develop strategies
that should allow you not only to resist the pull of current opinion
but to take advantage of it.

Dr. LeBon's Crowd

The potent force of massed human beings is a phenomenon recognized since antiquity, one often discussed by the philosopher or
portrayed by the dramatist. Still, a more scientific analysis of crowd
behavior, like many other such philosophical curiosities, was not
undertaken until the latter part of the nineteenth century. Only then
did rigorous investigation begin.

In 1895 a Frenchman, Gustave LeBon, wrote what continues to
rank as one of the most incisive works on mass psychology, *The
Crowd.* According to LeBon, "The sentiments and ideas of all per-
sons in a gathering take one and the same direction, and their con-
scious personality vanishes. A collective mind is formed, doubtless

transitory, but presenting very clearly defined characteristics. The gathering has then become . . . a psychological crowd."[2] In such situations, the actions of individuals may be quite different from those the same individuals would consider when alone.

One of the most striking features of the crowd to LeBon was its great difficulty in separating the imagined from the real. "A crowd thinks in images, and the image itself calls up a series of other images, having no logical connection with the first . . . a crowd scarcely distinguishes between the subjective and the objective. It accepts as real the images invoked in its mind, though they most often have only a very distant relation with the observed facts. . . . Crowds being only capable of thinking in images are only to be impressed by images."[3]

At times, as LeBon saw, the image evokes cruel behavior; the belief in witches and sorcerers sent tens of thousands to the stake in the sixteenth and seventeenth centuries, and the "isms" of this century have taken tens of millions of lives. At other times, the image can inspire heroism, as in the crowd that swept the Bastille or the Republican crowd that with bare hands stormed the fascist Montana Barracks in Madrid in 1936. With the benefit of hindsight, the image may become droll, as when London was abandoned to the Thames. But, to capture the crowd, the image must always be extremely simple. LeBon believed the individual regresses in a crowd and "descends several rungs in the ladder of civilization. Isolated, he may be a cultivated individual; in a crowd he is a barbarian. He possesses the spontaneity, the violence, the ferocity, and also the enthusiasm and heroism of primitive beings."[4]

LeBon was an astute, if not particularly sympathetic, observer of crowds, and his description of crowd behavior is strikingly applicable to what we can readily discover taking place in financial markets. Certainly all the elements are present: numbers of people, intense excitement, and that essential simple image. Indeed, few images are more simple and yet as beguiling as *instant wealth*. Each such image carries the crowd far into the realm of fantasy, and sometimes beyond the boundaries of sanity. Despite the assumption of the rationality and omniscience of investors claimed by our academic friends, the last word on the subject often seems to be the roar of the crowd.

Each time, as LeBon foresaw, the image was not only simple and enticing, but seemingly infallible. And, as he predicted, people lost their individuality. Crowd contagion swept intellectuals, artists, nobles, and businessmen in every period as easily as it did the common people. Actually, those who should have known best often led the way. And so, to see just how strong its pull can be, we might look a little more closely at the behavior of crowds in the marketplace.

The Mississippi Scheme

The French, usually pacesetters in fashion, launched one of the first of the gigantic speculative manias, beginning in 1716. The Mississippi Company, as the venture was dubbed, resembled in many ways the classic "South Sea Bubble," which was soon to develop on the other side of the Channel.

The central character in the Mississippi Company was John Law, the son of a Scottish banker. A tall, dashing figure, Law had fled to the Continent with a death sentence on his head, the result of his having killed a rival in a duel over a love affair. Having studied banking in Amsterdam, Hamburg, Vienna, and Genoa, Law had a fairly sophisticated understanding of the use of credit. He was able to convince the French Regent of the merits of using paper money to lower interest rates, increase employment, and expand business. A national bank was established, which issued paper money up to twice the value of the country's gold and silver. The beginnings proved sound enough, and the bank prospered.

Law's vision, however, was much grander. Two years later, in 1718, he secured the right to the development of the vast Mississippi basin, then a territory of France.

Under Law's orchestration, a gigantic speculative bubble began to take shape. The stock in the new venture was first sold to the public on very attractive terms. Three quarters of the payment could be made in Louis XIV *billets des états* at face value, although this particular currency then traded at an almost 80 percent discount.

To eliminate any doubt as to the prosperity of the scheme, Law promised a dividend of 40 percent of the face value of the stock in the initial year. Using the discounted Louis XIV notes to subscribe, a shareholder would receive 120 percent of his investment in dividends alone in the first twelve months! This, and the lure of the Indies, proved too much. Few were bothered by the fact that the company was just starting and had no assets. Enthusiasm easily checkmated logic; three hundred thousand applications were made for the first fifty thousand shares. Dukes and marquises and comtes, with their duchesses, marchionesses, and comtesses, jostled in the streets with prostitutes and peddlers, seeking to subscribe. Some of the nobility took apartments while waiting their turn in order to avoid rubbing shoulders with the "great unwashed" around them.

The demand for the stock seemed inexhaustible. Law issued a steady stream of new shares at progressively higher prices. Only months after the original stock sale, a new issue was offered and was oversubscribed at 5,000 livres—ten times the initial price.

Law was an expert at painting the canvas of concept. To make the potential even more dazzling, he acquired the tobacco monopolies, as well as the East China, India, and Africa companies, and merged them all into the Mississippi Company. Indians were paraded through the streets of Paris, bedecked with gold and silver, to demonstrate the wealth of the territories. Engravings showing Louisianan mountains bursting with gold, silver, and precious stones were widely distributed.

The price rise of the Mississippi Company was breathtaking and in itself became almost hypnotic. "The tendency to look beyond the simple fact of increasing value to the reasons on which it depends greatly diminishes," wrote John Kenneth Galbraith of investor behavior in 1929.[5]

Professor Galbraith's wry observation is as apt for the rue de Quincampoix, where the stock was traded. Large crowds became acclimated to prices working constantly higher—day after day, week after week, and month after month. Previous and now "old-fashioned" standards of value were left far behind.

It was difficult for anyone to escape the the scheme's almost irresistible appeal, and few did. At the height of the frenzy in 1720, the Mississippi Company had appreciated forty times from the initial offering price of 500 livres in 1716. The market price of the shares was now worth eighty times all the gold and silver in France.*

*Madness, perhaps, in retrospect, but only a few years ago the experienced senior investment officers of America's largest and most powerful financial institutions did almost exactly the same thing. They decided that there were only fifty or so stocks to buy out of a total of twelve thousand public companies, and they bid them up to astronomical prices. Avon Products, for example, was valued for more than the entire U.S. steel industry, although it was dwarfed in size and profitability. At the time, the heads of these institutions, including Morgan Guaranty, Banker's Trust, and Citibank, vigorously defended the course they were following

The rue de Quincampoix was packed with speculators of all classes. Every available space was used for trading. A cobbler rented his stall to traders for ten times his normal wages. The rents for houses on the street rose twelve to sixteen fold from previous levels. Fortunes, naturally, were made—a banker was said to have made 100 million livres, a waiter 30 million. The word *millionaire* came into use for the first time.

The wild speculation took on many of the aspects of a carnival. Tents were erected to trade stock, to sell refreshments, and even to gamble. One man set up a roulette wheel in the midst of the packed throng and did a thriving business. The major roads leading to Paris were made almost impassable because of the masses trying to reach the city. Over three hundred thousand people came from the provinces to participate in the trading!

Law was idolized by the crowd. So great were the surrounding throngs anywhere he went that the Prince Regent provided him with a troop of lancers to clear the way. Enormous bribes were paid to his servants to get an interview with him, and even members of the aristocracy had to wait for weeks for an appointment. One lady drove around Paris for three days looking for Law, instructing her coachman to upset the carriage when he was sighted. When at last they tracked him down, the coach was driven into a post. It turned over, and the lady screamed shrilly to attract Law's attention. As Law came to her aid, she confessed the ruse and asked to subscribe to the next stock issue, to which he smilingly obliged.

Although Law exaggerated the opportunities, he did make a genuine effort to develop Louisiana and was successful in increasing French shipping, establishing new industries, and sharply raising French commercial activity. Nevertheless, the soaring prices of the Mississippi Company stock had little to do with the situation. When this awareness began to spread, a panic followed, in both the paper currency and the Mississippi shares.

LeBon was well aware of how swiftly the image guiding the crowd could change. "These image-like ideas," he wrote, "are not connected by any logical bond or analogy or successor, and may take each other's place like the slides of a Magic Lantern."[6] And so they

before Congress as "most prudent." As in the case of the Mississippi Company, both expert and average opinion was convinced that they had found the new Golconda. The subsequent performance of some of the more popular stocks is found in table 4, page 81.

did. The Mississippi shares, which previously represented spectacular riches, now meant doom.

Law attempted to stem the tide. Anticipating Cecil B. De Mille
by several centuries, he staged a spectacular in the streets of Paris.
Six thousand of the city's poorest inhabitants were pressed into
service, given new clothes, picks, and shovels, and marched through
the streets, presumably on the way to mine Louisiana gold. However,
even this major production stopped the panic for only a few days.

When the Mississippi bubble burst, the aftermath was devastating. First a few investors, then gradually more, and within weeks
almost all realized that the speculative frenzy was insane. A desper-
ate rush to sell began, but few buyers could be found. People now
focused on the emptiness of the scheme. Rumor again spread
through the rue de Quincampoix, this time that the company had few
assets and would be forced to omit its dividend entirely.

The image had changed for good. By late 1720 the stock had
fallen to 200 livres, some 99 percent below its peak only months
before. Law left the country in disgrace and died in obscurity nine
years later in Venice. To the end, he loved risk. No longer gambling
the economic stakes of one of the two most powerful nations on
earth, he was content to wager his few available shillings with pass-
ersby on whatever local action moved him.

What Is Social Reality?

The vision of the jeweled and powdered French dukes, comtes, and
marquises frantically scurrying about the rue de Quincampoix,
breathlessly followed by their duchesses, comtesses, and marchionesses, décolletage aheaving, may be amusing, but are there
lessons to be learned that also apply to modern markets?

History has shown that group madness need not last for only
brief periods. The fear of the flooding of the Thames occurred over
many months, the Mississippi bubble was in full bloom for four or
five years, and the persecution of witches and sorcerers went on for
centuries. In each of these cases, the image created its own reality,
reshaping the perceptions, actions, and attitudes of the crowd. How
were such strange realities brought into being and nurtured, and why
should supposedly rational people succumb so easily to them?

Social psychologists tell us that our beliefs, values, and attitudes can be thought to lie along a continuum. At one extreme are those based on indisputable physical evidence—if I throw a crystal goblet against a wall, it will shatter; or if I point my skis straight down a long, steep slope, it's pretty unlikely I'll reach the bottom intact. Such outcomes, termed physical reality, are abundantly clear and don't require other people's confirmation.

At the other end of the continuum are beliefs and attitudes that, although important to us, lack firm support. What facts are available are sparse and difficult to evaluate. In this category are such questions as the existence of God, whether there is a "best" political system, or, of primary interest here, what a stock or the market is really worth at a point in time.

Psychologists have demonstrated that the vaguer and more complex a situation, the more we rely on other people whose intelligence we respect, both for clarification and as standards against which to judge the correctness of our own views. This helps us reduce the uncertainty we have toward our own beliefs. Most investors, for example, attempting to assimilate many contradictory facts in order to put a value on the Mississippi Company shares, undoubtedly sought the opinions of other intelligent investors to form their own assessments. When people use others as yardsticks against which to determine the correctness of their own views, they are utilizing what psychologists call social comparison processes.

We can do this in very commonplace ways, rarely giving it a second thought. I was once in a Middle Eastern restaurant in New York where the men's and ladies' rooms were marked with what to me were unintelligible symbols. I was momentarily puzzled, until a man who obviously knew where he was going strolled confidently through one of the doors, solving my problem. Or consider the case of the *Wall Street Journal* reporter who wrote of a recent dinner he and his wife had with a desert sheik. After the meal, two other distinguished Western guests sat back and belched heartily. The reporter and his wife, guessing that this was the proper sign of approval for the hearty fare, followed suit with gusto.

Similarly, a speaker may gauge the worth of his talk from the audience's reaction. After one of his speeches, Lincoln, judging from what he thought was the indifferent response of the crowd, turned to a friend and said, "It's a flat failure and the people are disappointed." The speech was the Gettysburg Address.[7]

The greater the anxiety is and the more indeterminate the situation appears to be, the more readily we rely on the behavior of others to gauge the proper course, treating much of the information we receive from them as being no less real than if we had directly observed it from physical reality. We thus forget its personal and tentative nature.

The term *social reality* refers to how a group of people perceive reality. As Leon Festinger, who first proposed the theory, described it: "When the dependence upon physical reality is low, the dependence on social reality is correspondingly high. An opinion, attitude, or belief is 'correct, valid, and proper' to the extent that it is anchored in the group of people with similar beliefs, opinions, and attitudes."[8] The ensuing social reality can then be a strange amalgam of objective criteria and crowd fancy. Facts, such as are available, can be twisted or distorted entirely to conform with prevailing opinions.

And this brings us back to the strange aberrations of people in crowds that we have seen in this chapter. In each instance, the information was vague, sometimes complex, and anxiety producing to the people of the time. Few standards existed to help them. Fortune-tellers may have been right in some of their earlier prophecies, establishing their credibility for the new auguries. During the Mississippi Scheme, one could see the substantial gains made by those who bought early, and that noblemen, confidants of the Regent, and shrewd businessmen were buying the stock—most said the price rise was only beginning.

People then as now were uncertain, sometimes anxious, and as a result wanted to compare their opinions with those of other individuals whom they respected. Great numbers were drawn by the need to verify their individual views into conformity with the group's beliefs; the larger the nucleus of the group, the greater the attraction of its beliefs to those who had initially resisted them.

Just how easily people's behavior can be influenced by others in uncertain and even mildly anxiety-producing circumstances can be seen from the following laboratory experiment of S. Schacter's.[9] Subjects were injected with a drug called epinephrine, which temporarily causes heart palpitations and hand shaking. The subjects were told that the drug was a vitamin supplement called "Suproxin." In each case, the subject was placed in a room with a stooge, planted there by the experimenters, who allegedly had also been injected with "Suproxin." With no forewarning, the subject searched for an explanation as his heart beat faster and his hands began to tremble. He started to watch the stooge, who, as you can guess, was not inactive. In one case, he behaved lightheartedly, singing, dancing, constructing and flying paper planes, in general acting in a high-spirited, zany way. Other subjects were each put in a room with a stooge who was gloomy and morose, made angry remarks, complained about a questionnaire both were filling out, and in a sudden fit of pique, ripped his up.

How did the subjects react? Feeling the effects of the drug, and watching the behavior of the stooges, the great majority adapted behavior patterns to match.

The record outside of the laboratory is not much different. Because there are so few objective guidelines, social reality has always had a merry time in the fashion world, for males and females alike. At the turn of the century, the dictate was for women's hemlines to drag along the ground; in other periods, they were well above the knee. In the late nineteenth century, to be *au courant* demanded an exceptionally narrow waist (seventeen or eighteen inches), and many a poor woman had her floating rib removed to conform to the dictate. In 1943 so many women tried to imitate the hairdo covering one eye of then-reigning film queen Veronica Lake that, according to United Press International, "the Federal Government branded her a menace to the war effort; it claimed too many lady airplane workers imitating her peek-a-boo bob had scalped themselves in the machinery."[10]

Crowd fashions and fads are no different today. Take jogging, for example. It may be healthy—the jury still seems out here—but it has certainly become contagious. It has mainly taken over from the previous physical fitness exercises, such as jumping rope (very "in" several years ago, but now advised against by some doctors because it may cause shin splints), yoga, and the RCAF-X4 plan.

Whether it's on a quiet Vermont byway or early morning in Riverside Park, there is a strong likelihood of meeting someone jogging these days. Many a poor middle-aged businessman or matron goes through the motions, panting heavily, tongue hanging out and eyes bulging, all supposedly in the name of physical fitness. Fashionable jogging outfits costing $175 or more are sold at Bergdorf Goodman and Saks Fifth Avenue. And the elegant ladies of the East Side now lunch at expensive restaurants while sporting their faultlessly tailored jogging wear, never for a moment meant to be sweated in.

Perhaps this isn't a fad—but already numbers of books on walking are being readied for release.*

Does the same hold true of past fashions in the marketplace? Uncertainty, anxiety, lack of objective reality, and sudden and violent shifts in the image of the group were certainly integral to crowd behavior here too. Each interpretation of what was realistic was established and maintained by the consensus of the group. In every mania the group was injected (in a manner not unlike the epinephrine experiment) with an image of spectacular wealth, which changed its behavior. This new social reality was fabricated of the dreams, hopes, and greed of many thousands of investors. Many watching a particular bubble saw as much clearly. Yet most could still believe that things really would be different this time . . .

The Reality of 1962

Let's next stop briefly at the Wall Street of 1962 to examine the workings of social reality on modern investment crowds. Are they any different from those of years past?

After the 1929 crash speculative fervor burned out for a generation. In fact, the Dow didn't break its 1929 high of 381 until November of 1954, at which time the nation was prosperous, industrial activity was increasing, and consumer income was rising, as were corporate earnings and dividends. The market, with only a few minor setbacks, continued to work solidly higher through the balance of the decade. "Time," Disraeli wrote, "is the Great Physician." And so it was. A new generation of investors, untutored in the lessons of disaster that their parents had learned, was now firmly at the helm. Confident of the future, they were intrigued with the tremendous investment opportunities that were present in the dynamic—pre-Arthur Burns—economy.

Just as the eighteenth-century investors were propelled by the unlimited wealth of the New World, so modern investors now saw the possibility of unlimited profits through modern science. Because of these expectations, the major technology companies of the time— IBM, Xerox, Polaroid, and Texas Instruments—commanded towering prices.

*One title: *Walk, Don't Run.*

Even more striking, when viewed with the hindsight of seventeen years, was the 1961–62 period's enormous similarity to the English South Sea Bubble of the early eighteenth century—in the willingness of people to buy almost any new venture. In 1720, companies that made wheels of perpetual motion or converted gold from lead were in demand. In 1961–62, esoteric technological companies exerted enormous appeal. Whether it was alchemy in the first place or science in the second didn't matter much, as investors understood the prospects of each equally well. The crowd on the cobblestones in Exchange Alley, where the bubble companies traded, or watching the action on luminous electronic tapes in the boardrooms of space-age America behaved the same.

The beginnings, as usual, were sound enough. Many small technological companies sold to the public in the 1950s showed spectacular appreciation. An investment of $1,000 in Control Data when it was first offered in 1958 was worth $121,000 by 1961. The same $1,000 put into Litton Industries in the mid-1950s moved up fiftyfold during that period. Seeing these profits and believing in the unlimited wealth to be gained in anything scientific, investors scrambled to buy the shares of any small company that was being offered to the public for the first time. A frenzied new-issues boom took place in 1960 and 1961. All that was required was that the company be in electronics, computers, medical technology, or pharmaceuticals. Any company ending in "ics" or "tron" was enthusiastically bid up. Nytronics, Bristol Dynamics, and Supronics shot to immediate premiums. Some of the gains were spectacular: Dynatronics was issued at 7 and rose to 25 instantly; Risitron Laboratories went from 1 to 3⅞. Simulmatics, a company incorporated only two years earlier and with a negative net worth of $21,000, was offered at 2 and immediately quoted at 9.

The public appetite for such stocks was almost insatiable. One elderly woman called her broker to buy shares in "Hebrew National Electronics." The broker explained that the company was not in electronics at all, but was a kosher meat packer and processor. She accepted the news with disappointment and a tinge of anger. Several months later, when the stock had also moved up, she again phoned the broker. "They are too in the electronics business!" she said indignantly. "They sell electronic salami slicers."[11]

As the fever spread, new issues were underwritten in many industries outside technology. The boardrooms were filled to overflowing, and the talk on commuter trains and in theater lobbies was of hot new issues and the best little underwriting houses.

Promoters, not really very different animals in 1962 from what they had been in 1718, understood the appetites of the crowd and scoured the countryside for acceptable merchandise. "Why go broke? Go public," the prospective underwriting client was told. Shopworn goods were rechristened with sparkling new space-age names. Many of the hottest underwriting firms were one- or two-man companies.

The mania was intensified by the underwriters' advertising of the success of their merchandise. One firm, Michael Lomasney and Company, ran an ad that stated that had an investor purchased $1,000 of each of the sixteen issues it had underwritten in the past eighteen months, he or she would have had $36,800 by September of 1961. This was topped by another small underwriting firm, Globus, Inc., with offices, appropriately enough, on Madison Avenue. "If you bought each of Globus' issues," their ad rang, "you would have tripled your money by late 1961." The froth danced higher and higher.

This was, of course, a house of cards, but nobody seemed to notice—or care. With money being made at every turn, a stream of how-to literature came off the printing presses. Nicolas Darvas, a gypsy dancer, wrote a book entitled *How I Made Two Million Dollars in the Stock Market.* Another writer published a book modestly promising *How to Make a Killing on Wall Street.* *

The realization came, as always, that this was a fool's paradise. By the latter part of 1961, speculative ardor had cooled noticeably. In the sharp break of April–May 1962, a panic enveloped the new bubble companies. While the market recovered in short order and went on to new highs, most of the underwritings traded at pittances of the former values. An SEC study of five hundred randomly selected issues offered in the 1950s and early 1960s showed that 12 percent had simply vanished, 43 percent had gone bankrupt, 25 percent were operating at a loss, while only 20 percent displayed any earnings whatever. Of the latter, there were only twelve which had

*Even the art world was unable to avoid the get-rich-quick craze. One service—the Art Market Guide and Forecaster—put together an average of five hundred artists and called it the AMG index, after its own initials. One ad read: "With the art market for paintings up 97 percent since the war—and 65 percent in the last year alone—you can lose immense profits by failing to keep informed of the monetary value of art, present and future."[12]

any real promise. Social reality had led the crowd down the same strange path in 1962 as it had in 1720.

The Compellingness of Crowd Opinion

Why do social comparison processes produce an investor consensus that is often so far off the mark? Part of the answer seems to lie in how easily people's opinions are drawn together under conditions of uncertainty.

An excellent experiment to show this was devised by psychologist Muzafer Sherif.[13] Sherif took advantage of the little-known autokinetic light phenomenon. A tiny pinpoint of light beamed for a few seconds in a darkened room appears to move, although in fact it is stationary. Sherif asked his subjects to calculate the extent of the movement as carefully as possible. (Since the light appeared to be moving, the subjects believed it actually did.) With no reference points upon which to anchor judgment in the blackened room, individuals gave answers ranging from a few inches to eighty feet—the latter subject believed he was in a gymnasium rather than a small room.

After one hundred trial sets, the median guess of each subject was recorded. Figure 12 on page 72 shows that it ranged from one to over eight inches (as the line on the extreme left of both charts indicates). However, when subjects were brought together, the judgments converged. Figure 12(a) indicates the amount of convergence there was in each succeeding one-hundred-test figure with two people present; figure 12(b) with three. In the latter case, from individual medians varying from under an inch to almost eight inches, the group's convergence by the third one-hundred-set test moved to slightly over two inches.

Sherif added another variable by including a confederate. If the subject estimated the light moved twenty inches, the confederate might estimate two. His influence was enormous. By the end of the trials, most subjects' estimates came very close to those of the confederates, which remained stable throughout.

Writing of these experiments, psychologist William Samuels noted: "The majority of subjects in such studies indicate little awareness that their perceptions have been manipulated by the estimates

Figure 12.
Convergence of opinion in light-movement experiment.

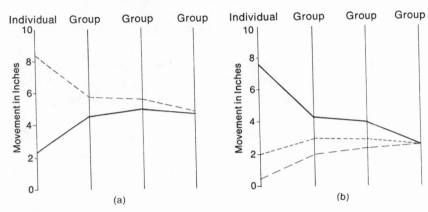

SOURCE: Figures from pages 208 and 209 in *Social Psychology* by Muzafer Sherif and Carolyn W. Sherif. Copyright © 1969 by Muzafer Sherif and Carolyn W. Sherif.

of others, for they maintain that they had previously made their own estimates *before the others spoke.* The influence process then may be a rather subtle phenomenon. Partners who are well liked, who have high status, who are reputed to be competent on the judgmental task, or who merely exude self-confidence when announcing their estimates are all especially effective in influencing a subject's personal norm of movements."[14]

It is also interesting to see how much a naive subject's judgment could be shifted under subtle manipulation—as much as 80 percent or more without pressure of any sort. Because one of the prime features of the stock market is uncertainty, opinions frequently move toward a consensus and, not unlike the autokinetic light experiment, toward the most authoritative-sounding or outspoken points of view available at the time—usually those of the experts, whose record we already know. Then throw in anxiety, another very powerful force leading toward consensus. During the best of times the stock market is uncertain and difficult, and in its worst moments can induce first-rate terror. People find it natural under such circumstances to take comfort and security in the opinions of savvy, smart money. Small wonder that the consensus of the many appears to be a refuge, not a trap.

Earlier, we saw just how elusive the anchor of objective reality and the concept of value on which it is based actually are. It is not surprising, then, given the nature of the psychological forces at work, that we too can often find ourselves dashing frantically down a rue de Quincampoix, an Exchange Alley, or a Wall Street . . . which brings me to the next wild adventure: the "go-go" market of 1967–68.

God Has Been Good to Solitron Devices

The fascinating yet disturbing aspect of financial manias, knowing what we know about social comparison processes, is that few lessons can be learned from the past. The same mistakes made in almost the same fashion inevitably crop up again and again.

Looking back at the bizarre speculative period of a decade ago, one might feel almost as though the clock had stopped at the height of the 1961 enthusiasm and only started ticking again in 1967. Investors resumed the previous speculation at an increasingly intensified pitch, with all memory of the previous crash seemingly erased. Remarkably an even larger new-issues boom commenced, and interest again focused on many of the now familiar technology stocks of 1962 —Xerox, Polaroid, Texas Instruments, and IBM.

This was the time when youth took over Wall Street. With youth came changes in the investment game: value was no longer to be found in the stodgy blue chips favored by their elders. The action now was with new issues, growth stocks, and concept stocks. A group of sideburned, flamboyantly dressed young men in their twenties and thirties came to the helm. They were the freewheeling, high-spirited embodiments of the times who were determined to clear out the dogma, error, and cobwebs of the past. Called "gunslingers," the new breed was out to change the world with the sureness of their instincts and the quickness of their reactions. They believed that rapid moves in and out of stocks led to exceptional results. Often entire portfolios would be turned over two or three times a year. This new style of buying or selling was called "go-go" investing. The sole objective was "performance," which meant achieving higher returns than the market averages and competing gunslingers.

In the deadly competition that soon developed, all bench marks of fiduciary responsibility were forgotten. Criticism that the new methods were highly speculative was tossed aside, in the words of one gunslinger, "as coming from the cultural alienation of an outdated generation."

On Wall Street a new tide of folk heroes moved in—Gerald Tsai, Fred Carr, Fred Mates, Fred Alger, and John Hartwell, to name a few. They were often treated with awe by the financial press and the public—at the time, it seemed, with good reason. Gerald Tsai, the initial go-go star, used rapid-fire trading to increase the Fidelity Growth Fund, which he managed, by 65 percent in 1965. Starting his own Manhattan Fund in 1967, he doubled the 20 percent rise in the averages. But Tsai's performance was dull when compared with many of the others. Fred Carr's Enterprise Fund rose 118 percent in that same year as he moved stocks in and out of his portfolio at a breathtaking rate. In one quarter Enterprise traded two hundred companies, more than some staid mutual funds turned over in a decade. In late 1968 the Mates Fund of Fred Mates was up a stunning 158 percent for the year.

Many of the new breed assiduously avoided the major industrial giants, "buggywhip companies," as they were sometimes contemptuously called. At the height of the go-go market in 1968, when numbers of concept companies had gone up twenty-five or even fifty fold, giant AT&T made an eight-year low. One money manager summed it up in *Forbes:* "Excitement, not solidity, is what makes stocks move now." Again social reality took hold and investors frolicked away, unfettered by the time-tested standards of the past.

The gunslingers bristled with confidence. John Hartwell, who in 1968 managed $425 million, ignored the prudent policy of wide diversification, stating: "If you have more than half a dozen positions in an account of, say, $500,000, it only means you are not sharp enough to pick winners."[15]

All eyes were focused on relative performance. The winners of the go-go derby would receive large flows of funds from the enthusiastic public, while the losers would have the money quickly taken away. In spite of its excellent record, Gerald Tsai's Manhattan Fund had net redemptions in 1968 as the public moved into better-performing vehicles, such as those of Fred Carr and Fred Mates. As one manager phrased it: "In this market, the crowd is betting on the jockeys, not the horses."

Outstanding fund managers could make a million dollars or more a year, and they lived high—gold faucets in bathrooms, fifteen-room penthouses on Park Avenue or in The Dakota, and summer homes on the Adriatic. Because of the public's obsession with them, performance rankings became the go-go manager's lifeblood. Fred Alger once flew to Europe to protest to Bernie Cornfeld, then running the vast International Overseas Fund network, that one month he was ranked number two rather than number one because of a typographical error. The mistake was immediately corrected.

Performance was achieved mainly by financial sleight of hand. Substantial gains were made by buying large blocks of thinly traded companies, pushing them higher. Legions of admirers usually followed in the wake of the go-go stars, making the price rise: a self-fulfilling prophecy for a while. Because of their tremendous ability to generate commissions, the major go-go managers would get large blocks of hot new stocks at the issue price, which immediately went to substantial premiums, generating instant profits on their books. The gunslingers would also buy letter stock—stock not authorized to be traded in public markets—at a substantial discount. The discount would often be two thirds or more of the going market price. The fund would immediately revalue the stock at a one-third discount from the market, and—*voilà*—a 100 percent profit.

It is a tribute to the power of a speculative frenzy that though these and many other practices were widely known and sometimes criticized at the time, very few people seemed to care how questionable the gains really were. Only the "bottom line" mattered—that the funds were performing well.

The rapid trading of huge blocks of stock made this the golden age of the brokerage firm. Many an institutional salesman who could scarcely distinguish an asset from a liability made six figures a year from his gunslinger clients, and most fully believed they deserved it. One fellow became a brief legend by leaving a hundred-dollar tip after a single round of drinks.

The gunslinger's mode of operation was simplicity itself. One merely had to have an exciting story and a record of rapid sales and earnings growth to substantiate it. Almost no attention was paid to how real the earnings actually were. And it was, again, the day of the black-box operation. Companies in technology were bid up to astronomical prices as investors envisioned futures of limitless growth. The chairman of one small technology company that had multipled tenfold in price told his annual meeting in 1968: "God has been good to Solitron Devices."

Money managers and clients alike became intoxicated by the gains. One investor, dazzled by the sensational promises of the go-go managers, went to his investment advisor, David Babson, a crusty old New Englander, and told him his objective was no less than 40 to 60 percent a year. For the previous ten years, Babson had increased his client's money at a not unimpressive 10 percent rate to $126,000. To illustrate the absurdity of his client's request, Babson showed him that a 40 percent rate of growth would have resulted in this sum becoming $100 million in twenty years, while a 60 percent rate of growth would have made it $1.5 billion!

For those of us playing at the time (I had come to Wall Street a year or so earlier), it was indeed the golden age. Everywhere the atmosphere was giddy with success. Almost any investment we tried, be it computer service, uranium exploration, or flight safety instruments, worked out, and many did spectacularly. With our stocks quadrupling, several going up tenfold, and one over fiftyfold, it was hard not to attribute the gains to our intelligence and surefootedness.

The longer the odds, the more sensational the payout. The favorites went up even more than the Mississippi Company over a similar period of time. With so much money being made so quickly, it was almost impossible not to be sucked into the speculative whirlpool, and not many resisted.

All around us, thousands of professionals wrote research reports condoning the current price movements and recommending a plethora of exciting new opportunities. As experiments have shown, the expert's support of a concept more firmly locks it into place. Very often people are persuaded by a message, not because of its compelling logic but because they consider the communicator an expert.* (Thus the old adage of the singer, not the song.) Not only were the experts bullish, but their record of success in the immediate past was good, further enhancing their credibility.

Once again, as in the 1920s, everybody talked stocks. One of my friends (let's call him Peter) was at the time in group therapy —he said to straighten himself out, but from our talks it seemed more likely to meet new, interesting women. Whatever the case, the red-hot market permeated the group. Peter, both intelligent and articulate and not in the least reluctant to express his views, quickly became the center of attention. The sessions, under the encouragement of the analyst, an avid investor himself, turned

*Those interested might see, for example, S. E. Asch, "The Doctrines of Suggestion, Prestige, and Social Psychology," *Psychological Review* (No. 55, 1948): 150–177; and C. I. Hovland, I. L. Janis, and H. H. Kelley, *Communication and Persuasion* (New Haven, Conn.: Yale University Press, 1953).

more and more into stock-picking seminars. One diffident middle-aged businessman had joined the group because he believed himself a financial failure. He bought one of my friend's suggestions, University Computing, and saw it rise fortyfold. Buying more and more on margin as the price shot up, he became the ultimate business success, a multimillionaire. The transformation in his self-confidence was amazing, so much so that Peter now had trouble maintaining his position as group guru. But the businessman's fantasy was most temporal—the stock eventually led him to bankruptcy, whereupon Peter was made to return the Piaget watch he had been given in appreciation. At this point, my friend wisely turned to computer dating, which he hoped would better provide self-realization.

Some authorities became alarmed at the level of speculation. The American Stock Exchange, on which many of the smaller and more speculative companies traded, published a list in February 1969 of 109 speculative companies in which it forbade members to trade for their own accounts.[16] Former SEC chairman Manuel Cohen said at the time: "Frankly, I would have liked the AMEX to have applied the ban to all of its securities." However, most defended the reality of the moment. As one market expert wrote in a major financial magazine:

NEW ENVIRONMENT

I would therefore like to propose the thesis that as the result of all that has been happening in the economy, the world, and the market during the last decade, we are at least in a different—if not a new—era and traditional thinking, the standard approach to the market, is no longer in synchronization with the real world.

Possibly the market ought to be considered as having gone into a sort of orbit in outer space, in the sense that while we can see how we got where we are, we really have never been here before, and therefore cannot be certain of what happens next.[17]

This seems to most clearly summarize the thinking of all investors in all manias. When the 1968 bubble finally burst, it was the most severe crash since 1929. Forty-seven billion dollars, or three times the amount lost on Black Tuesday, 1929, vanished in thirty highfliers alone. Most of the speculative favorites fared even more poorly. National Student Marketing dropped from 140 to 3½, Solitron Devices (whom the Lord apparently no longer favored) from

286 to 10¼, Parvan Dohrman from 142 to 14, and Four Seasons Nursing Homes from 110 to zero!

Gone were the performance stocks, along with most of the high-living performance managers. Many of my own friends lost not only their profits, which were sometimes thirty to forty times their original investments, but their initial stakes as well. I was luckier, but it did take some stomach-wrenching weeks of large losses to set off the warning bells of the imminent danger. Like everyone else, in spite of all I had read about crowd manias, I found it hard to believe that this wonderful orbit in outer space was over.

Last Year's Bubble

Finally, for those of you who might think that bubbles, even those of a decade earlier, are now ancient history, we might briefly look at one that has been taking place recently. The new mania is, appropriately enough, in gambling stocks, and investors have played it with as much gusto as any in the past.

With the legalization of gambling in Atlantic City, and the opening of the first casino there by Resorts International in late May 1978, speculative money poured into the gambling stocks. It didn't matter that the record of many was lackluster at best, and that some were operating deep in the red. People saw only large profits ahead. Again, all past standards of value were forgotten as the gambling

Table 3
GAMBLING STOCK COMPARISONS

	PRICE 12/30/77	SEPTEMBER 1978 HIGH	PERCENTAGE INCREASED FROM BEGINNING OF YEAR
Resorts International B	22¾	325	1,428
Resorts International A	22½	210	933
Caesar's World	6⅞	68	989
Golden Nugget	5¾	44⅝	776
Playboy	7½	32¾	436
Bally	17¾	71¾	412

NOTE: Adapted from "Up and Down Wall Street," *Barron's*, September 5, 1978.

stocks skyrocketed. Just how much some of them soared is shown in table 3.

Resorts International's A stock went up over nine times, and its thinly traded B stock rose fourteenfold.* As a bench mark, back in 1720 the English South Sea Company (considered by many to be one of the classic speculative outbursts) appreciated 813 percent in roughly the same period of time.

It didn't matter how many new casinos were to be built in Atlantic City—threatening Resorts International's highly profitable temporary monopoly. Speculators believed the more casinos, the better—a greater number would attract larger throngs, and each would coin gold. The players happily bid up any company that had any intention of building in Atlantic City, and many that did not.

It also didn't matter that stocks that had tripled, quadrupled, quintupled, or risen even more had only the remotest connection to gambling, if any at all. As *Barron's* editor Alan Abelson pointed out on September 4, 1978, Allied Leisure, whose stock had risen from 1½ on July 31, 1978, to 6⅝ one month later, was actually in Chapter 11 (bankruptcy proceedings) the previous year. Speculators were betting that the company, which made "some form of coin-operated amusement devices," would benefit if gambling was legalized in Florida. The price action showed few considered that even if gambling was sanctioned, Florida companies would have no monopoly on such devices and this one couldn't even earn a profit.

Even a maker of tombstones got into the act by announcing it was considering investing in a casino in Atlantic City. From a low of 2¼ in late December 1977, the stock moved as high as 25 before entombing numbers of investors as it again dropped well under 10 by November of 1978.[18] Despite numerous warnings, speculation continued to roll merrily along.

Once again, although valuations bordered on the insane, the speculation had a momentum all its own. Men who clearly saw the absurdity of current prices and moved too soon were stung as in manias past. One of the Street's ablest money managers, who reputedly ran up a personal fortune once approaching $40 million from six figures a decade earlier, quickly grasped the unsoundness and

*In no small measure due to a short squeeze: people who had sold the stock short could find no stock to borrow with the small amount of B stock outstanding, and were forced to buy it at much higher prices.

tried to profit from it by selling short. He lost an estimated $10 to $15 million.[19]

While the full story has not been played out to the time of this writing, it's likely that the current bubble will end like all of the others, with the image of instant wealth suddenly and violently disappearing.

Not Very Different

All manias, though separated by centuries, have had surprisingly similar characteristics. They started in prosperous economies, where people were looking for new investment opportunities and wanted to believe they existed. Each mania had sound beginnings and was based on a simple but intriguing concept. The rise in prices, in every case, became a self-fulfilling prophecy, attracting more and more people into the speculative vortex. Rumor always played a major role, at first of fortunes made and of good things to come, and later in prophecies of doom. In almost every case, the experts were caught up in the speculation, condoning the price rises and predicting much higher levels in the future. At the height of both the 1961 and the 1967–68 markets, money managers stated that the valuation standards of the past no longer applied—things really were different this time. And on both occasions, the statements were uttered shortly before the end.

Another point common to all speculative manias is the greater fool theory. Some of the more independent or cynical thinkers were not in fact overwhelmed by the consensus thinking of the time. They believed stocks should never have reached the preposterous levels that they had, that the crowd really was mad. But they thought it would get madder still (if a portfolio had gone up sixfold, why not eightfold or even tenfold?). There would thus be a chance to profit from the folly, which would only become more outrageous. Thus wrote British Member of Parliament James Milner in 1720 after being bankrupted by the South Sea Bubble: "I said indeed that ruin must soon come upon us but I owe it came two months earlier than I expected."[20] Not very different from the *Dun's Review* article at the height of the 1968 market, 248 years later: "The overriding question at the moment is: how long can a speculative boom go on? How

Table 4
MARKET FAVORITES FROM DIFFERENT ERAS

	HIGH PRICE	LOW PRICE	PRICE DECLINE FROM HIGH (IN PERCENT)
Holland, 1637			
Semper Augustus	5,500[a]	50[a]	99
(tulip bulb)			
England, 1720			
South Sea Company	1,050[b]	129[b]	88
France, 1720			
Mississippi Company	18,000[c]	200[c]	99
1929–32			
Air Reduction	233	31	86
Burroughs	97	6¼	94
Case	467	17	96
General Electric	201	8½	96
General Motors	115	7⅝	94
Montgomery Ward	158	3½	98
1961–62			
AMF	66⅜	10	84
Automatic Canteen	45⅝	9¾	79
Brunswick	74⅞	13⅛	82
Lionel	37⅞	4½	88
Texas Instruments	207	49	76
Transition	42⅜	6¼	85
1967–70			
ITEK	172	17	90
Leasco Data Processing	57	7	88
Ling-Temco-Vought	135	7	95
Litton Industries	104	15	86
National Student Marketing	143	3½	98
University Computing	186	13	93
1971–72			
Avon	140	18⅝	87
Clorox	53	5½	90
Disney	119⅛	16⅝	86
Levitz Furniture	40¼	3⅞	90
MGIC	97⅞	6⅛	94
Polaroid	149½	14⅛	91

[a]Florins.
[b]Pounds sterling.
[c]Livres.

many months, investors and dealers ask, before we see a repeat of 1962?"[21] Even knowing this, most found it impossible to stop.

As speculation grew more widespread, it became the major topic of the day. In almost every period, credit was abundant and cheap. Near the end, prices rose sharply and turnover increased markedly. Finally, there was a sudden shift in the social reality, resulting in a panic that carried prices far below those initially prevailing. It's also interesting to see the similarity in the declines in each of the speculative manias. As table 4 on page 81 shows, all are on the order of 90 percent.

Four general principles seem to emerge from a study of financial speculations. First, an irresistible image of instant wealth is always presented that draws a financial crowd into existence. Second, a social reality is created that blinds most people to the dangers of the mania. Opinions converge and become "facts." Experts become leaders approving events and strongly exhorting the crowd on. Overconfidence becomes dominant, and standards of conduct and the experience of many years are quickly forgotten. Third, the LeBon image of the magic lantern suddenly changes and anxiety replaces overconfidence. The distended bubble breaks with an ensuing panic. And fourth, we do not, as investors, learn from past mistakes—things really do seem very different each time, although in fact each set of circumstances was remarkably similar to the last.

As we have seen, even though the investors of the 1960s and 1970s were armed with exacting fundamental tools, these did not save them from behaving in a fashion almost identical to the frenzied English and French of centuries earlier.

Is there some way to resist the crowd? That was the question that led to the search for a new investment method on my part, a method based on psychological as well as financial principles, for the former are at least as important in handling the problems raised. As we'll see next, the trouble lies in the methods used by sophisticated investors. Rather than making them experts in handling speculative excesses, the techniques very often result in their leading the stampede.

CHAPTER FIVE

The Not-So-Expert Expert

We have just seen how easy it is under conditions of uncertainty to follow the prevailing uppers and downers of the crowd. But it is still unclear what launches these lemminglike drives and why experts, in spite of their training, prove as susceptible as (if not more so than) the average investor in leaping into the torrent. Warren Buffett, the highly successful money manager we met earlier, posed precisely this question in 1965 and concluded: "Curiously enough, there is practically nothing in the literature of Wall Street attacking the problem, and discussion of it is virtually absent at Security Analysts Society meetings, conventions, seminars, etc."[1] Almost a decade and a half later, there are still no good answers. We shall shortly see why.

Buffett's question had a much more universal ring than he may have perhaps thought at the time. Almost all of us have learned in our school days of classic miscalculations experts have sometimes made. Lord Cardigan hardly demonstrated the benefit of an extensive military background when he led the Light Brigade, well bedecked with blue ribbons for beautiful horseflesh, steeplechasing, and musical riding, into the barrels of three hundred Russian cannon at Balaklava. Nor was Yale economist Irving Fischer's comment "Stocks are now at what looks like a permanently high plateau," uttered a few days before Black Tuesday, 1929, the brightest financial statement of the century. The same might be said for the political judgment of Neville Chamberlain, standing at Croydon Airport upon his return from Munich, waving a document, and shouting, "I bring you peace in our time."

The illusion of expert invincibility is one that most of us put behind us long ago. What had not been known until recently is that under certain conditions, *experts err predictably and often.* There is a consistency to the mistakes made by professionals in fields as diverse as psychology, engineering, and publishing. And, as we shall see in this chapter and the next, the conditions for such errors are as fertile in the stock market as anywhere.

The problem of expert failure can be traced to man's capabilities as an information processor. Just how much information he can handle effectively under varying circumstances has come under intense scrutiny in recent decades, and some of the results are striking. We will see that the vast storehouses of data about companies, industries, and the economy that current methods require the investor to comprehend may not always give him or her an extra "edge." In fact, ingesting large amounts of investment information can lead to making worse rather than better decisions. Impossible? At the end of the chapter, you'll see that the favorite stocks and industries of large groups of professional investors, chosen by exactly the methods we are questioning, fared far more poorly than the averages over an almost fifty-year period.

To outdo the market, then, we must first have a good idea of the forces that time and again victimize even the pros. Once these forces are understood, the investor can build defenses and find routes that skirt the pitfalls.

The Not-So-Expert Expert

Just how good is man as a processor of information, and where does he run into trouble? Nobel Laureate Herbert Simon, one of the pioneers and leaders in the field, has studied both questions intensely over more than four decades. According to Simon, "Every human organism lives in an environment which generates millions of new bits of information every second, but the bottleneck of the perceptual apparatus certainly does not admit more than 1,000 bits per second, and possibly much less."[2] We react consciously to only a minute portion of the information that is thrown at us. But Simon states that even the filtering process is not a passive activity which provides a pretty reasonable representation of the real world, but "an active process involving attention to a very small part of the whole and the exclusion from the outset of all that is not within the scope of our attention."[3]

Simon notes: "The capacity of the human mind for formulating and solving complex problems is very small compared with the size of the problems whose solution is required."[4]

Researchers in many fields began to ponder whether such cognitive limitations actually existed, and if they did, how they might affect the decision-making process in their own disciplines. Could they, as Simon may suggest, result in a serious curtailment of the professional to carry out his responsibilities effectively in a complex field?

Some of the first experiments in cognitive limitation were conducted in the field of clinical psychology, which, like psychiatry, requires the practitioner to make complex diagnostic decisions if proper treatment is to be administered. One of the pioneer investigators was Paul Meehl. In the late 1940s and early 1950s, Meehl made twenty separate surveys of groups of clinical psychologists who, after thorough examinations, recommended treatment for psychotic and schizophrenic patients.[5] In each case the groups of psychologists made predictions of how they believed the patients would respond to the particular treatment they prescribed. These predictions were then compared with the average recovery rates based simply on the standard treatments in the past. Meehl expected the psychologists' diagnoses would undoubtedly improve the prescribed treatment and result in higher recovery rates. The past averages based on standard treatment would be the floor from which the effectiveness of the diagnoses could be gauged. But, in the words of one researcher, "This floor turned out to be the ceiling." The predictions of the groups of clinicians were inferior to the simple averages in eighteen out of twenty studies and as good only twice!

Further studies showed that there is no correlation between the amount of training and experience a clinical psychologist may have and his or her accuracy. One indicated rather surprisingly that psychologists were no better at interpersonal judgments than individuals with no training, and sometimes worse.[6]

Do such findings extend beyond the couch? Apparently so. A

group of radiologists reading X-ray films failed to diagnose lung disease 30 percent of the time, although the symptoms were clearly evident.[7]

And, in a classic study of tonsillectomies in the mid-1930s (a fashionable operation at the time), a sample of one thousand schoolchildren from the New York City school system were examined by a group of doctors. A total of 61 percent were found to have had their tonsils removed. The remaining children were examined by a second group of physicians, who stated that 45 percent needed tonsillectomies. Another set examining the diminishing group recommended removing 46 percent of the rapidly depleting stock of tonsils. A final examination was carried out on the survivors and, sure enough, the diagnosis indicated 45 percent of these children should have the operation. At this point, only sixty-five children remained. Fortunately, the doctors decided to call off further testing before tonsils became extinct in the New York City school system.[8]

Configural Who?

Dozens of such studies have made it clear that expert failure extends far beyond the investment scene. And the problems very often reside in man's information-processing capabilities. Current work indicates he is a serial or sequential processor of data who can handle information reliably in a linear manner—that is, he can move from one point to the next in a logical sequence. In building a model ship or a space station, there is a defined sequence of procedures. Each step, no matter how complex the particular technology, is linked to the preceding step and will be linked to the succeeding stage until completion.

However, the type of problem that proved so difficult to the professionals we just examined was quite different; here configural, or interactive, rather than linear reasoning was required for the solution. In a configural problem, the decision maker's interpretation of any single piece of information changes depending on how he evaluates many other inputs. Take the case of the security analyst: where two companies have the same trend of earnings, the emphasis placed on growth rates will be weighed quite differently depending on their respective industries and their financial strength. In addition, the assessment will be tempered by the dividend trend, the current payout ratio, profit margins, returns on capital, and the host of analytical criteria we looked at previously. The evaluation will also vary with changes in the state of the economy, in the level of interest rates, and in the companies' competitive environment. Thus, a successful investor must be adept at configural processing, integrating many diverse factors, since changes in any may require a revision of the total assessment.

Not unlike juggling, each factor weighed is another ball in the air, increasing the difficulty of the process. How good, then, are professionals, both within and outside of the investment field, at conducting this type of reasoning? Are they always as good as their methods demand?

A special technique using a statistical test called ANOVA (Analysis of Variance) has been designed that evaluates the configural capabilities of the experts. In one such study, nine radiologists were given a highly configural problem, that of deciding whether a gastric ulcer was benign or not.[9] To make a proper diagnosis, the radiologist must work from seven major cues either present or absent in an X-ray. These can combine to form fifty-seven possible new combinations. Experienced gastroenterologists indicated that a completely accurate diagnosis could only be made by configurally examining the combinations formed from the seven original cues.*

Although the diagnosis requires a high level of configural processing, the researchers found that in actual practice, it accounted for only a very small part of all decisions—some 3 percent. Over 90 percent came from serially adding the original individual symptoms.

A similar problem requiring a high degree of configural reasoning is found in deciding whether or not a psychiatric patient is to be allowed to leave the hospital for short periods. Here there were six primary cues that could be present or absent (for example, does the patient have a drinking problem?) and sixty-four possible interactions. The hospital staff included nurses, social workers, and psychologists. Again, the use of configural thinking was little in evidence, although it was essential for optimum solutions.[10] In another test thirteen clinical psychologists and sixteen advanced graduate students attempted to determine whether the symptoms of 861 pa-

*For those of a technical bent, these can combine into patterns ranging from fifteen possible two-way interactions, twenty possible three-way interactions, fifteen possible four-way interactions, six possible five-way interactions, and one six-way interaction.

tients were neurotic or psychotic, a highly configural task. The findings were in line with the first two examples.[11]

Curious about what results would be found in the stock market, Paul Slovic, a respected researcher in this area, devised a test to see how important configural (or interactive) reasoning actually was in the decisions of market professionals themselves. In one study thirteen stockbrokers and five graduate students in finance were given eight important financial inputs (trend of earnings per share, profit margins, outlook for near-term profits, etc.) that they considered most significant in analyzing companies. The optimum solution could only be found in a configural manner. As it turned out, configural reasoning, on average, accounted for only about 4 percent of the decisions made—results roughly equivalent to those of the radiologists and psychologists.

Moreover, the emphasis the brokers initially said they put on various inputs varied significantly from what they actually used in the experiment.[12] For example, someone considering the trend of earnings per share over time most important might actually place greater emphasis on near-term prospects. Finally, the more experienced the brokers, the less accurate the assessment of their own scales of weighting appeared to be. All in all, the evidence rather clearly indicates that most people are low-level configural processors, in or out of the marketplace.

Security Analysis—A System Designed for Bobby Fischer?

In light of what we have just seen, we might ask how dependable current investment methods actually are. To answer this question, let's look more thoroughly at the manner in which a company is evaluated by fundamental analysis. Suppose, for example, an analyst decides to examine Aetna Life and Casualty. How will he go about it?

Examining the company's financial statements, one sees it is a gigantic operation. In 1977 it had revenues of $8.1 billion, $408 million in net income after taxes, 30,700 home office employees, and 24,000 agents. It writes group insurance for one out of ten workers in the country, automobile insurance for 4.8 million drivers, as well as homeowner's insurance for 1.4 million dwellings. But these are only openers: it also writes twenty-seven other major property and casualty insurance lines, many dozens of different policies in life, health, and pension areas, and it is engaged in several other, non-related ventures as well.

Since chapter 3 indicated that the most important determinant of value is an assessment of the company's earnings power, the analyst will probably start here. To do his job properly, he'll have to look at many dozens and possibly hundreds of inputs.

In the case of Aetna, he normally will review in some detail the recent history and prospects of each of its major lines. He may, for example, begin with the property-casualty business, which accounts for about 57 percent of Aetna's income. The company has twenty-eight important lines in this area, with the largest—automobile insurance—accounting for 40 percent of overall divisional revenues. Since the results of these lines can have a significant bearing on the overall outlook, the analyst will probably try to get as thorough a picture of each operation as he can. He may take the auto insurance segment, for example, and subdivide it into commercial and private passenger; these in turn can be split between bodily injury and property damage.

But if he is the thorough type—and most of the dying species of institutional analysts are—he will go further, possibly getting breakdowns from management on how each of these lines is faring in important states.

But we're not finished with our friend yet. In fact, his most difficult innings lie ahead. Multiplying this information by the large number of other businesses Aetna writes extends the length and perhaps tediousness of the analysis manifold. However, if tediousness were his only concern, the analyst might happily accept it. A far more serious problem is that much of the information he is able to ferret out has a high degree of uncertainty attached to it.

Facts provided to him by management as the basis for his various estimates are partial or incomplete at best and sometimes prove to be entirely incorrect. Varying amounts of information are normally available about individual lines. Obviously, no company will relate all the necessary profit and loss and claim experience data to an outsider.

The analyst may be told that the automotive property line is "up nicely" or that automobile liability is "so-so" in the year to date. If he asks how one should translate a "so-so" or an "up nicely" into a reasonable earnings estimate, more times than not he'll be met with a shrug and told it's corporate policy not to divulge the information, and once in a while he'll be told, "That's your problem."

In any case, the analyst is left on his own. He must rely on personal judgment, deciding whether "nicely" means up 10 percent or 30 percent, or "so-so" means flat or down sharply. Checks can be made with trade sources and the competition, but the information provided will also be qualitative and sometimes misleading. Thus the analyst's judgment is extremely important at every stage of the assessment.

In analyzing an insurance company, it is also important to evaluate the appropriateness of the current rate structure. Because of competition and rising inflation, there is a large element of doubt about how good rates actually are. Even company officers, who spend years in a particular division, can often be wrong in their assessments. In the 1973–74 period, for example, the insurance industry badly misjudged the consequences of rising inflation in its property-casualty business and did not increase rates sufficiently, taking enormous losses as a consequence. Yet, at the time most managements believed their rate structures were sound.

Forecasting the earnings of a large industrial company is not much easier. Often operating in hundreds of different markets, many of which produce intermediate products,* sometimes in up to one hundred separate countries, the analyst is bombarded with vast amounts of difficult-to-quantify information on competitive conditions, capacity utilization rates, and pricing. What will be the effect on Ford of a new compact introduced by GM, or a sports car by Volkswagen? How badly will DuPont polyester operations be hurt if Celanese cuts prices on one or two grades of polyester tire cord? All pertinent information must somehow be synthesized and evaluated in order to arrive at the earnings estimate.

Earnings forecasting, then, depends on large numbers of underlying assumptions, many of which are rapidly changing and very hard to quantify, which means their accuracy is always in doubt.

In addition to the forecasting problems, the harried analyst must also assess the quality of management, the company's expan-

---

*These are the raw materials for another manufacturing process. Many plastic resins, for example, go into a thousand or more end products (ranging from carpets to tires). Estimating the outlook for the myriad of intermediate markets is an extremely difficult task.

sion plans, its finances, the probable dividend rate, the quality of its accounting, and dozens of other vital factors. And all estimates are contingent on general economic conditions, which means correctly gauging the level of interest rates, unemployment, inflation, industrial production, capital spending, and other important variables. Economists themselves are as often wrong as they are right in these estimates. (For details on the record of forecasting, please see chapter 8.)

Finally, even if the analyst could surmount all of the obstacles so far listed, he would still need to know as much about many other companies in order to determine whether the company he chose represented the best value.

The theory appears anything but undemanding on its poor adherents. The amount of information they are expected to process is staggering. And since a good part of it is qualitative and difficult to pin down, the money manager or analyst is required to use his judgment scores of times along the way. Ideally, the professional needs to have information-processing capabilities not dissimilar to those of a fairly large-scale computer. He must have a central storage file for the massive amounts of information of a political, economic, industry, market, and company nature he needs, and he must be able to update and cross-reference it as numerous new and sometimes contradictory developments occur. The Bionic Man might be capable of as much, but work in the behavioral sciences pretty clearly indicates that most human beings are not.

But the requirements of the theory do not end here. One also needs a very high level of configural, or interactive, reasoning ability in order to apply different weights to the scores of factors upon which the analysis is contingent. And we've already seen that man is simply not a good configural processor of information. The reach of conventional investment theory may very well exceed the grasp of many of us to use it properly. The method brings us well into the range of information overload. One of the things that can happen follows.

How Much Knowledge Do We Need?

Under conditions of complexity and uncertainty, experts demand as much information as possible to assist them in their decision making.

Seems logical. And naturally, there is a tremendous desire for such incremental information on the Street, because investors believe the increased dosage gives them a shot at extraordinary profits.

But as I've indicated earlier, that extra "edge" may not help you. A large number of studies have shown pretty conclusively that increasing the amount of information available to an expert decision maker doesn't do much to improve his judgment.[13]

In a study of what appears to be a favored class of guinea pigs, the clinical psychologists,* the subjects read the background information on a large number of cases. As the level of information increased, the diagnostician's confidence rose dramatically, but his accuracy continued to be low. In the test, the psychologists were given background information on a case and asked what they thought their chances were of being right. Thirty-three percent estimated they were correct; 26 percent actually were. When the amount of information was increased fourfold, 53 percent thought they would be correct; 28 percent proved to be.

Interestingly enough, the above findings seem fairly universal— no improvement with more information. The same results were obtained, this time using track handicappers. Eight experienced veterans of the racing forms were progressively given five to forty pieces of information they considered most important in picking winners. As figure 13 shows, the degree of confidence rose directly with the level of information, but the number of winners, alas, did not.[14]

The parallel between these examples and the investment scene is striking. Wall Streeters place immense faith in the detailed analysis of its experts. In-depth research houses turn out thousands upon thousands of reports, sometimes running up to a hundred pages or more and sprinkled with dozens of tables and charts. Washington listening posts have been set up to catch the slightest indications of impending changes in government policies affecting companies or industries,† and scores of conferences are called to provide the money manager with penetrating understanding in dozens of important areas.

The more detailed his level of knowledge, the more effective the

*Eight were clinical psychologists, eighteen were graduate students in psychology, and eighteen were advanced undergraduates.

†Sounds impressive, but, I think, a waste of the client's money. Many times it seems the primary source of the listening post is the *New York Times,* the *Washington Post,* the *Wall Street Journal, Business Week, Time,* or *Newsweek.*

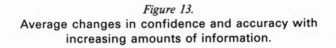

Figure 13.
Average changes in confidence and accuracy with
increasing amounts of information.

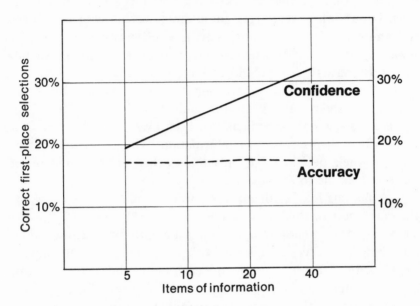

expert is considered. A few years back, for example, a leading investment magazine related the story of an analyst so knowledgeable
about Clorox that "he could recite bleach share by brand in every
small town in the Southwest and tell you the production levels of
Clorox's line number 2, plant number 3. But somehow, when the
company began to develop massive problems, he missed the signs."
As in the case of the psychologists and the experts of the racing
sheets, the amount of information available had little to do with the
outcome. The stock fell from a high of 53 to 11.[15]

This outcome is, unfortunately, no exception. The inferior investment results noted in chapter 1, as well as those that we will view
next, were based on just such detailed research. To quote a disillusioned money manager several years back: "You pick the top [re-
search] house on the Street and the second top house on the Street
—they all built tremendous reputation, research-in-depth, but they
killed their clients."[16] Perhaps a good point to note now is that
in-depth information does not mean in-depth profits.

I hope it is becoming apparent that these configural relationships are extremely complex. In the marketplace investors are dealing not with twenty-four or fifty-seven relevant interactions, but with an exponential number. We have already seen how experts working with far fewer inputs have proven remarkably inadequate at interactive judgments. Because these psychological findings are largely unknown on Wall Street, as elsewhere, investment experts continue to be convinced that their major problems could have been handled if only those extra few necessary facts had been available. They thus tend to overload themselves with information, which usually does not improve their decisions but only makes them more confident and more vulnerable to serious errors.

A famous market theorist of another era, Garfield Drew, saw the end result of this problem clearly. In 1941 he wrote: "In fact, simplicity or singleness of approach is a greatly underestimated factor of market success. As soon as the attempt is made to watch a multiplicity of factors even though each has some element to justify it, one is only too likely to become lost in a maze of contradictory implications . . . the various factors involved may be so conflicting that the conclusion finally drawn is no better than a snap judgment would have been."[17]

Under conditions of anxiety and uncertainty with a vast interacting information grid, the market can become a giant Rorschach test, allowing the investor to see any pattern he wishes. In fact, recent research in configural processing has shown that experts can not only analyze information incorrectly, they can also find relationships that aren't there—a phenomenon called illusionary correlation.

Trained psychologists, for example, were given background information on psychotics, and were also given drawings allegedly made by them. (These, in reality, were very carefully prepared by the experimenters.) With remarkable consistency, the psychologists saw cues in the drawings that they expected to see —muscular figures "drawn" by men worried about their masculinity, or big eyes by suspicious people. Not only were these characteristics not stressed in the drawings, in many cases they were in fact less pronounced than usual.* Because the psychologists focused on the anticipated aberrations, they missed important correlations actually present.[18]

The complexity of the marketplace naturally leads to an attempt to simplify and rationalize what seems at times to be unfathomable reality. Often investors notice things that are simply coincidental, and then come to believe that correlations exist when none are actually present. And if they are rewarded by the stock going up, the practice is further ingrained. The market thus provides an excellent field for illusionary correlation. The head and shoulders formation on the chart cuts through thousands of disparate facts that the chartist believes no man can analyze. Buying growth stocks simplifies an otherwise bewildering range of investment alternatives, just as the Kondratieff wave occurring every fifty years clarifies economic activity which to many might otherwise appear to defy analysis. Such patterns, which seemed to have worked in the past, are pervasive in the marketplace. The problem is that some of the correlations are illusionary and others are chance. Trusting in them begets a high risk of error. A chartist may have summed it up appropriately: "If I hadn't made money some of the time, I would have acquired market wisdom quicker."

Now, unquestionably there are people with outstanding gifts for abstract reasoning that permit them to cut through enormously complex situations. Every field will have its Bernard Baruchs or Warren Buffetts, its Bobby Fischers or Anatol Karpovs. But these people are decidedly few. In chess, for example, there is only one grand master for every few hundred thousand or so players. And even masters or experts, while more plentiful, still represent only a small fraction of those who pursue the game regularly. It seems, then, that as in chess, the information-processing capabilities and the standards of abstract reasoning required by current investment methods are probably too complicated for the majority of us, professional and amateur alike, to use to beat the market regularly.

---

*The belief that all paranoid patients accentuate certain characteristics in their drawings belongs in the category of psychologists' old wives' tales.

At this point, some of you might ask whether the problems in decision making, particularly in the stock market, are being exaggerated. The answer, I think, can be found by looking at the favorite investments of market professionals over time.

What is the record? Let's start with a large international conference of institutional investors held at the New York Hilton in February 1970. Over two thousand strong, the delegates were polled for the stock they thought would show outstanding appreciation that year. The favorite choice was National Student Marketing—the highest-octane performer of the day. From a price of 120 in February, it dropped 95 percent by July of that same year. At the same conference in 1972, the airlines were selected as the industry expected to perform best for the balance of the year. Within 1 percent of their highs, the carrier stocks fell 50 percent that year in the face of a sharply rising market. The conference the following year voted them a group to avoid.

Are these simply chance results? In my earlier book, *Psychology and the Stock Market,* I included seven surveys of how the favorite stocks of groups of large numbers of professional investors had subsequently fared. In all the surveys, the choices of the professionals did worse than the market averages. And this before adding on commission charges and advisory fees.

As I indicated at the time, these were the only samples I had been able to locate. Since publication, with further digging and an excellent research assistant—Ms. Nan Miller—as well as some luck, we have unearthed a large number of additional samples—some fifty-one encompass investment advice given over the almost fifty-year period between 1928 and 1976. The surveys show the favorite stock or portfolio of groups of professional investors. The number participating ranged from twenty-five at the low end to as high as several thousand. The median was well over a hundred. Wherever possible, the subsequent performance of the professional choices was measured against the S&P 500 for the next twelve months.*

The results are presented in table 5. The first column shows the time period for each set of surveys, the second the source of the

*Several studies used different averages or time periods. For details see Appendix I, pages 250–253.

survey, the third the total number of surveys conducted, and the final column the percentage of each set of surveys that outperformed the market in the next twelve months.

Table 5

EXPERT FORECASTS OF FAVORITE STOCKS AND INDUSTRIES

TIME SPAN	SOURCE OF SURVEYS	TOTAL SURVEYS	PERCENT OUTPERFORMING MARKET IN NEXT YEAR
1929–32	Cowles Surveys	3	0
1953–76	*Trusts and Estates*	21	33
1967–69	*Financial Analysts Journal*	1	0
1967–72	*California Business*	7	29
1969–73	*Institutional Investor*	7	0
1973	*Business Week*	2	50
1974	*Seminar* (Edson Gould)	2	0
1974	Callan Associates	4	0
1974–76	Mueller Surveys	4	25
Total number of surveys		51	
Percentage of professional surveys *underperforming* market			77

NOTE: Dividends excluded in all comparisons.

The findings startled me. While I believed the evidence clearly showed that experts make many mistakes, I did not think the magnitude of error was as striking or as consistent as the results make evident.

Seventeen of the studies measure the performance of five or more stocks the experts picked as their favorites. By diversifying into a number of stocks instead of just choosing one or two, the element of chance is reduced. And yet, the seventeen portfolios so chosen underperformed the market on fifteen occasions! This meant, in effect, that when you receive professional advice about stocks to buy, you would be given bad advice nine out of ten times. Throwing darts at the stock pages blindfolded or flipping a coin to decide what to buy would give you a fifty-fifty chance. Using a financial professional would reduce your odds considerably.

The other thirty-four samples did not do appreciably better. Overall, the favorite stocks and industries of large groups of money managers and analysts did worse than the market on thirty-nine of fifty-one occasions—or 77 percent of the time—as table 5 shows.

One of the first studies was done by Alfred Cowles,* among the earliest systematic students of markets, who made three separate studies measuring the forecasting record of investment advisors, large insurance companies, brokers, and bankers between 1928 and 1932. All underperformed the market.†[19]

Another important survey is based on polls conducted by *Trusts and Estates* over a twenty-one-year period. Each year a large number of investment officers with bank trust departments (as a group, the largest institutional common-stock investors) were asked to name their three favorite industries for the next year. Table 6 gives the results for the 1953–76 period.‡ The favorite industry of most bank portfolio managers did worse than the market in fourteen of the twenty-one years, or 67 percent of the time. It's also interesting, since there are dozens of industries to choose from, that one industry— office equipment—was favored so often.

Moving on to more recent times, a number of broad surveys have been conducted by *Institutional Investor,* a magazine widely read by the professionals. In late 1971, for example, the magazine polled more than 150 money managers in twenty-seven states, each of whom chose the five stocks he or she believed would show the best performance the following year. Different types of money managers were surveyed, ranging from the people who ran hair-trigger performance funds to conservative bank and insurance types. The magazine indicated that although four hundred stocks were selected overall, there was a remarkable consensus regarding the top ten favorites, which were weighted toward concepts popular at the time.[20]

The top ten fizzled in a rising market, gaining only 1.3 percent in 1972, a year the averages rose 15.6 percent. For the two-year period, the favorites declined almost eight times as much as the averages. After the top ten that year, fifty runners-up were named. They did even more poorly, declining an average of 5

---

*For those interested in more details of the samples, please refer to Appendix I.

†Cowles was a formidable researcher and a possible precursor of the random walk theory, coming as he did from the bastion of that theory, the University of Chicago. One of his many tests measured all the recommendations of William Peter Hamilton, who you may remember was the editor of the *Wall Street Journal* and cooriginator of the Dow theory. Cowles plotted Hamilton's entire forecasting record between 1904 and 1929 and once again found that if someone had followed each recommendation, he would have done worse than the averages.

‡The first poll took place in 1953; no polls were made between 1954 and 1956.

Table 6
TRUSTS AND ESTATES
Subsequent Twelve-Month Performance of Favorite Industry

| YEAR | FAVORITE INDUSTRY | PERFORMANCE OVER THE NEXT 12 MONTHS | |
		INDUSTRY	S&P 500
1953[a]	Electric and gas public utilities	1.0%	− 6.6%
1957	Oil	−16.0	−14.3
1958	Electronics and electric utilities	75.0	38.1
1959	Oil	− 9.7	8.5
1960	Auto and accessories	−26.6	− 3.0
1961	Office equipment and machine group	31.0	23.1
1962	Chemicals, office equipment, banks	−17.1	−11.8
1963	Electric utilities	6.9	18.9
1964	Chemicals	15.6	13.0
1965	Chemicals	4.3	9.1
1966	Oil	−10.6	−13.0
1967	Utilities	4.7	20.1
1968	Office equipment	− 0.9	7.7
1969	Office equipment	15.6	−11.4
1970	Office equipment	−17.5	0.1
1971	Building materials	5.5	10.8
1972	Retail	11.7	15.7
1973	Office equipment	−21.5	−17.4
1974	Office equipment	−37.0	−29.7
1975	Office equipment	27.7	31.5
1976	Petroleum	29.0	19.1
Percentage underperforming market		67 %	

[a]No surveys conducted in 1954, 1955, and 1956.

percent in 1972 and ten times as much as the market in the 1972–73 period.

Another survey was conducted the next year, 1973. It was a down year for the market and the S&P dropped 17.4 percent, hardly a ripple when compared with the average decline of 40.4 percent for the top ten, as shown in table 7 on page 100. Twenty-seven other stocks were also selected for performance that year, and again they did worse than the averages. The surveys were discontinued after 1973.[21]

A final survey, conducted by Callan Associates, a West Coast consulting firm, is worth noting. Three dozen investment managers were asked at the end of 1974 to pick both their favorite six stocks

Table 7
THE 1973 TOP TEN

COMPANY	PRICE 1/1/73	PRICE 12/31/73	PERCENT CHANGE	PRICE 12/31/74	PERCENT CHANGE FROM 1/1/73
IBM	321⅝	246¾	−23.3%	168	−47.8%
Polaroid	126⅛	69⅞	−44.6	185⅝	−85.2
ITT	60¼	26⅜	−56.2	14¾	−75.5
Teleprompter	33¼	3⅞	−88.3	1½	−95.5
Eastman Kodak	148⅜	116	−21.8	62⅞	−57.6
Gillette	63⅞	35⅞	−43.8	25⅜	−60.3
McDonald's	76¼	57	−25.2	29⅜	−61.5
Motorola	65½	49¼	−24.8	34⅛	−47.9
Digital Equipment	91¾	101⅞	+11.0	50¾	−44.7
Levitz Furniture	26⅞	3⅝	−86.5	1¾	−93.5
Average change			−40.4%		−67.0%
S&P 500					
(without dividends)	118.1	97.6	−17.4%	68.6	−41.9%

NOTE: All companies adjusted for stock splits.
SOURCE: Reprinted by permission of the publisher from *Psychology and the Stock Market,* by David Dreman, p. 154. © 1977 by AMACOM, a division of American Management Associations. All rights reserved.

Table 8
CALLAN ASSOCIATES SURVEY (12/31/74)
Performance Over the Next Twelve Months

Six-stock portfolio to buy	+20.7%
Favorite industry—drugs	+ 2.8%
Worst six stocks	+42.9%
Worst industry—electrical and electronics	+42.0%
S&P 500	+31.5%

and favorite industry and at the same time the six stocks and single industry they thought would do worst in the following year. Table 8 shows some rather extraordinary results. The "worst" stocks and single industry did better than the S&P, while the "best" did worse.

More recently, professionals have been reluctant to participate in such polls. When asked to name his favorites, one analyst replied tersely: "We don't make this information available free anymore."

What do we make of results such as these? The number of

samples seems far too large for the outcome to be simply chance. In fact, the evidence indicates a surprisingly high level of error among professionals in choosing both individual stocks and portfolios over a period spanning almost fifty years.

Such evidence, in the first place, is incompatible with the central assumption of the efficient-market hypothesis.* But far more important are the practical implications of what we have just seen: the discovery of a very plausible explanation of why fundamental methods often do not work. The theory demands just too much from man as a configural reasoner and information processor. Both within and outside of markets, under conditions of information overload our mental tachometers appear to surge far above the red line. When this happens, we no longer process information reliably. Confidence rises as our input of information increases, but our decisions are not improved. And from the evidence we've seen in the stock market at least, they appear to deteriorate.

While it is true that experts may do as poorly in other complex circumstances, the market professional unfortunately works in a goldfish bowl. In no other calling that I am aware of is the outcome of decisions so easily measurable.

The high failure rate among financial professionals, at times approaching 90 percent, indicates not only that errors are made, but that under uncertain, complex conditions, there must be some systematic and predictable forces working against the unwary investor to account for such extraordinarily poor results.

The next chapter will look at what these forces are, and how we may try to counter them.

*The hypothesis states that it is impossible to beat the market because of the competition among professionals, which results in prices always being about where they should be. But just as the theory holds that even professionals cannot outdo the market over time, it also holds that they cannot do substantially worse. After all, it is their very decision making that keeps prices at their proper level in the first place. The surveys, however, give us a different picture from the one assumed by the theorists. The massive underperformance in both up and down markets indicates that their most crucial assumption is inconsistent with a statistically significant body of evidence. Findings such as these appear to indicate that the hypothesis is built of straw.

CHAPTER SIX

Avoiding
Bad Market Odds

"It is a great advantage for a system of philosophy to be substantially true," Santayana once wrote. Similarly, it would seem a great advantage for popular investment philosophies to be essentially workable. Unfortunately, as the evidence to date indicates, their workability often appears as elusive as the "truths" of philosophy.

But perhaps even more striking is that the methods not only fail to provide any help to the expert, but prove a positive liability—judging from the record we just viewed. Indeed, the failures appear so widespread that there must be systematic reasons to account for them. And there are. Despite what many economists and financial theorists assume, people are not good intuitive statisticians, particularly under the difficult conditions previously described. Which means they simply do not calculate odds properly when they make investment decisions. Because they don't, repeated and predictable errors crop up in markets—errors that can be recognized and avoided. First, we must attempt to learn why such mistakes occur so frequently. Once their nature is understood, a set of rules can be developed to help monitor investment decisions and provide a safety net against serious mishap. After doing this, we can move into specific strategies that are built precisely upon these intuitive statistical limitations.

Researchers have found that people, in making many decisions, adopt shortcuts or rules of thumb rather than formally calculating the actual odds of something happening. Called judgmental heuristics, in technical jargon, these are the various learning and simplifying strategies people use to make the processing of large amounts of information possible. Experience over a lifetime shows that most such judgmental shortcuts work exceptionally well and allow us to cope quickly with and organize data that would otherwise prove overwhelming. Driving a car down Broadway, for example, one would (or should) concentrate only on operating the vehicle, other traffic, and pedestrians, screening out thousands of other distracting and disruptive bits of information. The rule of thumb is to focus solely on what directly affects our driving, and the rule is obviously a good one.

We also use selective processes in dealing with probabilities we are facing. In many of our decisions and judgments, we tend to be intuitive statisticians. We use mental shortcuts that work well most of the time. We think our odds of survival are better driving at fifty-five miles an hour than at ninety miles an hour, although few of us have ever bothered to check the actual numbers. A professional hockey team is likely to beat an amateur one, if the "amateurs" are not Russians or Czechs; a discount department store will probably sell TV sets more cheaply than Macy's or Bloomingdale's; and we might expect to get to a city six hundred miles away faster by air than by ground transportation. There are many dozens of such examples one could readily cite to indicate that such procedures are both valuable and immensely timesaving.[1] But being an intuitive statistician has limitations as well as blessings. The very simplifying processes that are normally highly efficient timesavers in most cases tend to lead to systematic mistakes in investment decisions. Here they can make people believe the odds in an investment situation are dramatically different from what they actually are. As a result, they consistently shortchange the investor.

The distortions produced by the subjectively calculated probabilities are large, systematic, and very difficult to eliminate even after people have been made fully aware of them, as we'll see next.

The Short, Happy Life of the "Hot" Advisor

We have already seen how quickly investors flock to better-performing mutual funds, even though financial researchers have shown that the "hot" funds in one time period very often turn out to be the poorest performers in another. Fred Mates was the top fund manager for most of 1968, and close to the bottom of three hundred fund managers in 1969. The subsequent records of Fred Carr and Gerald Tsai were also lackluster at best. Even so, investors are continuously enthralled by such "hot" performance for brief periods. Because of this susceptibility in most people, brokers or analysts who have had one or two stocks move up sharply or chartists who call one turn correctly are believed to have established a credible record and can readily find market followings.

Likewise, an advisory service that is right for a short period of time can beat its drums loudly. "Professor C," for example, is currently advertising week after week in numerous publications how his "market barometers" have never been more negative, and shows the reader how right he has been for one year. Or Hans Frinz, the Swiss monetary gnome and goldbug, runs banner advertisements proclaiming the correctness of his recent opinion on the upward movement of gold. The truth of the matter is that both Hans and the good professor have been wrong in their judgments far more often than either would like to remember. In 1974, near the bottom of the market, I remember Frinz telling a seminar of professionals that he felt gold would go to $600 within a year, the level at the time of the Dow. And the Dow in turn would go to 200, near the level at which gold was then trading. Shortly thereafter, gold dropped sharply, and the market increased by nearly 70 percent.

However, advisors understand—either intuitively or consciously—that the public is convinced that results over short periods are meaningful when they are more often than not simply chance happenings. And those in the public eye usually gain large numbers of new subscribers for being right—for a time. The principle is central to the subscription game.

This brings us to the first of the major probability errors that this chapter will examine, the one that Israeli psychologists Amos Tversky and Daniel Kahneman called the "law of small numbers."[2] Examining journals in both psychology and education, they found that researchers tended systematically to overstate the importance of findings taken from small samples. The statistically valid "law of large numbers" states that large samples will usually be highly representative of the population from which they are drawn; for example, public opinion polls are normally fairly accurate because of their ability to draw on large and representative groups. However, the smaller the sample used (or the shorter the record), the more likely the findings are mere chance occurrences rather than really meaningful. And yet the Tversky and Kahneman studies showed the typical psychological or educational experimenters gambled their research theories on samples so small that the odds that the figures were simply chance were much too high.[3] This is almost identical to the investor gambling on an excellent but all too brief record of an advisor. The psychologists and educators were far too confident that their results, based on only a few observations or a short period of time, were significant, even though they were trained in statistical techniques and should have been well aware of the dangers.

What is important to note is how readily people can overgeneralize the meanings of small numbers of supporting facts or statistics. Our intuitions seem to be satisfied with quite limited statistical evidence, which may not be at all representative of the real facts. Sometimes the evidence we accept may run to the absurd. I once heard two brokers at Elaine's, a popular New York café, agreeing that the best way of judging Coca-Cola's sales prospects was to talk to a few of the delivery men. Since the company has many thousands of such men scattered throughout the country, I felt a little sorry for the clients who were to benefit from such incisiveness.

Tversky and Kahneman's findings, which have been repeatedly confirmed, are particularly important to our understanding of some stock market errors and lead to a rule that investors should try to follow:

Rule I: Don't be influenced by a short performance record of a money manager, broker, analyst, or advisor.

The law of averages indicates that many—usually playing currently popular trends—will have excellent records, often for months and sometimes for a year or more, only to be followed by disastrous ones later. If you buy the record just after a period of spectacular performance, chances are that the manager will not sustain it.

This is the sad lesson to be learned from the "performance managers" of 1968, many of whom forlornly traded in smoking pistols for cab driver's medallions or bartender's aprons after decimating their clients' portfolios. And it was the same lesson that the English and French investors buying the South Sea and Mississippi companies were taught some 250 years earlier.

A Variation on the Previous Problem

A second error, in many ways parallel to the first, also indicates man's shortcomings as an intuitive statistician. People, in making decisions, appear to become overly immersed in the details of a particular situation and neglect the outcome of very similar situations from past experience. These past outcomes are called prior probabilities and logically should help to guide similar choices in the present.[4]

But they tend not to. An experiment showing this rather clearly was made with a group of advanced psychology students. The group was given a brief analysis of a graduate student, said to have been written by a psychologist several years earlier after conducting some tests. Psychology students are taught that profiles of this sort can be enormously inaccurate. And the one here was not only outdated but contained no indication of the subject's academic preference. The study, which follows, was intended to provide them with nothing of practical value.

Tom W. is of high intelligence, although lacking in true creativity. He has a need for order and clarity and for neat and tidy systems in which every detail finds its appropriate place. His writing is dull and rather mechanical, occasionally enlivened by somewhat corny puns and flashes of imagination of the sci-fi type. He has a strong drive for competence. He seems to have little feel and little sympathy for other people, and does not enjoy interacting with others. Self-centered, he nevertheless has a deep moral sense.

Tom W. is currently a graduate student. Please rank the following nine fields of graduate specialization in order of the likelihood that Tom W. is now a student in that field. Let rank one be the most probable choice:

    _____Business Administration
    _____Computer Sciences
    _____Engineering

————Humanities and Education
————Law
————Library Science
————Medicine
————Physical and Life Sciences
————Social Science and Social Work

Given the lack of substantive content, the graduate students should have ignored the study entirely, and made choices based simply on the percentage of students at the graduate school going into each field—information that of course had been provided for them, and that, it was assumed, they would act upon. At least, according to the laws of normative probability, this was what was expected of them. According to these laws, the more unreliable the available information is in a specific situation (called the case rate— in this example the profile of Tom W.), the more one should rely on past percentages (called the base rate—in this instance the percentage of students enrolled in each field).

Did the group look at the past percentages? No. This experiment and others like it demonstrated that the students relied entirely upon the profile and decided that computer sciences and engineering were the two most probable fields for Tom W. to enter, even though each had relatively few people in them. In spite of their training to the contrary, the psychology students based decisions on unreliable information, ignoring the more pertinent inputs.

A parallel example in the stock market is the emphasis people put on the individual outlook for exciting new issues and concept stocks (the case rate), even though the substantiating data are usually flimsy and uncertain at best. Still, investors rarely examine the high probability of loss in such ventures (the base rate). For example, most buyers of hot new issues in 1968, focusing on the individual story, forgot that over 98 percent of these issues had dropped in price after the 1962 market break. Here again, the prior probabilities, although essential, were ignored in the analysis. Which brings us to another rule of investment decision making:

Rule 2: Don't rely solely on the case rate. Take into account the prior probabilities.

The greater the complexity and uncertainty present in the investment situation you face, the less emphasis you should place on your current appraisal alone, and the more you should look to the success or failure of similar situations in the past.

Put another way, rather than attempting to obtain every fact and sliver of information about a difficult investment situation (much of which is contradictory, irrelevant, and difficult to evaluate correctly), the investor should, if it is at all possible, concern himself as much with trying to gauge the longer-term record of success or failure of a particular course of action.

We have already looked at new issues. The same rule could be applied to a number of similar investment situations. For example, if the investor likes a concept stock, he might take a cross-section of favorites of other periods and see how they worked out some years later, or if he decides to try his hand at market timing, examine how well the system he has chosen has worked over time.

In each instance, the information in the particular case being examined should, where possible, be supplemented by evidence of the longer-term record of success or failure of similar situations, the base rate, which should influence the decision made.

Regression to the Mean

The two previous investment biases play major roles in buttressing one of the most important and consistent sources of investment error. As intuitive statisticians, we do not comprehend the principle of *regression to the mean*. Although the terminology sounds formidable, the concept is actually quite simple. The statistical phenomenon was noted over a hundred years ago by Sir Francis Galton, a pioneer in eugenics, and will prove indispensable to the practical investment methods we are coming to next.

In studying the height of man, Galton found that the tallest group had sons whose mean height was shorter than the father's; conversely, in the shortest group of fathers, the mean height of the sons was taller. Since many tall men come from families of average height, they are likely to have children shorter than they are, while the opposite holds true for shorter men. In both cases, the height of the children was less extreme than that of the fathers and closer to the average.

The study of this phenomenon gave rise to the term *regression,* and the principle has since been documented in many areas.

Regression to the mean, although quite alien to us intuitively, occurs quite frequently.[5] Take the example of the reaction we have to a baseball player's batting average. Although a player may be a .300 hitter over some seasons, his record is anything but even. The player will not get three hits in every ten times at bat. There are times when he will be batting .500 or more, well above his average (or mean), and others when he will be lucky to hit .125. Over 162 games, whether the batter hits .125 or .500 in any dozen or so games makes little difference to the average. But rather than realizing that the player's performance over a week or a month is not usually in line with his season's average, we tend to relate only to the immediate past record. The player is believed to be in a "hitting streak" or a "slump." Fans, sportscasters, and, unfortunately, the players themselves place too much emphasis on brief periods and tend to forget the longer-term average.

Regression also occurs in many instances where it is not expected and yet is bound to happen. Air Force flight instructors were chagrined after they praised a fledgling pilot for an exceptionally good landing because it was normally followed by a poorer one the next time. Conversely, when they criticized a bad landing, a better one usually followed. What they did not understand was that at the particular level of training of these student pilots, there was no more consistency in their landings than in the daily batting figures of baseball players. Bumpy landings would be followed by smooth ones and vice versa. In effect, there was a pattern of regression to the mean. Correlating the landing quality to their remarks, the instructors erroneously concluded that criticism was helpful to learning and praise detrimental, a conclusion almost universally rejected by learning theory researchers.

And now, with some understanding of the principle, we can go back to how it works in the stock market. According to a major study made by Ibbotson and Sinquefield of the University of Chicago,[6] stocks over the last fifty years have returned 9.2 percent annually in price appreciation and dividends (see figure 14), against a return of about 4.1 percent for bonds. An earlier study by the Cowles Commission showed much the same stock return going back to the 1880s.

However, as the figure shows, the return has been anything but consistent—not unlike the number of hits a .300 hitter will get in individual games over a few weeks or a month. There have been long

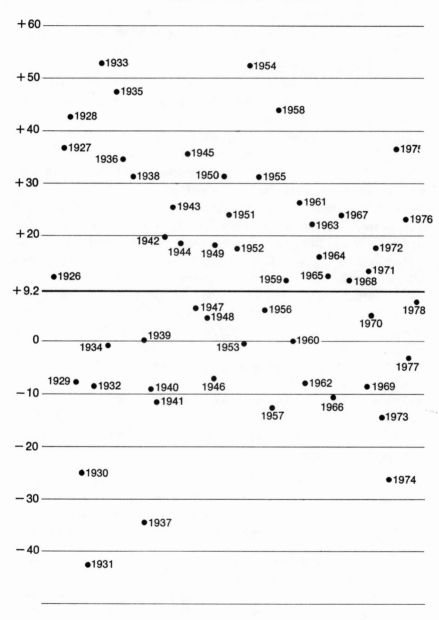

Figure 14.
Annual return on stocks, 1926–78.

periods when stocks have returned more than the 9.2 percent mean. And within each of these periods, there have been times when stocks performed sensationally, rising sometimes 50 percent or more in a year. At other times, they have seemed to free-fall. Stocks, then, although they have averaged 9.2 percent over a long period of time, have had their own periods of "streaks" and "slumps."*

For investors, the long-term rate of return of common stocks, like the batting average of a ballplayer, is the important thing to remember. However, as intuitive statisticians, we find it very hard, if not impossible, to do so. Market history provides a continual example of our adherence to current trends.

The investor of 1927 and 1928 thought that returns in the nature of 35 to 40 percent were in order from that time on, although they deviated far from the past mean; and in 1933 and 1934 he believed huge losses were inevitable, although they too deviated sharply from the long-term mean. The same is true of every major market peak and trough. As figure 1 (page 10) on investment advisor buying and selling indicates, most experts are closely tied, if not pilloried, to the current market movement. The belief that extreme returns, either positive or negative, will persist continues, rather than the far more likely probability that they are simply a remote point on the graph charting the distribution of returns and that succeeding patterns will tend to fall in line with historial standards.

The relevance of these long-term returns can be masked by detailed knowledge of the specific trend or fashion and by intense involvement in it.[7] Even those who are aware of these long-term standards of value for stocks often cannot see them clearly because of preoccupation with short-term conditions. And this leads to a third protective rule:

Rule 3: Don't be seduced by recent rates of investment return for individual stocks or the market when they deviate sharply from past norms. For investors, longer-term characteristics of stocks (the case rate) are far more likely to be established again.

Returns that are extremely high or low should be treated as deviations from long-term norms. The long-term return of the market might be viewed like the average height of men. It is unlikely that abnormally tall men will beget even taller men, just as it is unlikely

*As we'll see in chapter 12, this rate should rise with increasing inflation.

that abnormally high returns will follow already high returns. In both cases, the principle of regression to the mean will most probably apply, and the next series of returns will be less extreme. As chapter 8 will detail, even as returns deviate sharply from the market mean, dynamic forces on the investment and economic scenes are at work to reduce the deviations.

Because experts in the stock market are no more aware of the principle of regression than others, each sharp price deviation from past norms of value is explained by a new, spurious theory. This, together with other cognitive biases we will examine, leaves the investor vulnerable time and again to the fashions of the market-place, however far removed prices may be from intrinsic worth.

In bull markets, as Gerald Loeb noted, we tend to congratulate ourselves for boldness as prices move up, and we wish we had taken even greater risks. In bear markets, of course, we rue being in stocks at all. The pattern is ever-repeating.

The Input-Output Blues

Another powerful bias that usually leads to consistent error in the market and encourages investors to accept the biases just discussed is their intuitive belief that inputs and outputs should be closely correlated. Tests have shown, for example, that people are far more confident that a student will regularly have a B average if he has two B's rather than an A and a C. They believe that consistent inputs allow greater predictability than inconsistent ones, although the belief is not statistically valid.[8]

The direct extension of this finding is the manner in which investors equate a good stock with a rising price and a poor stock with a falling price. One of the most common questions analysts, money managers, or brokers are asked is, "If the stock is so good, why isn't it moving?" The answer, of course, is that its value (the input) is often not recognized in price (the output) for quite some time. Yet many investors demand such immediate, though incorrect, feedback—and can make serious mistakes as a consequence.

Another interesting aspect of the latter phenomenon is that investors tend to place high confidence in extreme inputs or outputs, which are often not valid. Computer service stocks in the 1967–68 market had sensational earnings growth (the input), which was confirmed when the price went up astronomically—as much as one-hundredfold (the output). The seemingly strong fundamentals went hand in hand with sharply rising prices for the South Sea Company or for that matter growth stocks in 1972 or early 1973. Extreme correlations look good and many people are quite willing to accept them as likely to continue, but as generations of investors have discovered the hard way, they aren't.

The same thinking is also applied to each crash and panic. Here the earnings estimates and outlooks (the inputs) became notably worse as prices dropped. Graham and Dodd, astute market clinicians that they were, saw this input-output relationship quite clearly. They wrote that "an inevitable rule of the market is that the prevalent theory of common stock valuations has developed in rather close conjunction with the change in the level of prices."[9] The consistency of this behavior leads us to our final market rule:

Rule 4: Don't expect the strategy you adopt to prove a quick success in the marketplace.

Demanding immediate success invariably leads to playing fashions or fads that are currently performing well rather than to investing on a more solid basis. An investment course, once charted, should be given time to work.* In reality, patience is a crucial but very rare investment commodity. The problem is not as simple as it may appear because studies have shown that businessmen and other investors abhor uncertainty.† Certainty to most people in the market is a satisfactory explanation of events within a condensed time frame; in short, quick input-output matching.

On Grizzly Bear Attacks and Stock Prices

Further evidence indicates that we consistently misread probabilities intuitively, and just as consistently we get into investment difficulties as a result. The ease and frequency with which we can recall an event affects the probability with which it is judged to occur.[10]

---

*I'll say more on this in chapter 9.

†See, for example, George Katona, *Psychological Economics* (New York: American Elsevier, 1975).

Now, this judgmental shortcut, or heuristic, works well most of the time because we normally recall events more easily that have occurred frequently. However, our recall is also influenced by factors in addition to frequency, such as how recently the events have happened and what their emotional saliency is.[11] People recall good or bad events out of proportion to their actual occurrences. The chances of being mauled by a grizzly bear at a national park are only one or two per million visitors, and the death rate is lower. Casualties from shark attacks probably represent an even smaller percentage of swimmers in coastal waters, although *Jaws* certainly resulted in a noticeable decrease in swimming off the Hamptons, Fire Island, and elsewhere for a time in 1976. However, because of the sensational nature of the dangers, most people tend to think the probabilities of such attacks are much higher than they really are.

And the actual occurrence of disasters, rather than the probabilities of their happening, has an important bearing on our purchase of casualty insurance. Earthquake and airline insurance purchases go up sharply after a calamity, as do purchases of flood insurance.[12]

Statements by experts, crowd participation, and recent experience strongly incline the investor to follow the prevailing trend or fashion in the marketplace. In late 1972 and 1973 the only stocks doing well were the highfliers, companies that month after month continued to climb steadily while more mundane companies dropped sharply. The experience was repeated and salient to the investor, while the disastrous aftermath of the 1961–62 speculation in highfliers or that of 1967–68 had receded far back in his memory.

A moment's reflection indicates that this judgmental bias reinforces the others. Recent and salient events, whether positive or negative, strongly influence judgments of the future. People, it appears, often become prisoners of such experience and view the future as an extension of the immediate past. The more memorable the circumstances, the more they are expected to persist, no matter how out of line with prior norms. As psychologists have pointed out, this is a difficult bias to shed.

The defense here, as in rule 4, is to try to take a longer-term view of events. While there is certainly no assured way to put such recent or memorable experience into absolute perspective, it might be helpful during periods of extreme pessimism or optimism to wander back to your library. If the market is dropping sharply, reread the daily and weekly financial periodicals during the last major break. If you can, pick up the *Wall Street Journal,* turn to the market section, and read how negative the opinion was of expert after expert in October, November, and early December of 1974, just before the market began one of its sharpest recoveries. Similarly, if we ever have another speculative market, it would not be a bad idea to check the *Journal* again and read the comments made during the 1967–68 bubble. While rereading the daily press is not an elixir, I think it will prove helpful.

We might briefly view two other systematic biases that are relevant to the investment scene and tend to fix investment errors firmly in place. They are also difficult to correct, since they tend to buttress the ones we've already viewed.

The first is known as *anchoring,* [13] another simplifying heuristic. In a complex situation, such as the marketplace, some natural starting point, such as current price, is selected as a first approximation of worth from which most people then make adjustments. Fairly typically, the adjustments are not sufficient. Thus, an investor in 1972 might have thought a price of 60 was too high for Levitz Furniture, and that 45 was more appropriate. But Levitz was grossly overvalued at 45, to which it dropped on the way to 5.

Again, the best defense against this bias appears to be in our earlier rule: *If the returns are particularly high or low, they are most likely to be abnormal.*

The final bias is an interesting one. In looking back at past mistakes, researchers have found that people believe that each major error made could have been seen much more clearly at the time than it was if only they hadn't been wearing rose- or dark-colored glasses at the time. The inevitability of what happened seems apparent in retrospect. Hindsight bias seriously impairs people's proper assessment of past errors and places a significant limit on what can be learned from experience. [14]

I remember sitting in an investment committee meeting of a large mutual-fund advisory group in 1971 when its members were particularly bullish on the market—naturally, it was going up at the time. The senior partner, looking at how sharply prices had risen from the depressed levels of 1970, asked, "How could we not have bought stocks then?" In 1975 he asked the same thing after the even sharper drop of 1974. And he'll likely ask it again after the next market rally.

This bias too is a difficult one to handle. That walk to the library appears here to be as good a solution as any. I think you will see that the mistakes made were far less obvious than they appear today.

Decisional Biases and Market Fashions

We saw in chapter 4 the seductiveness of current market fashions, how large numbers of rational and prudent investors could be swept away by the lure of profit from the New World, from bubble companies, or from go-go stocks. Now, with some knowledge of decisional biases, we can understand why the tug of fashion has always been so persistent and influential on both the market population and the expert opinion of the day.

Whatever the fashion, the experts could demonstrate that the particular choice performed in a manner superior statistically to other less favored investments in the immediate past. And sometimes the investment did so for fairly long periods of time. Tulip bulbs appreciated sharply for seven years prior to 1637. A Dutch expert in that latter year could easily show that for more than a decade tulips had yielded considerably more annually than did owning buildings, shops, or farms. The recent record was exciting and rising prices would seem to justify much more of the same.

The pattern continually repeats itself. A buyer of canal bonds in the 1830s or blue-chip stocks in 1929 could argue that though the prices were very dear, each had proved to be a vastly superior holding in the recent past. Along with the Crash and the Depression came the passion for government bonds at near-zero interest rates, which persisted for a decade and a half. A distinguished economist stated at a conference in 1948: "Never in the lifetime of anyone in this room will government two-and-a-halves sell below par." Barring the few unfortunates who, heeding these words, fell on their coupon clippers when bond prices nose-dived shortly thereafter, most found the prediction proved dramatically wrong.

In the 1950s investing in good-grade common stocks again came into vogue, and in 1962 and 1968 an excellent case could be and was made for buying concept stocks. By the end of the decade, the superior record of stocks through the postwar era had put investing in bonds in disrepute. *Institutional Investor,* a magazine exceptionally adept at catching the prevailing trends, presented a dinosaur on the cover of its February 1969 issue with the caption CAN THE BOND MARKET SURVIVE? The article continued: "In the long run, the public market for straight debt might become obsolete."

Stocks as a percentage of institutional portfolios rose dramatically, from 40 percent of assets in 1958 to 74 percent in 1972. So great was the demand for stocks that not only did pension funds—the largest institutional investor—put all new monies into them, they also sold off a portion of their bonds to increase their holdings further. The accumulation of stocks occurred just as their rates of return were beginning to decrease sharply. Of course, bonds immediately went on to provide better returns than stocks through 1978.

And with the poor results in the stock market in recent years, there has been a full swing of the pendulum. Through the end of 1978, stocks were being rapidly reduced as a percentage of total portfolios by institutional investors, and only a small part of new monies were being committed to them.* (Recently, I heard a well-regarded money manager tell an investment group that the last decade was only a prelude and that bonds would outperform stocks for the next twenty years.)

And behind the polls of expert failure we saw in the last chapter was the fact that the professionals tended to play the fashions of the day—concept stocks in 1968 and 1971, the top tier in 1972 and 1973, or "Smokestack America" in 1975 and 1976. In the *Institutional Investor* contest of 1972 for instance, the top-tier selections were weighted toward concepts popular at the time, including Bausch & Lomb, Levitz, and TelePrompTer. By early 1973 interest had shifted from concepts to growth stocks, and the top ten included IBM, Polaroid, ITT, Eastman Kodak, McDonald's, and Digital Equipment. One fund manager, noting the sharp rise in the price of large growth stocks at the time, said that their performance stood out "like a beacon in the night." Both the growth stocks and the concept stocks were clobbered shortly thereafter.

Although market history provides convincing testimony about the ephemeral nature of recent fashions, they have captivated generation after generation of investors. Each fashion has its supporting

*In 1978 only 15 percent of new pension fund money went into stocks, against 115 percent in 1972. In spite of large new cash inflows, stock holdings were cut back to only slightly more than 50 percent of these portfolios.

statistics, the law of small numbers. The fashions are salient and easy to recall and are of course confirmed by rising prices, the inputs and outputs again. These biases, all of which interact, make it natural to project the prevailing trend well into the future. The common error each time is that although the trend may have lasted for months, even at times for years, it was not representative and was sometimes far removed from the performance of equities or bonds over longer periods (regression to the mean). In hindsight we can readily see the errors and wonder why we did not see them earlier when they were so obvious.

Thus, it helps to have some rules in order not to be swept away by prevailing fashion. Let's briefly review the four don't rules:

1. Don't be influenced by a short performance record of a money manager, broker, or advisor.

2. Don't rely solely on the case rate. Take into account the prior probabilities.

3. Don't be seduced by recent rates of investment return for individual stocks or the market that deviate sharply from past norms. Longer-term characteristics of stocks, the base rate, are far more likely to be reestablished.

4. Don't expect the strategy you adopt to prove a quick success in the marketplace.

Frankly, the above four rules are going to be a lot harder to follow than you might think, because the cognitive biases are anything but phantoms. However, the effort to understand their pull should prove rewarding and help avoid many a serious error.

Shortcuts to Disaster

We find, then, that the information-processing shortcuts—called heuristics—which are normally both highly efficient and immensely timesaving in day-to-day situations, work systematically against us in the marketplace. Only in recent years has it been recognized that people simply do not follow the principles of probability theory under conditions of uncertainty. The tendency to underestimate or altogether ignore past probabilities in making a decision is undoubtedly the most significant problem of intuitive prediction in fields as diverse as financial analysis, accounting, geography, engineering, and military intelligence.[15] The implications of such consistent errors and cognitive biases are enormous, not only in economics, management, and investments, but in virtually every area where such decision making comes into play.

But the cognitive biases seem to flourish particularly well in the stock market and result in a high rate of investment error. These interacting biases systematically lead us into bad investment decisions. We are too apt to look at insufficient information in order to confirm a course of action, we are too inclined to put great emphasis on recent or emotionally compelling events, and we expect our decisions to be met with quick market confirmation. The more we discuss a course and identify with it, the less we believe prior standards are valid.

And so each trend and fashion looks unique, is identified as such, and inevitably takes its toll. Knowledge that none prevails for long is dismissed.

These cognitive biases, which affect each of us to a greater or lesser extent, are far more firmly locked into place by the group pressures described previously. Our own inclinations are powerfully reinforced when we see other people we respect interpret information the way we do. The failure of professional investors who are normally oriented to current fashions seems telling evidence of this point.

However, we should not be discouraged by these biases. In fact, as was suggested earlier, they can be harnessed to work in our favor. Let's turn to see how next.

PART III

A WORKABLE INVESTMENT STRATEGY

CHAPTER SEVEN

The Low Price/Earnings Ratio Investment Strategy: What Is It?

In Samuel Beckett's play Vladimir and Estragon sit endlessly waiting for Godot. Having come this far, you may have begun to feel that a sound and workable investment strategy, like Godot, may never appear. Certainly, the problems identified in the last three chapters suggest futility. Man's abilities as an information processor are imperfect, his limitations as an intuitive statistician are disheartening, and his investment decisions are all too often made under the influence of his fellow inebriates.

Fortunately, the story does not end here. Unlike Beckett's play, there is a good chance for a happier ending. Indeed, the very consistency of investor behavior patterns forms a crucial part of the strategy I'm about to propose. These patterns can be translated into a workable investment method that may very well pinpoint excellent opportunities for you.

The Quagmire of Visibility

One of the few things academics and financial practitioners agree on these days is this: earnings are a major determinant of stock prices.[1] Hence the ability to forecast profits with reasonable accuracy should give the professional a decided edge over the crowd. Little wonder, then, that an article of faith among Wall Street research departments has been that nothing is as important in the practice of security analysis as estimating the earnings outlook. The clearer the company's prospects and the better they look at a particular time, the better the visibility. Companies with the best earnings prospects and fastest growth rates are normally accorded higher price/earnings ratios, while companies with poor or lackluster prospects are banished to the lower-multiple tiers. Sometimes the disparity between the price/earnings ratios of the most favored and the least favored companies is immense. In early 1973, for example, investors valued each dollar of earnings of McDonald's or Disney at ten times a dollar earned by U.S. Steel.

In order to make such evaluations, as we have seen, forecasts extending earnings well into the future must be made with extreme accuracy. Forecasting is the heart of most security analysis as it is practiced today.

But from the evidence screened previously, the accuracy of such forecasts should be viewed with suspicion. Investment strategies so based have performed with a great deal of inconsistency, to say the least. What seems apparent is that the companies the experts liked best tended to be the wrong ones to buy. We must therefore ask another question: should one avoid the stocks the experts or the crowd are pursuing, and pursue the ones they are avoiding? The answer, as we shall see, is an unqualified yes. Here we will document the consistent success of an investment strategy over an almost forty-year period—a strategy that dramatically opposes much of conventional wisdom—and the reasons why it works.

For the findings show that *those companies that the market expects will have the best futures as measured by the price/earnings ratios they are accorded have consistently done worst subsequently, while the stocks believed to have the most dismal futures have always provided the best subsequent returns.* The foundation of the strategy is not without an element of black comedy. In fact, to some devotees of contemporary investment methods, the approach may appear to be a form of devil worship. What is believed to be "good" as an investment, according to P/E multiples, almost invariably turns out "bad"—and naturally, what is "bad" turns out to be very "good."

However, the findings are fortunately not in the least magical. For we know about the immense difficulties, and shortly we will see corroborating statistical evidence, of predicting earnings and economic events with any degree of consistency. Most investors do not recognize this, and when forecasting methods fail, aided in no small degree by the biases enumerated in the last chapter, a predictable psychological reaction occurs.

And here we confront the main irony: *One of the most obvious and predictable variables that can be harnessed into a workable investment strategy is the continuous overreaction of man himself when his assessment of a company's earnings (or the economy itself) proves incorrect.* This works just as surely with the investor today as it has with investors in all markets of the past. Let's turn to just how consistent this overreaction actually is.

The World Turned Upside Down

Beginning in the 1960s, researchers began to wonder if visibility— that crucial pillar of modern security analysis—was actually as solid as generally believed. One of the first to question how accurate the P/E ratio was as a measure of subsequent market performance was Francis Nicholson, who researched the problem while with the Provident National Bank.

In one comprehensive study done in 1968 measuring the relative performance of high versus low P/E stocks, he analyzed 189 companies of trust company quality in eighteen industries over the twenty-five years between 1937 and 1962. The results are given in table 9.

Nicholson divided the stocks into five equal groups solely ac-

Table 9
ANNUAL EARNINGS RELATED TO MEAN PRICES

P/E Quintile 1937–62	AVERAGE PRICE APPRECIATION PERCENTAGES OVER TOTAL PERIOD AFTER						
	1 Yr.	2 Yrs.	3 Yrs.	4 Yrs.	5 Yrs.	6 Yrs.	7 Yrs.
1st (highest)	3	11	21	31	46	65	84
2nd	6	14	24	35	50	65	83
3rd	7	18	30	43	60	77	96
4th	9	22	34	48	65	82	100
5th (lowest)	16	34	55	76	98	125	149

SOURCE: *Financial Analysts Journal* (January–February 1968).

cording to their P/E rankings. The groups (or "quintiles," in statistical nomenclature) were rearranged by their P/E rankings for periods of one to seven years. Recasting the quintiles annually on the basis of the new P/E information resulted in the stocks most out of favor (quintile 5) showing a 16 percent annual rate of appreciation over the total time span. Conversely, switching into the highest P/E's on the same basis resulted in only 3 percent annual appreciation over the period. Although the performance discrepancies were reduced with longer holding periods, even after holding the original portfolios for seven years, the lowest 20 percent did almost twice as well as the highest.

Similar results were turned up by Paul Miller, Jr., who used as his data base the companies on the COMPUSTAT 1800 Industrial Tapes with sales of over $150 million between 1948 and 1964.[2]

Like Nicholson, Miller divided the stocks into quintiles according to their P/E's. The findings are displayed in table 10. With remarkable consistency, investors completely misjudged subsequent performance. In both studies the results are completely uniform. The second most popular quintile had the second worst results, while the second most unpopular quintile had the second best results.

Miller also found that the lowest 20 percent of stocks according to P/E's did best in twelve of the next seventeen years. The highest 20 percent, by comparison, did best in only one subsequent year and worst in eight.

A third study, this one involving the thirty stocks in the Dow-Jones Industrial Average itself, is cited in *The Intelligent Investor.* The performance of the ten lowest and the ten highest P/E's in the group and of the combined thirty stocks in the industrial average was measured over five-year periods between 1937 and 1969. In each time span the low P/E's did better than the market and the high P/E's did worse. (See table 11.)

The study also calculated the results of investing $10,000 in either the high- or low-multiple groups in the industrial average in 1937 and switching every five years into the lowest P/E's (in the first case) and the highest P/E's (in the latter). Ten thousand dollars invested in this manner in the lowest P/E's in 1937 would have increased to $66,866 by the end of 1962. Invested in the highest

*All fiscal years in the study were between September 30 and January 31. All companies studied had positive earnings. The number of such companies increased from 110 in the former year to 334 in the latter.

Table 10
AVERAGE PRICE INCREASE PER YEAR, 1948–64

P/E QUINTILE	PRICE INCREASE
1st (highest P/E)	7.7%
2nd	9.2
3rd	12.0
4th	12.8
5th (lowest P/E)	18.4

SOURCE: Drexel & Co., Philadelphia, monthly review, 1966.

Table 11
AVERAGE ANNUAL PERCENTAGE GAIN OR LOSS ON TEST ISSUES, 1937–69

PERIOD	10 LOW-MULTIPLE ISSUES	10 HIGH-MULTIPLE ISSUES	30 DJIA STOCKS
1937–42	− 2.2	−10.0	− 6.3
1943–47	17.3	8.3	14.9
1948–52	16.4	4.6	9.9
1953–57	20.9	10.0	13.7
1958–62	10.2	− 3.3	3.6
1963–69	8.0	4.6	4.0

SOURCE: Benjamin Graham, *The Intelligent Investor,* 4th ed. (New York: Harper & Row, 1973), p. 80.

P/E's, the $10,000 would have appreciated to only $25,437. Finally, left in the Dow-Jones Industrial Average itself, the $10,000 would have grown to $35,600 by 1962.

A number of other studies through the 1960s came up with the same conclusion.* One by William Breen, published in the *Financial Analysts Journal,* used the fourteen hundred companies on the COMPUSTAT tapes for the 1953–66 period.[5] He eliminated all stocks with less than 10 percent annual earnings growth in the previous five years. He then selected a number of portfolios. The first consisted of ten stocks with the lowest P/E multiples relative to the entire market. The second portfolio also consisted of ten stocks, but

*Francis Nicholson, in an earlier test that eliminated companies with nominal earnings, measured the performance of high and low P/E stocks in the chemicals industry between 1937 and 1954.[3] The results strongly favored the low P/E stocks. James McWilliams used a sample of nine hundred stocks from the S&P COMPUSTAT tapes in the 1953–64 period and found strong corroboration of the better performance of low P/E stocks. McWilliams further discovered that while stocks having the highest individual appreciation in any given year appeared to be randomly distributed, those with the greatest declines were in the high P/E ratio group.[4]

in this case they had the lowest P/E multiples relative to their own industries. Each portfolio was assumed to be purchased in the first week of January and sold one year later. Both appreciation (or loss) and dividends were included in the return. Randomly selected portfolios were constructed and compared with the results of the two low-multiple portfolios. Table 12 indicates the proportion of randomly selected portfolios in each year that underperformed the low P/E groups. Again, the findings are dramatic. The low P/E's in both cases almost consistently outperformed a large percentage of randomly selected portfolios.

The conclusion of these studies, of course, indicated that low P/E stocks were distinctly superior investments over an almost thirty-year period. But theories, like sacred cows, die hard, and the findings created little stir at the time.

Table 12

PERFORMANCE OF LOW P/E STOCKS RELATIVE TO RANDOMLY SELECTED PORTFOLIOS

	LOW P/E RELATIVE TO MARKET		LOW P/E RELATIVE TO INDUSTRY	
YEAR	COMPOUND RETURN	PERCENTAGE OF RANDOMLY SELECTED PORTFOLIOS WITH LOWER RETURN	COMPOUND RETURN	PERCENTAGE OF RANDOMLY SELECTED PORTFOLIOS WITH LOWER RETURN
1953	19.3%	95%	13.3%	95%
1954	57.5	95	92.8	95
1955	45.2	95	35.5	95
1956	19.4	90	7.7	65
1957	−9.9	45	−15.6	20
1958	112.6	95	72.6	95
1959	102.9	95	61.1	95
1960	13.7	90	12.1	90
1961	155.2	95	36.1	70
1962	−4.2	95	−19.8	35
1963	25.5	75	33.8	90
1964	26.1	80	26.7	80
1965	50.5	80	22.0	15
1966	3.4	85	6.1	90
Average	37.5%	—	23.9%	—

SOURCE: *Financial Analysts Journal* (July–August 1968).

If the results were analyzed at all, they were criticized. For one thing, the growth school was still dominant among institutional investors during the first half of the decade. Even after the demolition of the two-tier market in 1974–75, many institutional investors could not bring themselves to believe the efficacy of the findings. After all, the results did seem to cavalierly toss aside our years of indoctrination (or perhaps brainwashing) to the contrary. When I published a paper in early 1976 summarizing some of the previous research, a number of professionals told me that such information was only history: "Markets of the 1970s are very different."

And the evidence, of course, was a mere transitory enigma to our financial friends in academe who in the late 1960s were adjusting the final nuts and bolts of the formidable efficient-market hypothesis. According to this university-launched dreadnought, such results simply could not exist because rational profit-seeking investors would not allow them to. Clever investors would immediately jump into the better-performing lower P/E stocks and stay clear of the trickier high P/E multiples until all the extra profits were extracted from the unpopular stocks.

Further academic criticism asserted that low P/E stocks were systematically riskier (in the parlance, had higher Betas) and therefore deserved to provide somewhat higher returns. And for the *coup de grace,* criticisms of the previous studies were wheeled into action. They were mostly hair-splitting and not convincing—at least to me. But recalling Einstein's dictum that the theory determines the observations, here indeed was evidence that *could not* exist if the dreadnought was to proceed merrily annihilating current investment practice.

Some Newer Work

Buying low P/E stocks appeared successful in studies of past performance. And, as a practical matter, it had worked for me, as I indicated—no small inducement to belief. Consequently, I thought it might be interesting to bring the findings up-to-date. Watching the collapse of the high P/E concept stocks through the early 1970s and finally the entire two-tier market in 1973–76,* it seemed that things had not really changed all that much. And a recent study which I undertook with the cooperation of Rauscher Pierce Refsnes Securities again demonstrated the low P/E case.† The work attested to the overall superior performance of such stocks through the current decade.

The experimental design tried to deal as thoroughly as possible with the problems of the previous findings.‡ The sample, the largest to date, was constructed from the COMPUSTAT 1800 Industrial Tapes, which contain data on the largest publicly held companies in the country. Included in the sample of 1,251 issues were 70 percent of the common stocks listed on the New York Stock Exchange as well as large companies on the AMEX and over-the-counter.§ The study covered the mid-1968–77 period. As in Breen's study, total return was measured—capital gains (or losses) and dividends paid—in each period analyzed.

The stocks were arranged by computer into ten equal groups (called deciles) strictly according to P/E's. The subsequent performance of each decile was measured. To determine P/E rankings, most recent twelve-month earnings were used to the end of each period, along with price on the last day of trading two months later. In effect, the earnings information was fully public at the time, and the P/E ratios were the ones currently available in the financial section of any newspaper.

A large number of different holding periods were used to get as many comparisons as possible of the performance of the various P/E groups. Portfolios were recast according to new P/E information as frequently as every three, six, or nine months, or held unchanged for as long as nine years.

Table 13 gives the results for the entire period of the study. *Even a glance at the record indicates the superior results of the low-multiple groups over the length of the study.* Recasting the deciles quarterly

---

*I've documented some of the evidence on the performance of concept stocks and the two-tier market in *Psychology and the Stock Market,* chapter 6.

†I was ably assisted by Kirit Patel, Jane Ruelfi, Bill Avera, and Clifford Atherton, among others.

‡For details, see footnote on page 135.

§All companies with five-year records and with fiscal years ending in March, June, September, or December were included. In the high P/E group, a maximum multiple of 75 was used to filter out companies with only nominal earnings, which were put into an eleventh group and included in the calculation of the overall sample return. Results of this group were erratic, partly because the sample size varied markedly in the different holding periods.

according to latest twelve-month earnings shows dramatic results. Had an investor put $10,000 evenly in the bottom 10 percent of P/E's at the end of August 1968 and switched quarterly thereafter to keep in the lowest P/E's continuously, he would have amassed $32,519 before commissions through August 31, 1977—and these returns occurred during an extremely poor period for the market. By comparison, had the investor switched quarterly on the same basis into the best stocks, the highest P/E's (decile 1), his $10,000 would have diminished to $7,708. In other words, the lowest P/E stocks did more than four times as well as the highest over the entire period of the study.

Had an investor switched annually, he would have received returns of 10.3 percent in the lowest P/E decile; by comparison, the returns in the top P/E decile were –1.1 percent. Even buying and holding the same stocks over the length of the study still distinctly favored the low P/E's. Ten thousand dollars in the bottom 10 percent of stocks in August 1968 held unchanged to August 1977 would have become $19,824; and $10,000 in the top 10 percent, $10,306. Although the superiority of the bottom over the top group is the most impressive, the eighth and ninth normally did far better than the second and third.

"But wait," the skeptical top-tier advocate might say. "What if you used a different starting point—for example, a starting date at

Table 13
ANNUALIZED COMPOUND RATES OF RETURN, AUGUST 1968–AUGUST 1977 (FULL PERIOD OF STUDY)

STOCKS RANKED BY P/E MULTIPLES DECILE	SWITCHING AFTER EACH				HOLDING ORIGINAL PORTFOLIO FOR 9 YEARS
	1 QUARTER	6 MONTHS	1 YEAR	3 YEARS	
1 (highest)	−2.64%	−1.06%	−1.13%	−1.43%	0.33%
2	0.92	1.62	0.56	−0.28	1.27
3	0.51	0.62	1.63	0.85	3.30
4	3.06	3.42	3.31	4.87	5.36
5	2.19	4.46	2.93	5.02	3.72
6	4.84	5.33	6.70	4.82	4.52
7	7.90	6.07	6.85	5.89	6.08
8	8.83	8.24	8.56	7.78	6.35
9	11.85	8.40	6.08	7.73	6.40
10 (lowest)	14.00	11.68	10.26	10.89	7.89
Average return of sample		4.75%			

the bottom of the 1970 market. Would the top tier (the high P/E's) do better from this point to the end of the 1974 bear market?"

Our numbers cruncher, a large Digital Equipment computer, had the answer in a flash; it is provided in table 14. The low P/E stocks far outperformed the upper deciles: the bottom 10 percent of P/E's over the full four-and-a-half-year period provided returns of 2.3 percent, while the top 10 percent of P/E's returned –1.5 percent. You might certainly ask why returns were so low. The answer lies in the fact that the bottom of the 1974 market was even lower than the bottom of the 1970 market. The S&P 500 (before dividends) was 9.1 percent under its May 1970 level in November of 1974. When allowances are made for sample composition and dividend reinvestment, results do not appear to be strikingly different.*

We next asked the computer to give us a snapshot of how the P/E investment strategy worked in another time period, this time from the top of the 1968 market to the market top in 1972, using the November 1968 to November 1972 period. Once again, the low P/E deciles produced superior overall results.

After reviewing these periods of bad markets, our tireless electronic colleague deserved a more cheerful question: how did the low P/E strategies work between the market bottom of August 1970 and

Table 14
ANNUALIZED COMPOUND RATES OF RETURN, MAY
1970–NOVEMBER 1974 (MARKET BOTTOM TO BOTTOM)

STOCKS RANKED BY P/E MULTIPLES	SWITCHING AFTER EACH				HOLDING ORIGINAL PORTFOLIO FOR
DECILE	1 QUARTER	6 MONTHS	9 MONTHS	2¼ YEARS	4½ YEARS
1 (highest)	−5.45%	−5.08%	−2.67%	−5.33%	−1.54%
2	0.68	0.80	0.59	−6.07	−0.98
3	−2.64	−0.99	−1.91	−2.84	−2.49
4	−1.52	−3.02	−0.82	−2.47	−0.73
5	−4.05	−2.84	−2.39	−2.02	−0.89
6	−1.74	0.87	−0.60	−1.78	−1.80
7	2.34	1.34	0.55	1.52	1.21
8	0.85	0.17	−0.35	4.04	3.32
9	2.00	1.50	−1.04	0.88	−0.65
10 (lowest)	6.01	3.12	2.54	5.04	2.27
Average return of sample			−0.60%		

*The larger equally weighted indices, such as the *Value Line* composite average of 1,684 stocks, were down more than the S&P 500 through this period.

the end of August 1976? The answer is found in table 15 (page 134), which shows the annualized returns for portfolios held for one to six years. Portfolios were held intact for the four- to six-year periods. As you can see, superior returns—and for a change, far above average ones—were provided for the low P/E stocks in all but the four- and five-year time periods. For example, turning over portfolios every three years provided 15.2 percent annual returns for the lowest P/E decile and 3.5 for the highest. Holding portfolios without switching for the full six years provided annual returns of 12.4 percent for the least-favored P/E stocks, compared with 7.1 percent for the highest 10 percent.

The four-year returns, and to some extent the five-year returns, are much lower than the rest. This is because we were near the bottom of the bear market in 1974, the worst of the entire postwar period, in the first case, and in the earlier stages of the recovery in the second.

Do low P/E strategies always provide superior results? No investment strategy should, and there was one period I was particularly curious about: namely, when it was pretty universally accepted that high-multiple stocks did do considerably better—during the height of the two-tier market between 1970 and 1973. Recall that at the time investing in high P/E stocks was almost obsessional with individual and institutional investors alike. To measure these results, we began at the bottom of the 1970 market once again, as this was the point from which the high P/E concept stocks and the growth stocks caught fire. The results are found in table 16, page 134.

As you can see, the high-multiple stocks did do relatively better than in the previous tables, particularly for the one-year holding period. In any case, however, even in a period where it was common belief that high P/E stocks were absolutely the buy, the table indicates that such was definitely not the case.

The superiority of the low P/E groups, then, is much more consistent than that of the higher P/E deciles. Although the bottom decile seems to have the best results in just about any period surveyed, the sixth, seventh, and eighth deciles have on occasion outperformed the ninth.

The findings presented here certainly make it appear that the advantage of a low P/E strategy is clear-cut. *In our work, it did not matter whether the investor started near a market top or a market bottom; superior returns were provided in any phase of the market*

Table 15
ANNUALIZED COMPOUND RATES OF RETURN, AUGUST
1970–AUGUST 1976

STOCKS RANKED BY P/E MULTIPLES	SWITCHING AFTER EACH			HOLDING ORIGINAL PORTFOLIO FOR		
DECILE	1 YEAR	2 YEARS	3 YEARS	4 YEARS	5 YEARS	6 YEARS
1 (highest)	6.10%	4.93%	3.50%	−1.45%	5.07%	7.07%
2	6.25	2.48	5.64	−1.42	6.47	8.03
3	8.01	6.72	10.07	−2.49	4.68	8.20
4	8.79	7.60	8.14	−4.95	3.33	7.26
5	7.49	9.52	12.00	−3.42	4.73	9.91
6	11.99	10.91	10.67	−2.81	5.58	9.91
7	12.36	13.28	11.67	1.21	7.69	11.99
8	12.79	12.70	11.64	−0.82	6.34	11.41
9	8.61	11.16	11.50	1.47	7.19	12.30
10 (lowest)	14.13	15.45	15.16	0.09	7.66	12.39

Average return of sample
	10.14%	10.14%	10.14%	−1.26%	6.22%	10.14%

Table 16
ANNUALIZED COMPOUND RATES OF RETURN, MAY
1970–FEBRUARY 1973 (TWO-TIER MARKET)

STOCKS RANKED BY P/E MULTIPLES	SWITCHING AFTER EACH				HOLDING ORIGINAL PORTFOLIO FOR
DECILE	1 QUARTER	6 MONTHS	1 YEAR	2 YEARS	2¾ YEARS
1 (highest)	13.07%	12.51%	15.78%	12.84%	12.40%
2	19.19	20.66	15.05	12.04	13.01
3	14.11	15.49	17.64	16.17	15.86
4	13.95	13.27	14.34	13.12	14.97
5	10.71	10.56	12.66	13.32	16.94
6	13.19	15.88	15.75	12.22	12.98
7	14.83	14.26	13.10	15.39	16.01
8	15.06	14.54	14.19	16.93	17.23
9	16.45	17.83	17.56	19.36	14.20
10 (lowest)	20.35	16.09	15.41	18.56	15.25

Average return of sample
	14.54%				

cycle (including the top-tier mania). And the cycle we measured showed the widest fluctuations of any in the postwar period. The average multiple of the S&P 425 varied sharply—from a high of 21 to a low of 7—yet the findings consistently and dramatically supported the strategy of buying and holding out-of-favor stocks.

The results in the study were certainly more striking than I had expected. If anything, they indicated patterns of investor behavior—and error—far more systematic than one would have believed possible.

But what of some of the past criticisms? Did any of them still have validity?* An efficient-market theorist would legitimately inquire about Beta—that somewhat discredited gauge of risk. "Low P/E groups are more volatile," he might say, "and should return more." We asked the computer this question, and fifty thousand or so calculations, or half a second, later, we had our answer. The Beta measurements indicated that, if anything, the low P/E stocks as a group were slightly less volatile than the higher deciles.† Low P/E stocks not only gave you better performance, but were marginally safer!

Our findings have also been confirmed by other new work in recent years. Two carefully prepared studies by Sanjoy Basu[6] came up with similar results. In his most recent study, published in the *Journal of Finance* in June 1977, Basu used a data base of 1,400 firms from the New York Stock Exchange between August 1956 and August 1971. He took 750 companies that had year-ends of December 31 and turned over the portfolios annually, using prices on April 1 of the following year. Like most of the previous studies, he divided the stocks into quintiles according to P/E rankings. The results (again using total return) are shown in table 17, page 136.

Basu's conclusions were similar to all the others: "The average annual rate of return declines (to some extent monotonically) as one moves from low P/E to high P/E portfolios."

Basu found, as we did, that the low P/E stocks provided superior returns, and were also somewhat less risky. Again, using his words: "However, contrary to capital market theory, the higher returns in the low P/E portfolios were not associated with higher

*Within the experimental design, we adjusted methodological criticisms of previous studies, such as hindsight bias—selecting stocks, as Nicholson did, that had survived to 1962, something an investor of 1937 could not have known; and not using year-end earnings and prices, as previous studies did, when investors could not know earnings until several months later. As I said, I did not think these would markedly change results, and our findings indicate they didn't.

†Average Beta, starting with the lowest deciles, was .9898, .9791, .9648, .9657, .9646, .9785, .9933, .9777, 1.3596, .9396. Average Beta for the bottom 40 percent was .9748; for the top 40 percent, 1.0667. An interesting by-product of this study appeared to be that Betas did not seem to be stable over time.

Table 17
PERFORMANCE OF STOCKS ACCORDING TO P/E RANKING,
APRIL 1957–MARCH 1971

P/E QUINTILE		BETA (SYSTEMATIC RISK)
A (highest)	9.3	1.1121
A*	9.6	1.0579
B	9.3	1.0387
C	11.7	0.9678
D	13.6	0.9401
E (lowest)	16.3	0.9866

A = highest P/E quintile.
A* = highest P/E quintile, excluding stocks with negative earnings.
SOURCE: As adapted from *Journal of Finance* 32 (no. 3, June 1977): 866.

levels of systematic risk. The systematic risk of portfolios D and E (the lowest) were lower than those for A and B (the highest)."

This work, updated and adjusted for previous criticisms through August 1977, thus provides new evidence that links to a chain extending over forty years, documenting the superior performance of low P/E issues.

Buying Out-of-Favor Stocks

The consistency of the previous studies is truly remarkable. Over almost every and any period measured, the stocks considered to have the best prospects (according to their P/E ratios) fared significantly worse than the low P/E stocks, using the same criterion. This leads us to a general observation, or rule if you like:

Rule 5: The evidence strongly supports an investment philosophy of buying solid companies currently out of market favor as measured by their price/earnings ratios.

It is the very unpopularity of such issues—because their visibility seems so poor when contrasted with the high enthusiasm displayed for the prospects of the "best" companies—that makes such an approach possible.

But if the record is so clear, why isn't everybody scouring the stock pages to bag these plump quarries—especially when the season is always open and there is no limit on the number you can bring home?

Needless to say, the reasons are not hard to find. Recall that these stocks violate just about every notion we have about proper investment theory.* In fact, some of the "good old boys" with impeccable backgrounds, faithful to the tried and failing methods of current investment practice, might, as I indicated, find this strategy borders on the heretical. "Do you know what's down there?" a major money manager once asked me, indicating by exhaling a touch more heavily than usual his considerable disgust. "How can any prudent man look at companies like these with such unthinkably poor visibility?" The high P/E's, on the other hand, present the best visibility money can buy. They are the real blue bloods of the investment scene. How, then, can one recommend such a reversal of course?

And here we run into the problem. Despite the record extending over four decades, people still believe they can accurately predict which stocks will perform well and which poorly. They are in no small measure aided by the cognitive biases. The high P/E companies have far higher than average earnings, sometimes for quite extensive periods, and prices advanced in line or ahead of their improving results. Many experts recommend these stocks—usually after they have already made a considerable move. As the P/E ratios move further and further away from those of average companies, many believe the divergence is justified, if indeed it should not be greater. The same factors apply in the opposite manner to the out-of-favor stocks.

People are too sure of their evaluations, which prove wrong often enough to lead to the results we have viewed. *The psychological consistency of the error is remarkable.*

This does not mean, of course, that there are not excellent stocks that justify their price/earnings ratios and others that should command only the slimmest of multiples. But, as the evidence indicates, these are relatively few, and, as we'll see next, the chances of knowing which they will be at the time are very small. Predicting the future is far trickier than most people imagine.

---

*Although not those of Benjamin Graham. He warned repeatedly, in both *The Intelligent Investor* and *Security Analysis,* of the dangers of overemphasizing visibility, which he also believed would lead to repeated investor errors.

CHAPTER EIGHT

Why Low P/E Strategies Work: The Failure of Forecasting Techniques

As the last chapter indicated, investors are too sure of their ability to judge how well or poorly a company will do. However, an impressive and growing body of evidence developed in recent years appears to demonstrate this conclusion. Earnings estimates and the forecasts of corporate executives and economists that often underlie them just aren't very reliable. Worse than that, the expert consensus about the outlook for the economy or estimate for an individual company is frequently far off the mark—so far off, in fact, that using such forecasts can often prove harmful to stock selection, portfolio performance, and investment health. I think it is important that we review these findings in greater detail, for they are at the heart of why low price/earnings strategies work and why the casualty rate among those using other contemporary methods is so high.

Chapter 5 showed that making earnings estimates is hardly a simple process. Because of our limited ability at configural, or interactive, reasoning and the vast amounts of information we are required to analyze, errors are very common. We have already seen that though they are not confined to the marketplace, the stock market appears to provide a hothouse environment for such errors because of the large number of inputs and assumptions required by the investor to forecast earnings correctly.

Yet reasonably good earnings estimates are essential to contemporary method. Just how important the differences between forecasts and actual earnings may be to the future performance of stock prices was demonstrated in a study by Niederhoffer and Regan. The researchers examined the fifty best- and worst-performing stocks on the New York Stock Exchange in 1970, and a random sample of one hundred other companies. Earnings estimates were taken from the Standard & Poor's Earnings Estimator (which specializes in tracking estimates of major retail and some institutional brokerage houses).

Figures were available for forty-four of the top fifty performers. The median projection called for a rise in earnings of 7.7 percent for the group. In fact, the actual increase turned out to be 21.4 percent. The forecast was off by 13.4 percent, enough to result in the median price of this group appreciating 48.4 percent!

The results in the bottom fifty companies are even more telling. Of the half-hundred worst-performing equities, thirty-four had published estimates. The median estimate was a rise of 15.3 percent. The actual reported earnings: a median decline of 56.7 percent. This "estimate gap" was accompanied by a staggering 83 percent drop in price.

Niederhoffer and Regan concluded that estimates were an important factor in performance: "In sum, the results of this study demonstrate that stock prices are strongly dependent on earnings changes, both absolute and relative to analysts' estimates. . . . It is clear that an accurate earnings estimate is of enormous value in stock selection."[1]

Enter the Economic Forecaster

Since fundamental earnings estimates rely on many underlying economic assumptions, the forecasting record of economists might be a good launching point to begin an analysis of the process.

Although economists have done dozens of excellent studies on the performance of financial institutions and the forecasting records of executives and analysts, they have surprisingly overlooked their own pronouncements. Perhaps judiciously, for while the evidence remains sketchy, what is available does not provide a picture of sibylic accuracy.

A survey of thirty-two major forecasters in December 1973, for example, discovered that only one had projected any decline in economic activity the following year—1974—which saw the worst recession of the entire postwar period.[2] In fact, at a conference called in the fall of 1974 by President Ford, the nation's leading economists resoundingly devoted their attention to the problems of curbing inflation. Newspapers pictured many of them happily wearing their large WIN buttons (Whip Inflation Now). They showed absolutely no awareness that the most critical phase of the recession was just about to start. It was almost like watching a professional football player pick up a loose ball, lose direction, and start rushing downfield the wrong way, followed by the rest of the team yelling encouragement. With the passage of time, and more detailed study of recent economic events, history may prove kinder to the economic advisors of Herbert Hoover.

But not to digress. What about the one man who proved correct in late 1973 and actually did see the recession coming? An article reported: "[Mr. X] stopped issuing stock market forecasts several years ago after being wide of the mark time after time."

Was this instance, striking as it is, simply the exception that proves the rule? Apparently not. Other evidence indicates that the forecasting record of the "dismal science" is dismal indeed. In 1947 a group of well-known forecasters predicted that U.S. economic activity would decline approximately 6 percent. The economy that year actually proved to be one of the strongest on record, showing an increase of 11 percent. And a survey of many dozens of economists and business analysts in late 1969, with business already in a downturn, disclosed that few believed a recession would occur in 1970.[3]

If you detect some not-too-subdued delight in such happenings, I am afraid it is the natural reaction of a professional investor. For in building random walk theory, economists have assumed that we professionals can make extremely accurate forecasts using most of the very techniques with which they themselves have floundered so often. I suppose it's always easier to analyze another's performance.

The problem again takes us to familiar ground: the more complex the level of decision, the greater the probability of a high level of error. Recently, albeit slowly, a part of the economic profession itself is questioning the value of forecasting.

These economists foresee the end of what they call "Newtonian economics," with its predictable cause-and-effect relationships. Too many things can go awry to base much faith on a simple one-figure forecast. According to Professor James B. Ramsey of New York University, "Almost all scientific disciplines have been moving in recent years from sure cause-and-effect relationships (deterministic) to (odds-on) 'stochastic' formulations of their theories."[4] Professor Lester Thurow of MIT adds that "to judge economics on its prediction record is to judge it in a way no other science is judged"[5] (except perhaps the way economists judge us poor market professionals). Professors Thurow and Ramsey see the end of simple single-figure estimates and the adoption of much wider ranges by economists to reflect the vast political and economic uncertainty the forecasts actually entail.

Management Forecasts

Since earnings estimates normally rely on many economic assumptions as well as dozens of factors unique to the industry or company, they too can often be far off the mark, frequently accompanied by the even wider swings in price that the Niederhoffer and Regan study indicated.

An article in the *Journal of Business* in October 1972[6] examined the estimates made by executives of fifty corporations published in the *Wall Street Journal* in 1968. Because the thorough analyst or money manager carefully interviews senior corporate officials in making his or her own projections, the results are illuminating. The executives missed actual company earnings by an amazing average of 20.1 percent. The error was downward-biased, since one company—Phoenix Steel, where the forecast of $2.50 in profits turned into a loss of $1.79, a difference of 139.7 percent—was excluded. Also telling was that the average forecast was for a period of under eight months (after eliminating the six forecasts made within a month or less of the end of the time, the average was still only 8.2 months).

An earlier study by Green and Segall (1967)[7] examined the accuracy of twelve company forecasts published during the 1963–64 period, again in the *Wall Street Journal.* Only seven precise dollar figures were given. Because of one large error (268.4 percent), the average absolute error for the seven was 50.3 percent. However, even after eliminating the figure, the mean error was still a formidable 14.0 percent.

A more recent study made by Basi, Carey, and Twark in 1976 measured the estimates of a group of executives of eighty-eight companies published in the *Wall Street Journal* in 1971–72, one of the calmer periods for business in recent years. It concluded: "Given the potential disruptive effects of poor forecasting on investing decisions as a result of current stock market mechanisms, perhaps it would be wise to declare a moratorium on pressures for mandatory published forecasts by firms until forecasting techniques have been refined sufficiently to assure considerably better accuracy than currently."*[8]

As table 18 on page 144 shows, the average error of four management studies was 14.5 percent, or as wide a miss as that of the estimates of the top fifty in the Niederhoffer and Regan survey. In fact, when one remembers that most investors consider earnings increases of 7 to 8 percent normal—and 10 to 15 percent in the above-average-to-growth category—executive forecasting errors of 10 to 20 percent make it impossible for the investor relying on them to distinguish the growth stock from the also-ran.

Analysts' Forecasts

The problem becomes even more complicated for analysts and money managers since most attempt to "fine-tune" earnings estimates well within a 10 percent range. As "Street-smart" investors know, even a 5 or 6 percent "miss" of the projection—particularly for stocks with supposedly excellent visibility, such as Avon, Polaroid, Xerox, or Franklin Mint—has unleashed waves of selling in the stocks, taking the prices down five or sometimes even ten times the amount of the forecasting error itself. Thus, an acuteness in predicting capabilities is called for on the Street that even managements well into the year and aware of their results (if indeed not exercising some control over them) cannot provide.

How well do analysts do at this game, where even slight errors often result in instant wipeouts? The aforementioned Basi, Carey,

*The Securities and Exchange Commission has been toying for some years with the idea of making it mandatory for corporations to publish earnings forecasts.

Table 18
FORECASTS, ANALYSTS VERSUS MANAGEMENT

Management Forecasts, One Year or Less[a]

STUDY	PERIOD STUDIED	NUMBER OF COMPANIES	MEAN ERROR[b]
Green and Segall, 1967	1963–64	7	14.0%
Copeland and Marioni, 1972	1968	50	20.1%
McDonald, 1973[c]	1966–70	151	13.6%
Basi, Carey, and Twark, 1976	1970–71	88	10.1%

Mean error in management studies: 14.5%

Analysts' Estimates, One Year or Less

STUDY	PERIOD STUDIED	NUMBER OF COMPANIES	MEAN ERROR[b]
Samuel S. Stewart, Jr., 1973[d]	1960–64	14	10–15%
Barefield and Cominsky, 1975[e]	1967–72	100	16.1%
Basi, Carey, and Twark, 1976	1970–71	88	13.8%
Malcolm Richards, 1976[f]	1972	93	8.8%
Richards and Frazer, 1977	1973	213	22.7%
Richards, Benjamin, and Strawser, 1977[g]	1969–72	50	18.1%
Richards, Benjamin, and Strawser, 1977[g]	1972–76	92	24.1%

Mean error in analysts' studies: 16.6%

[a]Managements' estimates taken from the *Wall Street Journal.*

[b]Minus signs removed so errors do not tend to cancel each other out. The last six analysts' studies use the S&P Earnings Forecaster exclusively or as a major source of estimates.

[c]C.L. McDonald, "An Empirical Examination of the Reliability of Published Predictions of Future Earnings," *Accounting Review* 48 (1973): 502.

[d]Samuel S. Stewart, Jr., "Research Report on Corporate Forecasts," *Financial Analysts Journal* (January–February 1973): 77–85.

[e]R. M. Barefield and E. E. Cominsky, "The Accuracy of Analysts' Forecasts of Earnings per Share," *Journal of Business Research* 3 (July 1975): 241–252.

[f]R. Malcolm Richards, "Analysts' Performance and the Accuracy of Corporate Earnings Forecasts," *Journal of Business* 49 (July 1976): 350–357.

[g]Richards, Benjamin, and Strawser, *Financial Management,* Fall 1977.

SOURCE: Adapted from R. Malcolm Richards, James J. Benjamin, and Robert W. Strawser, "An Examination of the Accuracy of Earnings Forecasts," *Financial Management,* Fall 1977, p. 82.

and Twark study also recorded estimates for the same companies from the Earnings Forecaster made by analysts at the same time. The analysts' error was some 40 percent higher than the executives', averaging 13.8 percent (errors ranged from an underestimation of 38 percent to an overestimation of 126 percent).

Another study, by Richards and Frazer (1977), used the S&P Forecaster for analysts' 1973 estimates on 213 companies, mainly on the NYSE. In addition, forecasts of six other analysts were collected from institutional, brokerage, and bank trust departments (the latter "high-powered" research estimates were not publicly available). The findings indicated that the mean forecast error was a cool 22.7 percent! Moreover, only minimal differences existed among researchers on any particular company. The investigators ended by stating that the small investor was not at a disadvantage because he could not afford the more costly research: "It is unnecessary to pay large sums for certain services when others are available at low cost."[9] The authors graciously did not add, "Particularly since both were so wide of the mark."

Probably the most devastating research spotlighting errant analytical forecasting is also among the most recent. Richards, Benjamin, and Strawser, writing in *Financial Management* (Fall 1977), evaluated analysts' estimates (again from the Earnings Forecaster) for ninety-two companies listed on the New York Stock Exchange. Each concern selected had annual estimates available for the 1972–76 period. For economic comparability, companies with fiscal years ending in the mid-calendar year were eliminated. A subsample of fifty of these companies was also used where estimates were available annually from 1969 through 1972. The results are shown in tables 19a and b, page 146.

Particularly striking is the high average annual error rate: 24.1 percent for the 1972–76 period, and 18.1 percent for the 1969–72 period. The analysts proved especially susceptible to changing economic circumstances. In the recessions of 1970 and 1974, the average estimate was off by a whopping 43.1 percent and 59.6 percent respectively.[10] (In fairness, however, it should be remembered that the analysts were ably assisted by the economic forecasters.)

Were the results due simply to the major errors of a few analysts' forecasts? No. Both Richards and Barefield and Cominsky in previous studies indicated the differential among forecasters on any one company was not significant. The consensus was far off target time and again.

Another shocker is presented in table 20 (page 147), which indicates the average industry forecasting error made by analysts annually for the 1972–76 period. Over the entire time span, the error ran to 26.2 percent annually. More significant, some of the industries supposedly with the "highest visibility," such as computers and retail

Table 19a
ANALYSTS' ESTIMATES ON FIFTY COMPANIES

YEAR	MEAN ERROR
1969	8.1
1970	43.1
1971	12.8
1972	8.0

Average annual error 18.1

SOURCE: Tables 19a and b adapted from R. Malcolm Richards, James J. Benjamin, and Robert W. Strawser, "An Examination of the Accuracy of Earnings Forecasts," *Financial Management,* Fall 1977, p. 82.

Table 19b
ANALYSTS' ESTIMATES ON NINETY-TWO COMPANIES

YEAR	MEAN ERROR
1972	7.8
1973	13.7
1974	59.6
1975	22.5
1976	16.7

Average annual error 24.1

stores, actually proved to have the worst estimates. The average annual analyst error in the office equipment and computer group was an astonishing 88.8 percent.

Since these two samples were taken from the S&P Earnings Forecaster, normally carrying the largest or most widely followed companies, and the companies covered had estimates from five to nine years, the results can scarcely be considered an aberration.

As table 18 indicates, analysts strayed wide of the mark in virtually every study—the mean error of all studies was 16.6 percent, and these studies were for one year or less!

However, investors, notably professionals, attempt to extend their earnings projections out well beyond one year, particularly if the stocks involved sport above-market multiples. The higher the multiple, the greater the visibility of earnings demanded. At the height of the growth mania in 1972–73, the growth rate for the highfliers was projected out for five or ten years or longer to justify the prevailing P/E ratios—60 for Avon, 90 for Electronic Data

Table 20
ANALYSTS' FORECASTS BY INDUSTRY

| | | PERCENT MEAN ERROR | | | | AVERAGE YEARLY PERCENT MEAN ERROR |
INDUSTRY	1972	1973	1974	1975	1976	1972–76
Banking	5.5	2.3	6.4	6.5	3.7	4.9
Building	12.0	13.7	35.8	28.2	28.1	23.6
Chemical	5.9	17.2	26.4	39.8	14.5	20.8
Drugs	3.3	6.2	10.1	10.7	8.6	7.8
Electrical equip.	13.3	17.5	20.2	30.6	8.4	18.0
Electric utilities	2.9	5.5	13.5	11.6	10.8	8.9
Office equip. & computers	17.1	14.1	391.8	13.1	8.1	88.8
Paper	19.7	20.2	16.1	32.1	10.0	19.6
Petroleum	4.9	19.4	40.6	40.7	10.7	23.3
Retail stores	9.1	7.1	182.6	24.3	10.2	46.7

SOURCE: Adapted from *Financial Management,* Fall 1977.

Systems, and 100 for Polaroid. If one-year estimates were off 10 to 20 percent or more, the more distant projections, as you might expect, were certainly no better.

One of the earliest studies analyzing longer-term projections was done by Cragg and Malkiel and published in the *Journal of Finance* in March 1968. The two professors studied the earnings projections of large groups of security analysts working for five important and highly respected investment organizations, including two major New York City bank trust departments, a mutual fund, and an investment advisory firm. Estimates were made for 185 companies for periods of from one to five years. *The researchers found that most analysts' estimates were simply linear extrapolations of current trends, and that the correlations between the actual and the predicted earnings turned out to be very low.* Cragg and Malkiel state that in spite of the vast amount of additional information analysts have, supplemented by frequent company visits, estimates are based on a continuation of past trends: "The remarkable conclusion of the present study is that the careful estimates of security analysts . . . performed little better than those of (past) company growth rates."[11]

In addition, it was discovered that had the analysts made the simple forecasting assumption that the sample companies' earnings would continue to grow near the long-term rate of 4 percent annually, the projections would have resulted in smaller overall errors in the five-year period than the analysts actually made.[12]

Similar results have been found in other studies. One by Edwin Elton and Martin Gruber compared mechanical forecasting techniques (a number of formulas based on the extrapolation of current trends) against the forecasting records of institutional analysts. They found such techniques "do about as good a job of forecasting as security analysis."*[13]

Reviewing the evidence makes it appear that forecasting is far more art than science and, like the creative fields, has as few masters. Excluding the highly talented exceptions, people simply cannot predict the future with any reliability. It seems extremely dangerous, then, for us to depend on methods that require the exceptional.

Et Tu, Earnings?

Some remarkable new research also shows that forecasting earnings provides an extremely wobbly crutch for investors. Oxford Professor I.M.D. Little revealed, in a paper appropriately entitled "Higgledly Piggledly Growth," that the recent earnings trends of a large number of British companies were of no use in predicting their future course.[14] Little's work proved uncomfortable to theoreticians and practitioners alike, and was promptly criticized on methodological grounds. The criticisms were duly noted, the work was carefully redone, but unfortunately, the outcome was the same. Earnings appeared to follow a random walk of their own, with past and future rates showing virtually no correlation. Recent trends (so important to security analysis in projecting future earnings) provided no indication of their actual future course.[15]

The research was repeated in a number of major studies in this country,[16] with the same conclusions: changes in the earnings of American companies also appeared to follow a random walk from time period to time period.

*You may recall here the Meehl studies of clinical psychologists, where it was shown that simple mechanical techniques performed as well as or better than the complex analytical diagnoses in twenty separate studies of trained psychologists. In fact, mechanical prediction formulas have been suggested in a number of fields, primarily psychology, as a direct result of these problems, and they will be a part of the strategies proposed in the next chapter.

Richard Brealey, for example, examined the percentage changes of earnings of 711 American industrial companies between 1945 and 1964. As in the other studies, he too found the directions of the earnings trends were not sustained but actually showed a slight tendency toward reversal. The only exception was for companies with the steadiest rates of earnings growth, and even here the correlations were only mildly positive.[17]

Thus once again and from quite another tack we see the precariousness of attempting to place major emphasis on earnings forecasts. *In short, it is impossible in a dynamic economy with constantly changing political, economic, industrial, and competitive conditions to use the past as a basis for estimates of the future.*

The Altar of Visibility

We have just seen that an imposing body of evidence demonstrates just how unreliable the future estimates of analysts are. *If one cannot forecast with any degree of accuracy, then the range between high and low P/E multiples should be much narrower.* * *But the range usually is not, and because it is not, the road to investment opportunity is wide open to us.*

Even though the evidence seems convincing, most of us feel intuitively that something has to be wrong. After all, we can name companies with years of uninterrupted and predictable earnings progress—Johnson & Johnson, Automatic Data Processing, and Burroughs come to mind easily. However, a few years back this list would have included Polaroid, Avon, Xerox, and Honeywell—companies that were once considered to have outstanding prospects but have since been downgraded by investors.

Polaroid, one of the classic growth stocks, seems to be a particularly appropriate case. The company had an unbroken string of earnings growth between 1964 and 1970. The market anticipated spectacular earnings ahead with the introduction of its revolutionary

---

*Additional evidence demonstrates that P/E ratios are poor predictors of future earnings growth. Stocks trading at low P/E multiples will have the same probabilities of large positive earnings as stocks trading at high P/E multiples.[18] The experiment discovered that in 76 percent of the cases, there was no significant correlation between the P/E multiple and the future rate of earnings growth.[19] Other work questions the market's ability to make accurate earnings expectations.[20]

SX-70 camera, and accorded it a gravity-defying P/E multiple of 100 times earnings in 1972.

I remember clearly the enthusiasm at that time among professionals at a major conference. One of the Street's foremost experts on the stock gave us his best thinking on Polaroid's price parameters for the next eighteen months. He believed the stock, then trading at 100, would be a minimum of 125 by the end of this time period and a maximum of 200. At worst, he said, "you should make 25 percent on your money." He had just put out a bulky research report documenting the earnings explosion he expected.

Unfortunately, problems with the SX-70, the introduction of a competing camera by Kodak (which at the time many photography analysts said would only expand the market), and a badly breaking stock market resulted in the minimum price parameters proving high. The stock dropped to under 15 within twenty-four months. Its vaunted and well-documented visibility had disappeared entirely.

For years, DuPont traded at well-above-average P/E ratios as investors saw the demand for polyester and nylon synthetic fibers outstripping supply indefinitely. It didn't, and the large premium in its P/E multiple was whisked away. The same proved true of Xerox, another exceptionally fine growth company. With the expiration of its plain-paper-copier patents, it began to experience increasing competition, which led to a slowdown in its growth rate and a drastic decline in its multiple.

The two-tier market of 1972–73 saw the stress on the visibility phenomenon carried to an extreme. Not long afterward, the vaunted visibility of not a few of these "religion" stocks was shattered, and the top tier collapsed dramatically.

But Why?

There are many reasons why a company may show outstanding sales and earnings growth for a period of years, followed by succeeding periods of slower expansion. Sometimes an excellent earnings record may be traced simply to accounting legerdemain: National Student Marketing, Memorex, and University Computing might be gruesome reminders to some of you.

In every market there are scores of concept companies, some

formed by creative accounting and others by short-lived competitive advantages. Invariably the market, enraptured by the high growth rates, mesmerizes itself into believing this to be a permanent joyride. The showroom-warehouse concept of Levitz Furniture was such a case. At the height of its popularity in 1971, the company sold at one hundred times earnings—before being crippled by management and competitive problems. It then dropped 97 percent in price.

In fact, the more successful a company becomes, the more difficult the task of maintaining its momentum. Competition, government controls, and market saturation all play roles in damping down returns. Safe patents—such as those of Polaroid and Xerox—are suddenly circumvented. Products and markets seemingly invulnerable to competition for years are suddenly inundated with it. Costs rise and cannot be passed on. Management teams skilled at running rapidly expanding companies with $100 or $200 million in sales may prove totally inadequate when volume reaches $300 or $500 million, and so on. Unexpected socioeconomic events, such as the energy crisis, wreak havoc on the soundest of company visibilities.

Within a dynamic and relatively free competitive economy, there are forces at work such as these, which tend to bring down above-average sales, growth, and return on capital over time. Such other forces as reduced competition, improving managements, and tighter financial controls tend to improve returns for companies going through difficult periods. These pressures are always moving companies toward average sales and profits rather than abnormally high or low returns.

And here we might refer again to the principle of regression to the mean, which we looked at in chapter 6. Company progress rarely runs in a straight line. In a dynamic, changing environment there will be periods of excellent growth and profitability, which create the seeds that foster greater competition and lower growth sometime in the future. On the other hand, for companies and industries undergoing current difficulties, the very elements of their lowered expansion, reduction of overhead, and belt tightening often bear the fruit of above-average growth once again.

In *Security Analysis* Graham succinctly summed up the problems of analyzing corporate fortunes: "The truth of our corporate venture is quite otherwise [than investors think]. Extremely few companies have been able to show a high rate of uninterrupted growth for long periods of time. Remarkably few also of the large companies suffer ultimate extinction. For most, this history is one of vicissitudes, of ups and downs, with changes in their relative standing."[21]

The push toward average returns is a fundamental if not the fundamental principle of competitive markets. And yet it is one that never seems to have been learned on the investment scene.

The lessons of chapter 6 about our limitations as intuitive statisticians help to explain why it is so hard to recognize the principle. The cognitive biases we reviewed—the law of small numbers, recency and saliency, inputs matching outputs, and hindsight—all combine to make us believe that this time the record of the good or bad company is different . . . this time it will persist. Looking at the case rate—the visibility of the individual company itself—we consistently ignore the base rate—the overall record that visibility is more often than not illusive. Doing so makes the situation seem unique each time and leaves us wide open to exactly the same errors.

Investor Overreaction

And the push toward average returns is precisely why the superior performance of the low P/E stocks and the inferior returns of the high P/E's are so consistent. The phenomenon, though clear and well documented enough, is simply not recognized by investors at large. Thus, great emphasis is placed on forecasting, although indeterminable economic, political, and company-related events make it impossible to pinpoint the future with any degree of accuracy—the reason, of course, that earnings follow a random walk of their own.

Because this is so, the disparity between high and low P/E stocks, as indicated, would be much smaller on average if the investor were the unfailingly rational man the academics think him to be. Unfortunately, he is not. When disappointments take place in the group of stocks whose earnings supposedly have the highest visibility, there follows a negative reaction from disillusioned investors. This occurs often enough for the group to consistently underperform both the market averages and the low P/E stocks.

And with the low P/E stocks, the reaction is the opposite. Such stocks languish in investor doghouses, if not tiger cages, because of their poor near-term visibility. Our analytical tools indicate that these companies offer only the poorest of value on a continuing basis. And we tend to overemphasize the importance of the adverse circumstances they are currently encountering. Because visibility is not nearly as predictable as we would like to believe, enough pleasant surprises occur in these groups (earnings, after all, follow a random walk) to lead to their above-average performance.*

Both the high and the low P/E cases represent extremes.† The probabilities are very strong that future returns will be more in line with those of more average companies. But most investors do not see it this way. Instead, they tend to see the current trend as the norm, no matter how extreme the present situation might appear within a probability distribution. The consistent overreaction to current trends opens up a great opportunity for the investor—putting him ahead of the crowd, so to speak. Which brings us back to the theme of the last chapter, and to an important rule:

It is far safer to project a continuation of investor reactions on the basis of what we now know psychologically than it is to project the visibility of the companies themselves.

From the prior performance of the low P/E stocks we have seen this approach work with remarkable reliability over an almost forty-year period.

It is true, of course, that there are excellent companies that will continue to chalk up above-average growth for many years or even decades to come, and there are especially talented investors who will find them at reasonable prices. But for most of us, whether individual or expert, the odds of winning at this game are pretty slim.

The *Low P/E Investment Strategy*

All of these findings lead very naturally to the strategy of buying companies out of favor as determined by their current P/E ratios.

---

*It is also important to note that the sharpest reactions to news, both good and bad, occur in the shortest time periods after it becomes known. The best performance for the low P/E and the greatest disappointments for the high P/E occur in the quarterly returns, followed by those for six and nine months.

†Paradoxically, at the time of this writing, the disparity between the two groups is about as low as it has been in years.

The investment strategy is built on the assumption that most investors will continue to value stocks as they always have, placing the most stress on how good or bad the company's outlook or visibility currently is. And, if this is the case, investor expectations will continue to change frequently, often to a far greater extent than changing company fortunes. The investor has only to be aware of this psychological phenomenon and act on it.

It's like betting on a marathon race where a prize is given to all who finish. We know that the great bulk of a thousand or more major competitors (the large corporations in this case) will do so, although most will run unevenly—the pace quickening or slowing for each at different times. But the crowd, surprisingly, isn't able to remember what the race is really about. Forgetting that most will finish, they concentrate only on those ahead at the moment, betting heavily on them and heavily against the marathoners doing poorly at the time. We have seen that the evidence strongly favors betting against the crowd. The low P/E approach is the first instrument that appears to be reliable and systematic enough to guide us successfully through the market dangers by now so obvious. Perhaps there are other and better strategies yet to be devised that will make this one look crude by comparison. Nevertheless, this strategy works where nothing else appears to. Knowing that it works, we can now safely move on to outlining how to use it in detail.

CHAPTER NINE

How to Use Low P/E Investment Strategies

In markets, as in the world of espionage, there is a flood of information to cipher through, most of it inconsequential, misleading, or even contradictory. The separation of the monumental from the trivial is no easy task. In fact, the intelligence services of World War II conspicuously demonstrated how good information could be totally ignored. We know today that the Germans had information on the exact time and place of D day. And, closer to home, there were advance and repeated warnings of a probable attack on Pearl Harbor.

And so with the information that was described in chapter 7. The conclusion was clear. Buying low P/E stocks would have provided above-average returns over the last forty years. However, as we have seen, although a good part of the evidence has been available for well over a decade, many a sophisticated investor who has viewed the results didn't really believe them.

Such conclusions, after all, seem too easy—too pat. Low P/E strategies are simple, in many respects mechanical, downgrading or eliminating entirely complex judgmental factors. Can the complexity of the modern investment scene be reduced to such an approach?

Common sense says no. There must be any number of methods that should provide superior returns to the investor. But if we examine the actual results, such methods are not in evidence. No other system appears to work as consistently, or for that matter, at all.

This is not to say that there are not numbers of investors who have run up large gains, sometimes fortunes, investing in growth or concept stocks, selling short, or a dozen other ways. But their success rests far more on their judgmental abilities than on the systems themselves.

Although it translates into a relatively simple and easy-to-follow method, we have seen how the low P/E investment strategy is rooted in new and fairly complex psychological and statistical findings that, even if well documented, are antithetical to most security analysis as it is practiced today—with its heavy emphasis on presumably accurate forecasting.

In the present chapter, we'll examine the practical application of the low P/E strategies in building a stock portfolio. There are a number of possible approaches. Some totally disregard security analysis because of its inherent problems with forecasting, information processing, and decisional biases. Others rely on some of its traditional principles that have demonstrated their value, while de-emphasizing or excluding entirely those that have proven problematical.

In short, the work will be laid out in a manner that I believe will make it possible to use low P/E strategies to improve your investment results.

Some *Rules for the Low P/E Investor*

The initial problems confronting any investor are how to select individual stocks and the number of stocks he should hold in his portfolio. Let's start with a few simple rules that have proven their worth over the years:

1. *The investor should buy only low P/E stocks because of their superior performance characteristics.* However, he has a number of choices in exercising this rule, which will be discussed later.

2. *Ideally, a portfolio should be invested equally in fifteen to twenty stocks, diversified among ten to twelve industries.* This is important if your means allow it.* Diversification is essential to con-

*For investors with very limited capital, alternative strategies will be discussed later in the chapter.

duct the low P/E strategy properly. Because returns among individual issues will vary widely, it is dangerous to rely on stocks in only a few companies or industries. By spreading the risk, you have a much better chance of getting a return fairly similar to the average for the quintile or quintiles chosen, rather than one substantially above or below this level.*

In our 1968–77 sample, for example, exactly half of the 3,870 stocks in the lowest decile over the entire period performed better than the S&P 425.

3. *The low P/E investor should attempt to buy medium or large-sized companies* (such as those on which the studies have been based), which means stocks listed on the New York Stock Exchange, or larger companies on the American Stock Exchange or traded over-the-counter.

Such companies are usually subject to less accounting gimmickry than smaller ones, which provides some added measure of protection. Accounting is a devilishly tricky subject and has taken a heavy toll of investors—sophisticates as well as tyros.

The larger and medium-sized companies also present another advantage to the investor: they are more in the public eye. A turn-around in the fortunes of Bethlehem Steel (which did occur recently) is far more noticeable than that of a publicly owned five-store auto-parts chain buried in the snows and pollution of Buffalo. And finally, the larger companies have more "staying power." The failure rate among them is substantially lower than among smaller ones or start-up situations.

Should We Abandon Security Analysis Entirely?

As we have seen, selecting stocks strictly because of their low P/E multiples, with no reliance on security analysis, has turned up better-than-average returns over long periods of time. Should we, then, consider abandoning security analysis entirely? A pertinent question, I think, for the evidence we've seen certainly shows it doesn't help much. However, I would not go quite this far (and not just because

*Financial studies have indicated that well-diversified portfolios of as few as sixteen stocks have an excellent chance of replicating approximately 85 to 90 percent of the return of the group from which they are selected, even if the group is the stock market as a whole.

I've been thoroughly steeped in the doctrines of the Old Church). I believe parts of it, which we'll look at next, can be valuable within the low P/E framework. Too, using the low P/E method eliminates or downgrades those aspects of traditional analysis, such as forecasting, that have been shown to be consistently error-prone. By recognizing the limitations of security analysis, the investor, I believe, can apply it with a good chance of achieving even better results within the low P/E universe.

In the next sections, I'll attempt to show in some detail how these fundamental screens can be used to supplement the three basic rules of low P/E investing we just looked at. Following this analysis, we'll examine other P/E methods that do not depend on security evaluation at all. These too should provide above-average market results. After viewing the various methods, you should be in a position to decide for yourself which seems to suit you best.

An Eclectic Approach

In my own application of the low P/E approach, I have used the bottom 40 percent of stocks according to P/E's for stock selection. The four lowest deciles provide a broad universe to apply the ancilliary selection criteria that follow. The analysis of the results that we saw in the last chapter indicated that this group, when viewed together, has shown consistently superior returns.

For those of you who are brave enough to dabble in security analysis after what you've seen, here are the ancilliary criteria which I believe are most helpful:

Indicator 1. A company should have a strong financial position. This is easily determinable from information contained within its financial statements. (The definitions of the appropriate ratios, current assets versus current liabilities,* debt as a percentage of capital structure, interest coverage, etc., can all be found in any textbook on finance, as well as in material provided free of charge by some of the major brokerage houses.†)

---

*Previously defined in chapter 3.

†Merrill Lynch publishes a thirty-one-page booklet, entitled "How to Read a Financial Report," which provides a brief introduction to corporate accounting and outlines most of the important financial ratios the average investor would require.[1]

A strong financial position will enable the company to sail unimpaired through periods of operating difficulties, which low P/E companies sometimes experience. Financial strength is also an important factor in deciding whether a company's dividends can be maintained or increased.

Indicator 2. A high-dividend yield, which the company can sustain and possibly raise. (This is dependent, of course, upon its financial position.) The high yield should provide protection against significant price deterioration as well as be an important contributor to overall return.

Indicator 3. As many favorable operating and financial ratios as possible. This would help to ensure that there are no structural flaws in the company. The definition of such ratios again can be found in standard financial textbooks.

Indicator 4. A higher rate of earnings growth than the S&P 500, both in the immediate past and projected into the near future. Such future estimates are an attempt to pinpoint not earnings, only general direction. We must remember that we are dealing with stocks in the bottom deciles, for which only the worst is expected. By assessing industry and company conditions, we can point to the path of earnings movement. We do not require precise earnings estimates like those of conventional forecasting methods; we should merely note their direction, and for short periods of time, usually about a year or so. If we are wrong, there's probably little downside risk, since the market has already discounted the worst, but if we are right and earnings are growing faster than the averages, the stock may well outperform the lower P/E groups in general. On a risk-reward basis, there is little cost for error and a good deal of upside if you are on target.

The important distinction between forecasting general direction of earnings and trying to derive precise earnings estimates is that the former method is far simpler and therefore more likely to be successful.

Indicator 5. Earnings estimates should always be made to lean to the conservative side, which ties in with Graham and Dodd's "margin of safety" principle. By relying only on general forecasts, and keeping them conservative, you are reducing the chances of error even further. If these standards can be met and the company still looks as though its earnings are growing more quickly than the S&P's for a term such as a year or so, this may prove to be an excellent ancilliary criterion.

• • •

Next, let's look in some detail at how to make stock selections
by this approach. To do so, I'll draw on actual written recommendations I made at the time.* The recommendations all followed a report
outlining the low P/E strategy for a multibranch investment house.[2]
While one can be accused of telling "war stories," forgetting setbacks
(not to mention routs), I think it is important to present the investor
with practical examples of how the criteria elucidated were often
very clear-cut at the time—not in retrospect. The overall record of
how all such recommendations fared, updated to April 1979, is
presented in table 24, page 173. The first example is General Tire.

General Tire and Rubber (GY)

General Tire was recommended, using the low P/E criterion as the
major guideline, in late April 1976 at 19⅜. This stock was then
trading at a multiple of 6.3 times latest twelve-months earnings,
about a 40 to 45 percent discount from the overall market. My
recommendation ran in part:

General Tire is a company that appears to particularly suit the policy
of purchasing issues with low price/earnings ratios. The tire industry trades
at a discount to the market multiple, and General Tire trades at a discount
to both Goodyear and Firestone, the industry leaders.

General Tire is the nation's fifth largest tire manufacturer. In the past
five years, as the table below demonstrates [table 22, page 164], its earnings
record and its return on capital [indicator 3] compared favorably with
Goodyear and Firestone, and are significantly superior to those of Goodrich and Uniroyal.

Another measure of the company's success is its dividend record. Since
1961 General Tire has far outdistanced the industry in its rate of dividend
increase. The dividend has been raised every year with the exception of
1967. In the 1961–1975 time span, dividends rose 276 percent. By comparison, Goodyear's have increased 144 percent and Firestone's 134 percent—
about one-half as fast. The second-tier companies, Uniroyal and Goodrich,
showed a gain of 14 percent and a decline of 24 percent respectively in this
time. General Tire also pays out the lowest percentage of its earnings in

*I conducted the low P/E strategy first as an investment strategist and later as consultant
to Rauscher Pierce Refsnes, Inc. Table 24 on page 173 gives the results of a "buy and hold"
strategy (allowing no changes) against the performance of the Dow-Jones average. These
results were published periodically during 1977 and 1978.

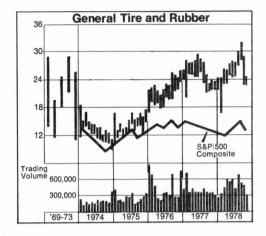

General Tire and Rubber

Per-share data ($) Year-end November 30	1977	1976	1975	1974	1973
Book value	37.27	33.40	29.78	27.92	25.77
Earnings[a]	5.09	4.59	2.71	3.40	3.37
Dividends	1.19¼	1.05¼	1.03¼	1.01¼	0.94½
Payout ratio	23%	23%	38%	28%	28%
Prices—high	29¼	25⅞	17¼	16¾	25¾
low	21⅜	16⅞	9¾	9⅛	10¾
P/E ratio	6/4	6/4	6/4	5/3	8/3

[a]Adjusted for 2 percent stock dividends in March 1978, 1977, and 1976; April 1975, 1974, and 1973. After $1 a share reduction from the extension of LIFO accounting in 1974; before special charges of $0.03 per share (net) in 1973.
SOURCE: Reproduced by permission from *Standard & Poor's Stock Reports*.

dividends. With the probability of significantly higher earnings in the current year, it is likely that the dividend could be boosted again.

Thus, with a large and growing dividend, General Tire ranked well by our second indicator. At the time of the recommendation, it yielded 5.3 percent (on the basis of its $1.08 annual dividend). As the previous statistics indicate, it had the fastest-growing dividend of any of the major tire companies through the 1961–75 period. Moreover, it paid out a lower percentage of earnings (see the dividend payout ratio in table 21, page 162). A low payout ratio as a percentage of earnings—barring large new expenditures for plant and equipment—indicates that the company is usually in a position to raise the dividend again if earnings continue to improve. And this turned out to be the case. GY raised its dividend several times since the report. By early 1979 the annual dividend rate was $1.50.

Table 21
TIRE COMPANY COMPARISONS

COMPANY	1971–75 ANNUAL EARNINGS PER SHARE GROWTH	1961–75 DIVIDEND GROWTH	1975 DIVIDEND PAYOUT RATIO	1971–75 AVERAGE ANNUAL RETURN ON NET WORTH
General Tire	8.5%	276%	39%	11.0%
Firestone	6.5	134	47	10.4
Goodrich	5.5	−24	70	6.3
Goodyear	3.0	144	49	10.5
Uniroyal	−2.5	14	96	7.0

GY had shown a superior record of earnings growth through a major diversification program that lessened its dependence on the highly competitive tire industry. For example, its RKO General subsidiary (20 percent of net earnings), which owns a number of major radio and television stations, bottling plants, as well as other businesses, increased earnings at a rate better than 20 percent annually in the 1970s.

In GY's tire business, the company de-emphasized the highly competitive branded replacement lines (which had produced large losses for Goodrich and Uniroyal), concentrating instead on stable but lower-margined original equipment and the less competitive private brands (such as those made to specification for the oil companies). General Tire also increased its share of the truck and off-the-road vehicle markets, areas of somewhat less strenuous competition.

In analyzing the company, it appeared that not only was it trading at a low P/E ratio, but it would very probably show sharp gains in its tire, chemical, and plastics businesses in 1976 (about 60 percent of consolidated revenues). Overall, earnings were likely to rise substantially in 1976 and probably again in 1977, lowering the multiple further if the estimates were reasonable. Income was projected to rise from the depressed $2.82 of 1975 to $3.80 a share in 1976 and $4.80 in 1977. These estimates were intentionally made conservatively, in accord with indicator 5. Actual reported earnings turned out to be higher.

The company's financial position (indicator 1) was also good and improving. At the time of the report, General Tire had a current ratio of 2.3 to 1, which was noticeably better than a year earlier and was quite acceptable, as was the fact that the long-term debt was only 34 percent of the capital structure.

Summing up, General Tire not only traded at a substantial discount from the average P/E but seemed to be entering a period of rapidly expanding earnings from a depressed base, had a good dividend yield (one that seemed likely to increase), and held a solid financial position.

King's Department Stores (KDT)

King's, a discount department store chain (114 stores), was selected in late May 1976. The company had a low P/E ratio (less than eight times earnings at the time), with earnings expected to be up fairly sharply in 1976 and again the next year. The recommendation ran in part:

King's, a moderate-sized discounter, has displayed an impressive growth record over the last decade while consistently earning a higher

Per-share data ($) Year-end January 31	1977	1976	1975	1974	1973
Book value	11.00	9.31	8.12	7.32	6.76
Earnings[a]	2.21	1.70	1.26	0.93	1.11
Dividends	0.60	0.52½	0.40½	0.37½	0.30
Payout ratio	27%	31%	32%	40%	27%
Prices—high	14½	13⅝	9¼	6½	13¾
low	11	8⅝	5½	4	4¾
P/E ratio	7/5	8/5	7/4	7/4	12/4

[a]Before special charge of $0.08 a share in 1977; before special credit of $0.01 a share in 1973.
SOURCE: Reproduced by permission from *Standard & Poor's Stock Reports.*

return on its shareholder's equity than any of the major retailers. Management has limited its expansion to smaller cities and larger towns, where competition is less severe. The company has also compiled one of the most impressive balance sheets in the retailing industry. Its strong financial position is essential to its mode of operations. King's has a long record of buying troubled discounters for cash and markedly improving their operations. Its excellent financial position has also allowed it to rapidly increase its dividend. Since 1970, cash payout has risen 150 percent from 20 cents to 50 cents a share. At 32 percent, the payout ratio is still modest and the dividend rate is likely to increase further with improving earnings. The stock currently yields 5.17 percent.

Rising consumer disposable income, which should be reflected in higher retail activity through the balance of the current year and again in 1977, should result in good earnings gains for the company in both years.

Statistically, King's record compares favorably with both Kresge and Sears, as the following table indicates [table 22].

Table 22
DEPARTMENT STORE COMPARISONS

	YIELD	1975 PRETAX MARGINS	5-YEAR AVERAGE RETURN ON EQUITY	1974 CURRENT RATIO	PREMIUM OF MARKET PRICE OVER CURRENT BOOK VALUE	P/E 1976 EARNINGS
King's	4.8%	6.1%	15.9%	8.1/1	27%	7.0
Kresge	0.9	5.9	14.9	2.2/1	265	19.2
Sears	2.3	5.9	11.9	1.5/1	90	20.0

While average earnings growth is well below Kresge's, it is better than Sears. It has both the highest pretax margins of the three and the highest return on equity. It also has by far the strongest current ratio. King's trades at only a 27 percent premium to its book value compared with almost triple for Kresge and double for Sears. While such comparisons must be treated with caution because of the smaller size of King's and its different retailing thrust, they do give some idea of how well the company has fared vis-à-vis the leading retailers.

Here again, a number of important fundamentals I favor along with a low P/E multiple were present:

Indicator 1. One of the strongest relative balance sheets in the retail industry—giving the investor a high degree of safety. (The report speculated that because of the company's exceptionally strong financial position, it was in an excellent position to make a major acquisition, something it actually did in mid-1977, taking over Mammoth Mart, a forty-unit discount department store chain. That should eventually improve KDT's earnings growth.)

Indicator 2. A high dividend yield (5.1 percent). Because of its strong financial position and the anticipated earnings increase that was projected, we believed it would be upped again. The dividend was in fact raised from a 50-cent rate to 60 cents annually in late 1976 and to 80 cents by spring 1978.

Indicator 3. Excellent pretax margins and returns on capital when compared with the industry leaders. (The higher the pretax margins and return on equity, the better.)

Indicator 4. Accelerating earnings expansion in the near future. (As indicated, the estimates had been made conservatively.)

Naturally, you won't find all of these indicators favorable all of the time. Stocks don't trade at low P/E's under A-O.K. conditions. Still, if you look, you'll be surprised at how often you will find many of these favorable indicators, as the King's example demonstrates.

To end this episode, King's outperformed the market in the thirty-five months following the recommendation.

General Cinema (GCN)

Shortly after King's, General Cinema was recommended, a stock particularly appealing to me because it had taken a classic "round trip." Several years earlier it had been a major institutional favorite, trading at a P/E of over thirty times earnings. At the time of the report it was very much on the outs with the institutions and the rest of the market, at a P/E of only 6.6 times latest reported twelve-month earnings, again well below that of the S&P 500. And yet, in spite of the fact that it was in the market doghouse, the analysis indicated it was still the exciting company it had been earlier.

General Cinema is the nation's largest operator of movie theaters, most of which are located in or near shopping centers, as well as one of the major bottlers of Pepsi Cola and Dr. Pepper. In its 1975 fiscal year (ending October 31), bottling operations accounted for approximately 60 percent and theaters 30 percent of earnings. The company also had smaller investments in two radio stations and a furniture warehouse.

Although General Cinema had a long record of earnings growth

Per-share data ($)[a]

Year-end October 31	1978	1977[b]	1976	1975	1974
Book value	NA[c]	10.46	9.14	7.37	5.27
Earnings[d]	4.43	3.64	3.04	2.68	1.93
Dividends	0.94	0.73	0.57½	0.46½	0.41
Payout ratio	21%	20%	19%	17%	21%
Prices[e]—high	45¾	31¼	26⅝	24	14
low	26½	20½	17	7½	5⅜
P/E ratio	10/6	9/6	9/6	9/3	7/3

[a]Data as originally reported.
[b]Reflects merger or acquisition.
[c]Not available.
[d]Before special item(s) of +0.09 in 1974.
[e]Calendar year.
SOURCE: Reproduced by permission from *Standard & Poor's Stock Reports.*

(in the last decade, it was 20 percent annually), the stock suffered severely after the 1974 credit crunch. Investors were alarmed by the fact that debt constituted a high percentage of the capital structure. The P/E dropped from 32 in 1972 to as low as 3 in 1974–75 (although earnings were actually 53 percent higher in the latter year, indicating once again how dramatic shifts in investor sentiment can be).

Evaluating the company in mid-1976, I thought that rapid earnings growth would continue in spite of the company's abnormally low P/E ratio. As important, not only was it reducing its debt absolutely, but it was doing so more quickly as a percentage of the capital structure because of the fast pace of earnings growth. By 1975 debt had declined to a more acceptable 47 percent of the capital structure from 60 percent in 1972, and by fiscal year-end 1976 it had dropped to 39 percent (the earnings buildup made it apparent that this was occurring at the time of the report). Indicator 1 was turning convincingly positive.

Thus we had a situation where the P/E was again low, the financial position was improving rapidly (indicator 1), and earnings were expected to outpace the market (indicator 4). For added measure, the company was very well managed.* The stock also proved to be a rewarding holding.

Aetna Life and Casualty (AET)

A final example using the eclectic approach was the giant Aetna Life and Casualty Company,† the nation's largest publicly owned insurance company, recommended in August 1977. Company earnings had grown at a 15 percent compound rate over the prior ten years —albeit growth had been anything but in a straight line because of the inherently cyclical nature of the property-casualty business.

The recommendation was made as the domestic property-casualty industry was undergoing a dramatic recovery from the 1973–75 debacle, the most traumatic on industry record. Overcompetition and an exceptionally high rate of inflation resulted in staggering operating losses for most of the industry in these years—$2.4 billion in 1974 and $4 billion in 1975. The huge losses caused capital impairment for some companies. The capital squeeze became so intense that a number of larger insurance companies were forced to liquidate major portions of their stock portfolios to raise cash almost at the precise bottom of the 1974 market.

Because of these problems, the industry instituted large rate hikes commencing in late 1975, and these increases continued through 1976 and part of 1977. Since it takes almost two years on average for new rate hikes to filter to the bottom line in the property-casualty industry, the significantly improved operating situation was expected to continue to produce sharp earnings gains in 1977 and again in 1978.

*I suppose I could add management as a further criterion, but the assessment is almost metaphysical—like the input-output relationships of chapter 6, it seems we all consider companies well managed when the stocks are going up.
†Discussed in evaluating analytical techniques in chapter 5.

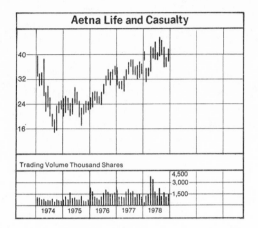

Per-share data ($)

Year-end December 31	1977	1976	1975	1974[a]	1973
Book value	38.00	32.47	28.10	25.19	28.96
Earnings[b]	7.76	3.91	1.90	2.85	3.66
Dividends	1.40	1.08	1.08	1.06	0.92½
Payout ratio	18%	28%	57%	37%	25%
Prices—high	38⅜	36¼	29⅜	39¼	41
low	28⅜	22½	17¼	15⅛	28¾
P/E ratio	5/4	9/6	15/9	14/5	11/8

[a]Adjusted for two-for-one split in 1974.

[b]Excludes capital gains/(losses) per share of $0.05 in 1976, ($0.14) in 1975, $0.03 in 1973; also excludes special credits of of $0.01 a share in 1976, $0.25 ($0.19 from accounting change) in 1975.

SOURCE: Reproduced by permission of *Standard & Poor's Stock Reports.*

Aetna reacted more quickly than most companies to the problems facing the industry during the 1973–75 period. Management introduced tighter controls and responded faster to the accelerating inflationary conditions. As a result, its property-casualty losses were far less severe than those of the industry at large. (In 1976 AET's combined ratio was 95.8 compared with 102 for the industry.*)

Faster rate adjustments and quicker claim processing also made Aetna's reserves adequate to meet rising claim costs. The necessity of having to increase such reserves had been a major fac-

*The combined ratio is the addition of the loss and expense ratios. The combined ratio of 95.8 indicates that Aetna recorded 95.8 cents of expenses and claim costs for every $1 of premiums written and brought 4.2 cents down to pretax underwriting profits. For the industry, the ratio of 102 indicated that it lost 2 cents for every $1 of premiums it wrote. This fits under indicator 3, as a low combined ratio for an insurance company is like a high profit margin for an industrial corporation.

tor in the poor industry underwriting record in recent years.

After a $5.9 million pretax loss in 1975 (and a combined ratio of 106.3), AET's property-casualty earnings rebounded to $243 million in 1976 and represented 60 percent of total earnings—the remainder of income coming from life, health, annuity, pension operations, and other businesses. Even sharper earnings improvements were recorded in 1977, with earnings rising 98 percent to $7.75 a share from $3.91. (This perhaps indicates the importance of direction rather than precision—the original 1977 earnings estimate made in June of that year was $6.50, undershooting the actual by 16 percent.)

Once again, most of the major indicators were strong. The stock had an extremely low price/earnings multiple, a reasonable and increasing dividend (at the time, the dividend yield was 4.3 percent), and the probability of continued increases in earnings.*

Old Republic International (OLDR)

For investors who enjoy being higher rollers, there is one subcategory of the low P/E strategy that might be considered—buying companies after they have reported losses. According to what we have learned about investor reactions to bad news, we might expect overreactions to companies reporting current losses—and as table 23 (page 170) indicates, this is precisely what happens.

Investors have always shunned stocks reporting losses, and as a result these stocks have consistently outperformed the S&P 425. As table 23 shows, if all stocks reporting deficits had been purchased one year after the loss, they would have appreciated 25.4 percent on average in the next twelve months, and 158.1 percent for the full five-year period compared with 12.1 percent and 69.3 percent respectively for the S&P 425.†

Which brings me to Old Republic International. This company was originally a pioneer in credit life insurance (insurance taken out on major installment purchases, such as cars or home durables).

---

*In 1978 earnings increased to $8.70 and the dividend was raised to $2.20, where the stock yielded 6.1 percent on the basis of the original recommended price.

†A bias probably exists in this table, since only surviving companies are selected. If insolvent companies were also included, the comparisons for the deficit companies might be less striking. However, because of the rarity of insolvencies among major companies, I do not think such differences would be significant.

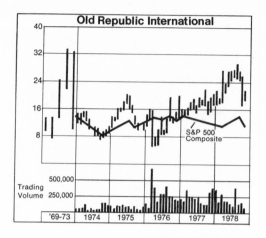

Per-share data ($)

Year-end December 31	1977	1976	1975	1974	1973
Book value	19.79	15.16	7.39	9.75	11.63
Earnings[a]	5.21	4.48	(3.90)	2.88	2.30
Dividends	0.56	0.28	0.49	0.49	0.47
Payout ratio	11%	6%	—	17%	20%
Prices—high	20⅜	17⅜	14⅞	19⅞	32¼
low	14⅛	5⅛	7⅛	10	9⅞
P/E ratio	4/3	4/1	—	7/3	14/4

[a]Adjusted for three-for-two stock split in September 1977, 1 percent stock dividend in February 1977, and 1 percent stocks dividends in August and November 1976.

SOURCE: Reproduced by permission of *Standard & Poor's Stock Reports.*

Table 23
COMPANIES IN S&P 425 REPORTING DEFICITS, 1948–67

HOLDING PERIOD	S&P 425 % CHANGE	STOCK PURCHASED DECEMBER 31, YEAR OF DEFICIT % CHANGE	STOCK PURCHASED DECEMBER 31, YEAR AFTER DEFICIT % CHANGE
1 year	12.1	23.2	25.4
2 years	25.5	47.9	49.6
3 years	38.1	78.9	100.0
4 years	52.0	116.9	127.1
5 years	69.3	159.7	158.1

SOURCE: Courtesy of Marine Midland Bank, November 1968.

However, through the 1970s, it became a major entity in a new and rapidly growing business—workmen's compensation for the coal-mining industry. With changes in federal and state legislation in 1971, giving miners greater coverage, these premiums skyrocketed. OLDR, by far the largest factor in this field, saw this business rise from3 percent of its premiums in 1972 to 33 percent in 1975 (the business was almost 50 percent of revenues in 1977, a phenomenal rate of growth of over 75 percent annually since 1972). Indicators 1, 3, and 4 were all quite positive.

However, as we have seen time and again, in a dynamic economy nothing is certain, and in 1975 the company incurred substantial losses in its small accident and health line—which it immediately decided to dispose of. After doing so, it lost $3.90 a share in 1975 versus a profit of $2.88 in 1974.

A number of large funds responded to the news in rather predictable fashion by attempting to sell (the more appropriate term is "dump") large amounts of OLDR stock. In this case, approximately 150,000 shares were placed on the market, which normally traded about 5,000 shares a day. The price, not surprisingly, plummeted. The stock dropped from 16 to under 7 the day the news was released.

When the smoke had cleared, it seemed to me that the company's appraisal of its losses was very probably correct, and that there would be no other write-offs forthcoming—statements, incidentally, that the management made publicly.*

The stock appeared to be quite attractive. It had the potential of large earnings in 1976 and still had considerable financial strength.

Part of the recommendation ran as follows:

Some of the most profitable investment opportunities have arisen from companies with good records that have stumbled temporarily. Our Investment Strategy Report of April 1976 indicated that companies reporting deficits subsequently outperformed the S&P 500 with regularity [table 23]. While the danger exists that an unfavorable change in a company's fortunes is permanent, for larger corporations in the vast majority of cases it is not, and a resurgence in earnings power normally occurs, resulting in the better performance of the deficit group.

Old Republic, a medium-sized life insurance company, appears to us to provide investors with an excellent opportunity to benefit from this

*It indicated that the sale of most of the accident and health line had already been negotiated.

phenomenon. Our analysis leads us to conclude that the problems that caused it large 1975 deficits have been resolved and earnings of $3.30 per share are estimated for 1976. Currently trading at only three times this estimate, and with the likelihood of continuing earnings buildup over the next several years, we believe the stock presents a particularly attractive speculation.

Earnings of $3.30 a share was a conservative estimate, much too conservative as it turned out. (Under such circumstances, however, a very cautious projection is called for.) OLDR reported net earnings of $4.48, and in addition tax and other credits of $2.00 a share, bringing total cash flow to $6.48 for 1976, which was more than the stock traded for at the height of the institutional dumping. (The low reached was 5½.) The next year, 1977, the stock earned $5.21 a share before special credits.

Upon examination the company looked too good to be true. Here was the classic investor overreaction in the face of good fundamentals. I wondered, more than half seriously, if this might not be the exception that proved the rule. Fortunately for me, it wasn't. The stock proved to be an extremely rewarding holding, rising 184 percent by April 1979. Even after this appreciation, the stock traded at a modest 3.8 times earnings and, I believed, continued to represent good value—this time as a straight low P/E investment.

Indicator 5. As noted previously, buying stocks showing losses is of course considerably riskier than simply buying low P/E stocks. An investor doing this must be very sure of the company's financial strength and should use only a small portion of his portfolio for this purpose, while diversifying into a number of issues to spread the risk.

An Overview of the Eclectic Approach

Indicators 1 through 3 used in accordance with the low P/E rules are all clear-cut and require reasonably straightforward calculations, avoiding the major portion of the configural and information-processing problems previously discussed. And indicator 4, which projects only general direction of earnings, is much simpler and safer to use, and consequently should have a far better chance of success than the type of precise estimates ordinarily made by security analysts.

Table 24

LOW P/E INVESTING VERSUS "THE MARKET," APRIL 1976–APRIL 1979

DATE RECOMMENDED	COMPANY	PRICE ON DATE RECOMMENDED[a]	DJIA	PRICE 4/23/79	% CHANGE IN STOCK PRICE	% CHANGE[b] IN DJIA
4/30/76	General Tire & Rubber	19⅜	996.85	26	+ 34.6	− 13.7
5/24/76	King's Department Stores	9⅝	971.53	13¼	+ 35.9	− 11.5
5/26/76	Old Republic International	9⅜	970.83	26½	+183.9	− 11.4
6/14/76	General Cinema	9⅜	991.24	20⅜	+117.3	− 13.2
12/9/76	Macmillan, Inc.	8½	970.74	18¼	+114.7	− 11.4
2/11/77	Dennison Manufacturing	12⅞	931.52	20	+ 55.3	− 7.7
8/3/77	Aetna Life and Casualty	37⅛	886.00	44⅜	+ 19.5	− 2.9
12/22/77	Mohasco Corporation	12⅝	821.81	13⅛	+ 4.0	+ 4.6
4/28/78	Honeywell, Inc.	51	844.33	68	+ 33.3	+ 1.9
7/13/78	Burlington Industries	18	824.76	17¾	− 1.4	+ 4.3
				Average change	+ 59.7	− 6.1

DJIA was 860.10 on 4/23/79.
[a]Prices adjusted for stock splits and stock dividends through 4/23/79.
[b]Dividends not included.

The eclectic low P/E approach that I presented worked well through the 1976 to early 1979 period. While I would be the last to argue that the record is definitive, it does indicate the successful performance of this strategy even through a period of moderate market decline. The results also fit in with the above-average success other money managers have had using very similar approaches.* Although the degree of success will certainly vary among different individuals and for the same individuals over differing time periods, the eclectic low P/E approach seems to be an extremely workable investment strategy, eliminating most complex judgments. Obviously, this is the method that I most favor.

However, as an investor, you may choose either to follow this strategy as I have laid it down, or perhaps to use a variety of mechanical low P/E approaches that avoid security analysis entirely, yet should show superior performance over time. Let's look at some of these strategies next.

Other Approaches Using the Low P/E Strategy

Since tables 9 through 17 indicated pretty conclusively that the low P/E's normally provided the best returns and the high P/E's the worst, the investor might reasonably ask why mechanical strategies based solely on buying stocks below the market multiple couldn't be used without any of the screening criteria described previously.

I believe such strategies are quite feasible, but once again general rules 2 and 3 apply: namely, the portfolio should be made up of fifteen to twenty stocks, diversified into ten to twelve industries; and the low P/E investor should attempt to buy medium- or large-sized companies.

Buy-and-Hold Strategies

First, we might consider a strategy remarkably similar to one advocated by our efficient-market friends—that of "buying and holding" a well-diversified portfolio of securities over a long period of time. Their strategy took no notice of P/E multiple. However, since

*In particular, a number of pension fund managers in the top 2 or 3 percent of the Becker ratings.

the record shows that low P/E stocks provide better returns over long holding periods, why not buy and hold portfolios of low P/E stocks instead?

As table 25 indicates, both the Nicholson and the Miller studies showed superior performance for the low P/E stocks for periods ranging from three to seven years. The periods tested in our work, from three to nine years, came up with very similar results.

From the table you can see that buying the lowest 20 percent of stocks in this manner and holding them gives you a very good chance of outdoing the market. Buying the bottom 40 percent of stocks according to P/E ratios should still give you superior performance, albeit probably reduced from the bottom 20 percent. However, there is an added measure of safety in the latter case because the investor has double the number of large, high-yielding companies to choose from.

The buy-and-hold strategies eliminate all commissions, transaction costs, and capital gains taxes. *For the ultraconservative investor, they would be the safest way to apply the low P/E strategy.*

You might ask how one determines P/E deciles and quintiles. Brokerage firms, advisory services, and financial publications often advertise long lists of low P/E stocks (the *Value Line* survey, for example, runs lists of high-yielding stocks with P/E ratios under 5

Table 25

AVERAGE ANNUAL RETURNS FOR HOLDING PERIODS OF THREE YEARS OR MORE

	SWITCHING AFTER EACH				HOLDING ORIGINAL PORTFOLIO FOR		
	3 YEARS[a]		5 YEARS[a]		7 YEARS[a]	8 YEARS[b] 1968–77 STUDY	9 YEARS[b] 1968–77 STUDY
	MILLER[c]	NICHOLSON[d]	MILLER[c]	NICHOLSON[d]	NICHOLSON[d]		
Highest 20% of P/E's	8.5	6.6	9.3	7.9	9.1	−1.3	0.8
Second 20%	8.9	7.5	9.8	8.5	9.0	3.0	4.4
Third 20%	11.4	9.2	10.9	9.9	10.1	2.7	4.1
Fourth 20%	12.5	10.3	12.0	10.6	10.4	5.5	6.2
Lowest 20%	16.6	11.6	14.1	14.7	13.9	7.2	7.2
Sample return	11.6	9.0	11.2	10.3	10.5	3.5	4.8

[a] Appreciation only.
[b] Total return.
[c] 1948–64.
[d] 1937–62.

almost weekly at the present time). However, if there isn't one available, some simple rules of thumb should suffice. First, take a broad market index, like the S&P 500, for which the current P/E ratio on latest twelve-month earnings can easily be found from a variety of sources, including brokers, newspapers, and the S&P stock guide. The current ratio of the S&P 500 is about 8. We next pick well-established companies paying good dividends and trading below this multiple. One rule of thumb might be to use a 20 percent discount or more from the S&P 500 (6.4 times earnings and down at the present time). The deeper the discount from the S&P 500, the further down you are moving in the low P/E range.

There is nothing magical about picking the bottom 20 or 40 percent. For a computer, it was simply a good cutoff point. And, as we found in the most recent study, at times the returns in the second lowest quintile were better than those in the bottom one.

This simple method should work fairly effectively if you do not have the actual deciles of low P/E stocks. Next, how do you find the P/E ratios themselves? This too is easy: the *Wall Street Journal, Barron's,* and the financial sections of most major daily newspapers will have the P/E ratio right next to the stock, calculated on latest twelve-month reported earnings. It is a relatively simple matter to run down the column and find stocks at a 20 percent discount from the market multiple (more or less as you choose).

Making Changes in the Low P/E Portfolio

Another twist on this approach, which also appears quite workable, would be to buy a portfolio of low P/E stocks and weed it periodically as stocks move up to the market P/E multiple or above, or if they fail to perform as well as the market over a certain period of time.* An overview of the studies indicated that returns normally diminished with longer holding periods. Thus, some method such as the above would serve to enhance overall return above that of the simple buy-and-hold strategy.

While this strategy introduces transaction costs, they should be quite small, since the investor should, on average, have only a few trades a year. The pruning process should also allow the investor to maintain a portfolio of low P/E stocks with above-average yields.

But once again, remember the two important rules of portfolio

*For sell rules, see page 180.

construction: diversification into fifteen or twenty stocks, and medium- to large-sized companies. As noted earlier, the deeper the discount from the average, the more you are moving into the lower deciles.

In any case, whichever of the mechanical strategies you choose, you should have a good chance of outdoing the market with minimal time spent making selections and with only average risk, if that.

Turning over the Bottom 20 Percent of Low P/E's Annually

For those who are willing to take some additional risk and who can get a list of the bottom quintile, the analysis of the findings in chapter 7 indicates that purchasing the bottom 20 percent of stocks and turning them over annually enhances return.*

Table 26 shows the superior performance of the bottom 20 percent of stocks in each study compared with the average return of all stocks in the samples. In all cases, the stocks were turned over on an annual basis. The four studies were conducted in time periods overlapping a forty-year period. Viewing the findings over the entire 1937–77 span, it would certainly appear that an investor could buy a portfolio of the bottom 20 percent of P/E's and turn them over annually.

Table 26
AVERAGE PERFORMANCE OF BOTTOM P/E QUINTILE VERSUS SAMPLE MEAN

TIME PERIOD	NAME OF STUDY	AVERAGE ANNUAL RETURN OF BOTTOM QUINTILE	AVERAGE ANNUAL RETURN OF MEAN	SUPERIORITY OF BOTTOM QUINTILE RELATIVE TO SAMPLE MEAN
1937–62	Nicholson[a]	16.0%	8.2%	+45%
1946–64	Miller[a]	18.4	12.0	+53
1957–71	Basu[b]	16.3	12.1	+35
1968–77	Recent study[b]	8.2	4.8	+71

[a]Figures reflect appreciation.
[b]Figures reflect total return.

*Investors without such a list who are willing to put up with an hour or two of work can approximate the bottom 20 percent fairly easily from the stocks on the New York Stock Exchange. There are approximately 1,450 common stocks listed on the exchange, so 140 would be the bottom 10 percent and 280 the bottom 20 percent. Running down the column of P/E ratios, start with the lowest multiples (the 1s, 2s, 3s, and 4s) and tick off the number of each multiple on a sheet of paper. In this manner a data base can be accumulated that should approximate the bottom 20 percent (although not absolutely the same, it is quick and should approximate the sample we are looking for). This need be done only once or twice a year.

"Ah!" you might say, "but what about recent years? Certainly some of your own tables in chapter 7 show that if you tried this method, transaction costs would eat you alive because of the low returns."

It is true that returns will vary widely with different time periods, from the 18.4 and 16 percent returns of the Nicholson and Miller studies to the 8.2 percent return we received in table 13 (not to mention the 2.0 percent of the May 1970–November 1974 period).

In the final chapter I'll present arguments I hope will convince you that returns should prevail at higher rates than those of the overall past and certainly will be above those of the last twelve years. Ibbotson and Sinquefield, the financial researchers whose evidence we viewed in chapter 6, have projected future rates of return for stocks of 12.5 percent for the next several decades. Suppose we accept this figure and assume a continuation of approximately 50 percent superiority in the returns of the bottom 20 percent of P/E's. This would lead to a total return approximating 18.5 percent annually.

Next, let's look at the specter of turnover costs. We found that 54.4 percent of the bottom decile turns over annually. However, from our observations, most stocks normally move into an adjoining decile. This should reduce turnover somewhat, but to be conservative, let's assume it continues to stay relatively high for the lowest 20 percent, say 45 percent annually. Remember that past annual turnover strategies generated appreciation as high as 18.8 percent, and if we are on target about better future markets, we should be in a position to absorb some added transaction costs, particularly when some brokers have discounted commissions to as low as 10 to 20 cents a share.

Now, let's make some assumptions to see how large the annual transaction costs would be. First, let's assume a portfolio of $100,000 and an average stock price of $25 a share, equally placed into twenty positions. (Each holding would then be two hundred shares.)

Using the 45 percent annual turnover rate, we would buy and sell nine positions a year on average. If we go to our neighborhood discount broker and are able to wangle 20-cents-a-share commission on our transactions,* the cost and commissions would be $360 to sell and an additional $360 on average to replace the positions. If we

---

*At the time of this writing (February 1979), some discount brokers were giving the public commissions as low as 12.5 cents a share on two-hundred-share lots.

assume other transaction costs at double these figures, total costs would be $1,440, or 1.44 percent annually.

Using the 12.5 percent rate of return as the future mean, we see that the portfolio average return would be $18,750, less the $1,440 in transaction costs, or $17,310. In other words, the net return would be 17.3 percent, versus 12.5 percent, or some 38 percent more. Obviously, this is a strategy that could only work for individual investors —the size of institutional blocks would markedly increase transaction costs because of their effect on market price.

Remember, again, that these are only assumptions, but I think they are practical ones, and they are based on studies of the returns of low P/E stocks over a forty-year period. The evidence indicates that superior results should be garnered from an approach such as the one just recommended.

On the Drawing Board Only

One potential strategy that intrigues me is based on turning over portfolios on latest twelve-month earnings on a quarterly basis Quarterly turnover resulted in by far the best returns in the lowest P/E decile and the worst in the highest in virtually every test we ran. For example, even though our studies covered an exceptionally poor period for markets, the average return on the lowest decile on a quarterly basis was 14.0 percent over the nine years of the study. This compared with a return on the highest P/E decile of −2.64 percent on the same basis and a long-term average return on common stocks of 9.2 percent. Returns of up to 20 percent were achieved in some of the better time periods through this interval, which makes me wonder just how high such returns could be in a bull market. Even adjusting for the significantly higher portfolio turnover on a quarterly basis (about 120 percent per year for the lowest decile) using our prior portfolio and transaction cost assumptions, this would reduce returns by only 3.3 percent annually on average. In more normal markets, quarterly turnover might certainly prove to be an exciting strategy.

However, I must caution you that the strategy is far too wild for my blood. It's based simply on our findings, which cover a single nine-year period, as well as on the assumption that similar results would hold in the future. It would also require a large number of transactions and extensive bookkeeping. To avoid Valium (or at the least increasing your intake), I think I'd leave this approach to a mutual fund to try first.

Realistically, then, there are a number of approaches to the low P/E strategies, all of them with substantial statistical documentation, in addition to the eclectic approach that I personally favor. While I don't believe low P/E investing need necessarily be the final answer to stock selection for everyone, it has consistently provided better performance in both good and bad markets.

To the present time it is the only system I know of that effectively and systematically checks investor overreactions—by far the largest and most important source of investor error.

However, there are still a number of questions that must be answered before you use these strategies, not the least important of which is deciding when to sell.

When to Sell

Regardless of the investment strategy you use, one of your most difficult decisions is when to sell.

There are almost as many answers to the problem as there are investors, but even among professionals the number who follow their own sell rules scrupulously is very limited. Psychological forces appear to impact most sell decisions, often with disastrous consequences. Given what we know of the subject, it seems that the safest approach is once again to rely on mechanical guidelines, which serve to filter out much of the emotional content of the decision.

The general rule that I have been using is that *stocks should be sold when their P/E ratio approaches that of the overall market, regardless of how favorable prospects appear.* These stocks should then be replaced by other low P/E stocks. For example, if the market P/E today was 9 and one of our stocks, say General Cinema, went up to the multiple, it should be sold and replaced by another low P/E stock.*

A further question may at times arise with sell strategies using the eclectic approach. Suppose an investor has a portfolio of twenty stocks and finds a new one that ranks much higher by the indicators

*Naturally, as prices change over time, the weightings of stocks in the portfolio will differ. When stocks are sold, the effort should be made to bring the weightings more into balance with one another.

previously outlined while also trading at a lower P/E ratio than a number of stocks he owns. A switch might then be made, but he must keep in mind the principle of a fixed number of stocks in the portfolio: each time one is purchased, another one should be sold. And, because he is bringing in more judgment in switching, changes of this sort should be relatively rare in order to avoid the danger that overtrading inhibits results.

A supplementary rule is that a stock that attains a high P/E multiple solely because of a decline in earnings should not be sold. It is true that by using the low P/E approach a number of clinkers will be acquired which, whether because they are cyclical or for other reasons, are approaching peak earnings and will incur earnings declines. However, we know the overall superior record of the low P/E group, which contains numbers of such companies. Thus, if you have adequate diversification, both by the number of stocks and by industry, this should not be a major problem.

Also, the price drop will often be an overreaction to the anticipated decline in earnings. Take the case of General Motors in the high 40s in 1973. At the time it was trading at a P/E of 5, well under the S&P 500. Earnings declined in 1974, and GM's multiple rose above the market's as the stock fell to 29. However, by late 1975, the stock was over 60, and by early 1976 it had moved up to 74—rising far more than the S&P over the period.

Another question is how long an investor should hold a situation that has not worked out. Again, there are many partial answers to this problem. The one that seems to work best is to adopt a two-year holding period.* My criterion is that if the stock has not done at least as well as the market after this time, it should be sold and replaced with another.

What the Low P/E Strategy Won't Do for You

Whether you opt for the eclectic low P/E strategy or take the bit between your teeth and head straight for low P/E methods without any form of security analysis, keep in mind that the strategies are relative rather than absolute. This means, in effect, that they won't

---

*For a cyclical stock with a drop in earnings, this might be stretched to two and a half or three years.

help you decide on when to get in or out of the market. Whether the market is very high or very low, you will receive no warning signals to sell in the first place or buy in the second.

What the low P/E strategy should do is give you the best relative opportunities for the money you have invested in the stock market. Which means that in a rising market, your stocks ought to do better than the averages, and in a falling market they should decline less.

Alternatives to the Low P/E Philosophy

Some investors may wish to participate in the stock market but for various reasons do not wish to make their own investment decisions. Others believe their capital is too limited to get a fully diversified low P/E portfolio.

With a limited amount of funds, the best approach would seem to be to purchase a no-load or low-load mutual fund with a broad portfolio. Select a fund that has come at least reasonably close to the market averages over a period of years (which probably means that it has not done an excessive amount of trading). This should provide you with results pretty much in line with returns received on common stocks in general.

Since studies have shown that no-load funds and low-loads have performed as well over the years as full-load funds, it is silly to pay the extra commission, which goes not to management but to the fund salesman. Brokers are not happy to recommend no-load funds, since those up-front sales charges run as high as 8¾ percent and are their bread and butter. If you do have trouble, as many investors have, finding one that suits your needs, you can get further information on no-load funds by writing to the No-Load Mutual Fund Association, 475 Park Avenue South, New York, New York 10016.

A broad portfolio can also be acquired by purchasing a closed-end investment company. These companies, unlike mutual funds, do not continuously issue and redeem shares: their number of shares outstanding is fixed. The larger closed-end funds are usually traded on the New York Stock Exchange, normally at a discount from the value of their assets. Table 27 indicates the average discount over the last five years.

Table 27
CLOSED-END INVESTMENT COMPANIES

COMPANY	ASSET SIZE[a]	AVERAGE DISCOUNT 5 YEARS, 1978
Adams Express	$217.8	20.5%
General American Investors	120.5	20.1
Lehman Corporation	451.2	21.7
Niagara Share Corporation	98.4	10.6
Tri-Continental Corporation	594.8	18.2
U.S. & Foreign Securities	115.7	25.3

[a]In millions of dollars.

SOURCE: Wiesenberger Investment Companies Service. Copyright 1979 by Warren, Gorman & Lamont, Inc., Boston, Mass.

The discounts provided on a weekly basis in the *Wall Street Journal, Barron's,* the *New York Times,* and various financial publications usually vary between 10 and 20 percent. If the discounts are larger than the average, as they tend to be during periods of market decline, interesting buying opportunities are available.*

Dollar Cost Averaging

As you receive new money over time, and assuming you've decided the proper percentage to allocate to equities, simply follow the low P/E philosophy. However, suppose you receive a large sum at one time. What should you do? In such cases, you might try a simple and effective method called dollar cost averaging. As an example, take the pleasant case of having just inherited $50,000. After reviewing your financial position, you decide you can afford to put almost all of it into the market.

To be prudent, you should do so over a period of time, possibly two or three years. You might invest each quarter over a two-year period in eight equal installments. When the market is high, you will buy fewer shares; when it is low, more. You will thereby avoid the risk of getting in entirely at the top—and the euphoria of buying at the lows. However, it is a safer approach, since your purchases will more closely reflect market movements over a two- or three-year

*In April 1979, with widespread market disillusionment, the discounts on many of the leading closed-end funds ran well over 20 percent, making them appear particularly attractive relative to equity mutual funds at that time.

period. The guessing game is something you should leave to the market timers—and you've already seen their record.

In this chapter we have reviewed some of the practical variations on the low P/E approach. Next, let's turn to some widely discussed investments outside of the stock market—how some can benefit you, and what, if you're not careful, others might do to your capital.

CHAPTER TEN

Your Broker
and the Fastest Games
in Town

The last three chapters laid out the strategies that I believe provide the average investor with the best chances for success. While the low P/E approach is certainly not an investment panacea, it does appear to solve many of the problems of selecting the right equities—in a stock market which, as the final chapter will attempt to show, provides excellent value today.

Still, the poor performance of stocks in the past decade and a half hardly qualifies for LeBon's image of instant wealth. Not surprisingly, then, after what we've seen of crowd reactions and cognitive biases, interest has shifted elsewhere. Because the psychology of markets is basically the same, many of the traps and pitfalls that we have already viewed are also present in these other arenas.

In the following sections, we'll look at a number of the other investments that have become very popular today and what your chances are in playing them. Some, fast-paced and barely regulated, are extremely risky. And, as we'll see, although enormous returns are promised, the odds at times are not quite as good as those offered by the old Ponzi scheme.

However, on a more refreshing note, there have been other investment developments in recent years that can be of real help to you, both in rounding out your portfolio and in providing tax savings.

While the examination necessarily will be brief, it should help you delineate some of the new investments you should examine and others you would be well advised to stay clear of.

Before beginning our survey of the investments themselves— not infrequently called "products" in the trade—we'll look at what role the principal merchandisers should play in helping to screen them.

The Role of Your Broker

Your friendly broker knows only too well that stocks have not been the most exciting investment ploys to attract new clients. His management is even more aware of the problem. Many a brokerage firm now states proudly in its annual report how little, not how much, it depends on stock commissions. The more important its other "products" to its total revenues, the better.

Should you rely on a broker primarily for his advice? The answer here, I think, is by and large no. There are many outstanding exceptions, of course (and almost every broker will tell you he is one of them). But how do you spot them? Certainly not by appearance, dress, or manner. Brokers are paid for the commissions they generate, not for the performance of their clients' accounts. They may look successful, but Gucci shoes, Polo suits, and Pierre Cardin ties have far more to do with good merchandising than with ability in the marketplace. The real exceptions, and this applies to all advice givers, should be able to document a successful record of performance, supplying you both with the performance of all stocks and investments they have recommended over an extended period and with the results of a number of their major clients' accounts (make sure they are not relatives or friends).

I don't mean to be cynical. Many salesmen will try to do an honest job, not just to keep the account but to get referrals from the client's friends and associates—essential to expanding business. But even if he is not affected by current fads, his clients undoubtedly are. The account executive's lifeblood is commissions, and because of this, except for those rare exceptions, he is dealing in fashion no less than a high-style boutique, which nudges him toward selling products that are currently "in."

Some brokers will sell anything that has a large commission attached to it, no matter how ill-suited it may be to the client—bad new issues, slow-moving secondaries, or other high-commission products. But is this really much different from the clothing salesmen who try to pocket extra commissions by selling you slow-moving, ill-fitting items? And it would be hard to make the case that the business ethics of insurance or used-car salesmen are much better. In any event, the customer's man can always argue that he gave the account a "shot" at making money, which of course does sometimes pay off.

You should be aware that despite federal statutes and stock exchange regulations going back to the 1930s, there really is no way of stopping an unscrupulous salesman from generating large commissions from the unwary. Unless he has gone to incredible extremes, as sometimes happens, such as "churning" a widow's portfolio from $100,000 to $8,000 in a couple of years while pocketing $150,000 in commissions, he won't be caught. You have to be careful because many a dishonest type can be extremely soft-spoken, articulate, and dress and act like a banker.

When the exchange does discipline its brokers, the connection between the offense and the public interest is sometimes mystifying, as Alan Abelson once wryly noted:

As a frequent critic of the Big Board, we must, in fairness, bow to its new and uncommon zeal in protecting the nation's investors. Last week, for example, it disclosed a number of disciplinary actions against errant brokers and other wretches whose activities come within its purview. We are particularly heartened by the Exchange's suspension of one fellow who allegedly committed the heinous crime of engaging in an outside business without approval: he was engaged in—grip the arms of your chairs now—a trout hatchery. The poor fish got a year's suspension. We were also relieved to see the powers-that-be at the Big Board crack down on brokers who agreed to share their customer's losses. Imagine if that sort of thing proved contagious. It would destroy a two-hundred-year tradition of sharing everything of your customer's—except his losses.[1]

Remember that the nature of the game makes it necessary for many brokers to turn over their accounts fairly rapidly. Account upgrading, as it is sometimes called, is a common maneuver for many brokers in a slow market or when commission business is slipping.

"Upgrading" means upgrading the broker's commissions, with the probability of only a questionable change (and possibly one to your detriment) in the composition of your portfolio. Some firms expect a minimum turnover in commissions from each salesman, depending on the size of the client's account. So unless there really is a good reason for making a suggested change, be careful.

More recently, with the rising interest in the faster-paced newer games, the commissions the broker can make have increased substantially. A tremendous amount of trading can be generated, much of which is old-fashioned "churning" but disguised in a highly sophisticated manner through the buying and selling of various computerized spreads.*

The salesman is an independent producer, after all, and must exist on his commissions. Recently I attended a meeting of a large national brokerage firm. One of two conflicting themes was presented by all the major speakers, and sometimes the same speaker presented both: first, always work in your client's best interest (which often means doing a minimal amount of trading); and second, your client always needs your help, his portfolio always needs some revision (in other words, a good salesman can find an opportunity to trade, or discover a new product). It's not hard, then, to see the danger that the unsophisticated investor has to face.

Unless you really think you can find that ideal broker who both is independent and has an excellent record, you had better use yours in the following manner:

1. As a source of information as to the credit worthiness of various fixed-income securities. He'll know call provisions, bond ratings, available yields, and information of this sort, and he can be useful in doing the bond shopping for you. But watch him; he can also lock in very large commissions on your bond transactions, especially if they are not New York Stock Exchange- or AMEX-listed.†

2. As a source of investment information on companies. He can probably supply you with long lists of high-yielding low P/E stocks and perhaps the lower deciles or quintiles themselves. If you don't

*See page 201.

†Particularly with infrequently traded issues, he may buy them at 95 and sell them to you at 98. Shopping around various brokerage houses is not a bad idea. In any case, let your broker know in your conversations that you are aware of such markups. You'll probably save yourself a good deal of money by doing so.

subscribe to a comprehensive statistical service, such as *Value Line,* very likely he does, and he can send you detailed information on the industries and companies you are interested in. He also has the Standard & Poor's statistical sheets. S&P prepares these on all companies on the New York Stock Exchange, American Stock Exchange, and also on major companies traded over-the-counter and on regional exchanges. The sheets contain excellent background data and brief synopses of the companies' major businesses, as well as recent developments. The broker should also be able to provide you with detailed information in any area that interests you. In short, he or she has statistical backup and information-gathering capabilities that can be invaluable aids to you. Brokerage firms spend substantial amounts in obtaining such information, so it certainly pays you to avail yourself of the sources.

The Discount Broker

If you already receive a comprehensive advisory service, you might decide to save on commissions by using a discount broker, particularly if you try some of the mechanical trading strategies mentioned in the last chapter.

In using a discount broker, you should remember a number of points. First, you can't be an odd-lotter. Usually a discount broker charges $25 to $30 minimum commission per transaction, so your volume has to be large enough to warrant the expense.

Second, he offers few or no frills. His only responsibility is prompt execution of orders, which is on a par with brokers charging regular commissions.

It's also important, if you are a large account, to make sure he has federal insurance up to $300,000. Most do, but a few carry it only up to $50,000. You can ask to see his financial statements, which he must provide on request. If a firm "bellies up," your account, even though insured, can be frozen for months, which could cost you dearly if you have to take immediate action. If you glance at the *Wall Street Journal,* Sunday *New York Times,* or *Barron's,* you will see numerous ads for discount brokers. The rates vary markedly, so it will pay you to shop around.

Next, let's turn to some of the games themselves and your odds if you choose to play.

Investing in Junk Bonds

Before we move on to the more popular games, some of which appear at times to have hawkers at every street corner, let's start with one that is not popular and for this reason may present some good opportunities for you—the interesting but more speculative one of investing in low-quality bonds. This form of investment has never gained a wide following.

Just as low P/E stocks have unfavorable outlooks, so junk bonds, as this group is appropriately named, are considered the poorest of corporate credit ratings*—investors are not sure that the issuing companies will be able to make future interest payments and eventually pay back the face value of the debt.

Such companies are at the bottom of the barrel of corporate credits—firms too small to be given credit ratings by S&P and Moody's, the predominant rating agencies;† those which have low credit ratings because of large amounts of debt outstanding, poor or cyclical operating records, or deteriorating financial positions; and at the very lowest tier, companies that are in bankruptcy proceedings. They're anything but hot items, so you won't often worry about a salesman trying to market them to you.

However, it is precisely because of the poor conditions existing or anticipated for such bonds that attractive opportunities often exist. Having watched these markets over the years, I've found that investor overreactions to such bonds seem very similar to overreactions to low P/E stocks. Let's look at a few examples of how psychological influences may play into the bond market.

One example is the enormous widening in yield spreads between higher- and lower-rated bonds in periods of extremely tight money, or when fears of a liquidity crisis are voiced. In the credit crunches of 1970 and 1974, for example, bonds with a BB rating yielded 13 or 14 percent. When credit reins were loosened, some

---

*If you are unfamiliar with the characteristics of bonds and debentures, please refer to Appendix II, which provides details of contractual obligation, types of risk, etc.

†Again, for details on credit ratings, please refer to Appendix II.

fairly significant gains were made on these issues, as they appreciated substantially more than higher-grade bonds. Yield and appreciation together might often total 30 percent or more. In fact, one major management firm, BEA Associates, put out a study showing the significantly superior returns such bonds have produced over time.

Investors also appear to overreact to bad news about a company without checking whether the developments will affect the bond itself. Often a bond is well secured by company assets so that adverse developments may only partially affect the issue, if at all. Even a bankrupt company's bonds may have a strong prior lien on assets before other creditors, often many times the size of the bond issue itself. One such example was Interstate Stores, which went into Chapter 11 proceedings in the early 1970s. One of its debentures, due in 1987, was secured with liens on inventories as well as by a general obligation. With the credit crunch and panic in both the bond and stock markets in 1974, the debenture traded at under 10 cents on the dollar,* although the company actually made $13 million that year. Earnings continued to increase, and by 1976 the bonds traded at 75, a market appreciation of over 650 percent.†[2]

Another case is the serious overreactions that sometimes occur when the agencies cut the credit rating of issues. In early February 1974 New York City's Con Ed 9⅜ of 2,000 were rated as BBB and were trading at 106.[3] In April the company, because of earnings difficulties, eliminated its quarterly common dividend, sending the stock plummeting from 20 to below 7. Standard & Poor's downgraded the company's bond shortly thereafter to BB, while Moody's suspended its ratings entirely. The result: the bonds dropped to a low of 57½ by September, a decline of nearly 50 percent, in spite of the fact that the company never stopped paying the interest on them. The bonds provided a cash yield of 17.4 percent at their low. Con Ed's earnings situation improved rapidly thereafter, and it restored its dividend. By late 1977 the rating had been raised to A–, and the bond moved back over par—to 102. Had an investor caught this

---

*Ten cents on every dollar the company was obligated to repay on the debenture.

†An interesting phenomenon observers first noted and capitalized on in the 1930s was that "bad bonds," those approaching bankruptcy or in bankruptcy proceedings, were always sold out of portfolios immediately by major financial institutions, with little investigation of the situation and almost no consideration of price—which often meant a pittance at best. Institutional investors still continue to act in much the same way today. An explanation of why will be given in chapter 11.

swing, the total return, including interest, would have been 170 percent in three and a half years.

Although it seems that psychological reactions very often do exist in bond markets (and possibly at times in the rating agencies too), unfortunately rules cannot be formulated nearly as systematically here as in the stock market. Unless you become well trained in assessing credit risk, I would advise you against playing junk bonds on your own. You might find a good advisor who specializes in this area and has a long-standing record of success, or perhaps you could place a small percentage of your portfolio (because of the added risk to come from the equity portion) in a junk bond fund that will give you a widely diversified portfolio of such issues. Two no-load funds investing in junk bonds are listed in table 28.

Table 28
JUNK BOND FUNDS—NO-LOAD

MUTUAL FUND	TOTAL RETURN	MINIMUM INITIAL INVESTMENT	SIZE OF FUND
American Investors Income P.O. Box 2500 Greenwich, Conn. 06830 Telephone: (203) 622–1600	16.0%[a]	$400	10.5 million
Fidelity Aggressive Income 82 Devonshire Street Boston, Mass. 02109 Toll-free number: (800) 225–6190	13.4%[b]	$2,500	71.5 million

NOTE: Includes dividends, capital distributions, and assumes reinvestment of all income.
[a] Annualized return, June 30, 1975, to March 31, 1979.
[b] Total return, November 1977 to April 1979.

Now let's turn to some of the more popular games.

Commodities

In recent years, the prices of gold, silver, platinum, and diamonds have skyrocketed. Other commodities, industrial as well as agricultural, have also moved up sharply. Not surprisingly, tens of thou-

sands of investors see commodities as the road to instant wealth*—
once again, that simple but effective image.

What are your odds in this game—certainly one of the most
spectacular in town? I think it is useful to examine the question in
some detail, for while commodity markets are soaring and may very
well continue to do so, the majority of investors are not making
money; indeed, most take losses. The reasons for failure are not
terribly different from those that apply to many other fast-paced and
seemingly unbeatable games, from high P/E stocks to options.

There are two principal tiers of commodity speculation. One
consists of the large and legitimate firms that are members of the
various exchanges and thus are subject to some regulation, particularly if the firm is a member of the New York Stock Exchange. The
second group is comprised of a wide range of firms often belonging
to no exchanges and governed by minimal regulations, if any at
all.

The legitimate brokerage firm normally deals in futures contracts. Margins in these contracts are quite low (usually under 10
percent of the total value of the commodity itself), resulting in highly
leveraged profits and losses. Expiration dates are brief, running from
a day or two to about a year. Because of the short period of time
involved, trading techniques have traditionally been based on technical analysis and market timing. From what was seen of the success
rate of these methods, you might guess that the scorecard is not good.
If you do, you're right.

My father is a commodities futures broker. In the late 1920s, his
first job was as a bookkeeper for a commodities brokerage firm.
Watching the eager if not sometimes frenzied trading of the firm's
clientele and listening to their boasts of profits, he began to examine
the record to determine how well they had actually done. He was
amazed to find that almost without exception none of them made
money over time. His advice is that if you are an outsider, stay out.
Unless you have that one expert in a thousand to advise you (and
you can't know beforehand), you are headed for trouble.

His experience is not unique. One commodities broker quoted
recently in *Forbes* said he had had one thousand clients over a period
of years; not one of them made money. And an article in *Money*
magazine estimated that 90 percent of small investors lose money,

*One source estimates that commodities futures trading will be $2 trillion in 1979.

with the life span of the average individual account only four months.[4]

Commodities are an excellent, almost ideal, revenue source for brokers. Contracts, as noted, are short, there are innumerable spreads,* and thus commissions (the rates are high in themselves) relative to client investment are usually many times those generated by the average stock account. Small wonder there has been such a rush by the brokerage houses to get into this excellent profit center.

However, most legitimate brokers at least try to give the client the best of their insight—whatever such "value added" is actually worth. But in recent years another breed of operator has moved into the game who is not unaware of hype, as the advertisements here, taken from *Commodities* (a magazine dedicated to commodities trading), indicate.

The goals of other new entrants are even more straightforward —find as many customers as you can, dazzle them with the thought of quick gains, and take them for every cent they can be persuaded to put up. As commodities regulation is only in its embryonic stage, such schemes are quite within the law.

Without regulation the smooth operator of "products" from commodities to Persian carpets can bilk you for all or most of your investment.† People who will carefully examine matters when committing relatively small amounts for a car or a television set will often invest $10,000 or $20,000 based on no more than a salesman's pitch.

Let's turn to one commodities scheme very popular recently as an example. Hundreds of salesmen sold the "product"—and why not? If the plan is properly executed, the commodity house is virtually guaranteed 100 percent of the customer's investment.

Although these plans go under a variety of names, the schemes are all fairly similar. One firm calls its plan "Limited Risk Forward."

---

*Buying or selling one month in a commodity (or one commodity against another) and hedging this by doing the opposite in another month or commodity. This limits profit but also limits loss.

†Even the formidable Mr. and Mrs. Henry Kissinger, while on a visit to Iran, were taken. Nancy was shown Persian carpets at the home of the U.S. ambassador by one of the country's supposedly most reputable dealers. She bought several beautiful carpets, investing more than $11,000, after being told they were over fifty years old. On returning to the United States, she had them reappraised; the embarrassed appraiser told her that they were in reality only ten to twenty years old, and that chemical rather than natural dyes had been used. The value was only about one third of the price they paid.

The literature begins by impressing customers with the inherent dangers of speculating in commodities:

LIMITED RISK FORWARD

Commodity markets are notoriously volatile. They can rise or fall the equivalent of thousands of dollars in the matter of a few days, even a few hours. It is just this volatility and its attendant *open-ended risk* which keeps conservative investors out of commodity positions. However, volatile price action can mean windfall profits to those aligned on the right side of any given market. The *question* is: How can a conservative investor enter the commodities market and not risk any more than a set, up-front amount? The *answer:* By taking a position in *Limited Risk Forwards.* [Italics theirs.]

It then goes on to advise the investor:

[We] believe that the trend of the markets favor those commodity speculators who assume medium or long-term positions in a particular market (like coffee, sugar, or copper) and then hold on. It is our experience that fast, in and out, jiggle trading creates lots of commissions for a broker and very few profits for the client. Since LRF's *cannot* be traded on a daily, in-out basis, we believe they are highly suited to a winning trading strategy. This fact coupled with their inherently limited risk makes them an *ideal* trading vehicle for the uninitiated or conservative commodity speculator.

It certainly sounds prudent enough; in fact, the company appears to be trying to save you from those naughty brokers who conduct "jiggle trading," creating lots of commissions for themselves at the poor client's expense. Here we seem to have a firm dedicated to your best interests, especially if you're "uninitiated." Now, what does this LRF do for you? Well, first of all, the client's risk is limited to only 100 percent of his investment, *"the purchase price he pays for the LRF, not a penny more* [their italics]." If 100 percent loss of investment is considered conservative, this plan is conservative indeed.

Moving on to the mechanics of the LRF itself, the company allows you to buy or sell any commodity contract you choose, domestic or foreign (including foreign exchange). They then immediately buy an offsetting one. Using their example, suppose you placed an order to buy sugar—then trading at 8 cents a pound—for one year, purchasing two contracts for $9,000 (110,000 pounds per contract). The company, at the time of your purchase, would offset your two contracts with two sales for the same time period of one year.

By so doing, the company guarantees you will not be called for further margin, because of the hedge. If sugar dropped a cent, it would cost you $1,100 in a regular commodities contract or $2,200 for the two. Sugar would have to drop 50 percent for you to lose your entire equity in a standard contract, as contrasted to an LRF. The only advantage of an LRF is that it protects you against an additional margin call (in this example, if sugar drops more than 50 percent) and maintains your position throughout the further decline. Thus, if the market nose-dives, you will never be sold out.

What is the cost of the privilege? Simply 100 percent of your capital—the amount the company automatically deducts for its service. If the market goes down or stays even, you lose everything. If it rises 2 cents, or 25 percent from the 8-cent price, you still lose. In this case, the $4,400 profit would be deducted from the $9,000, so you would show a $4,600 loss, *or over half your capital.* In other words, although you've made almost a 50 percent profit on the actual investment (as you would in a regular commodities contract*), you realize a greater than 50 percent loss because of their charges. Not particularly exciting odds in your favor. The company then asks:

WHY NOT SIMPLY BUY THE FUTURE ITSELF WITH NO AVAILABLE OPPOSITE POSITION, IF YOU THINK THE PRICE WILL GO UP?

Good question. The answer:

LRF's have many advantages over buying commodities with no available opposite position, but the principal advantage LRF's offer are *increased leverage* and *limited risk. . . .*†

The many advantages are not spelled out, with good reason. They don't exist. The only way you can benefit is to have a very sharp drop in the commodity, putting you deeply into the additional margin the company provides, followed by a far sharper recovery, which not only offsets the loss and then your entire original investment but also leaves some to spare. And all this in a relatively short period of time! A very rare flight pattern indeed.

You may ask if the house doesn't have some risks. After all, if additional losses are incurred above the original investment, the firm

---

*Commissions on the standard contract would be several hundred dollars.
†Which means, as we've seen, you can lose only 100 percent of your capital.

must make them up. But as you may guess, these people are no fools. If the firm is shrewd, why should they bother taking any risk at all?

Salesman A may think London gold futures contracts a year out are a good buy, and he relates this to Dr. A or Lawyer A. At the same time, Salesman B surprisingly arrives at the opposite conclusion, and believes gold has shot up far too quickly. He then advises Dr. or Lawyer B that it should be sold twelve months ahead. In short, the house can be fully hedged and pocket 100 percent on both sides. The commission scale, running up to 35 percent and sometimes more on this type of sale, would of course fail to influence the salesman's advice.*

Are the salesmen low-keyed? The question is only rhetorical. With commissions being what they are, and with the lack of regulation, a client can be told virtually anything with little danger. Financial reporter Kathryn Welling wrote of the hype delivered by one salesman (in a scheme as zany as the one described here—buying gold options issued by a New York metals dealer). She was repeatedly phoned by the eager promoter, who was unaware of her real purpose. One version of the hard sell: "Most of my clients have doubled their money in gold options in the last six or eight weeks, and that's just the beginning. I want to get your $5,000 up to $10,000. I feel the worst we should do is 100 percent in a year . . . but the timing is critical. We really have to make a move by Friday."[5]

The previous examples should give some idea of how dangerous it is to enter any game with which you are unfamiliar, particularly one governed by minimum legislation. Barracuda are always looking for you, the next victim. Are the odds any better in options?

Trading Stock Options

Options became the hottest game around after the 1974 break. There are now three or four dozen books out on them, some telling investors how to use them and others of the breathtaking returns possible by following the writers' strategies. First, I'd advise you to avoid the get-rich techniques. Like all others, from commodities to stop-loss orders, they don't work and you'll probably wind up on the losing

---

*In recent months a number of indictments have been brought in against a few of the many operators in the field.

end. If they are played like commodities, you have about the same chance of success.

But there are, I think, a number of secure ways of using options that, rather than increasing your market risk, should actually decrease it and quite possibly enhance your overall return.

A call contract gives the buyer the right to buy (at his option) a stock at a specific price, called the striking price, for a specific period of time. For selling the contract the seller gets a premium based on such factors as its length, nearness of striking price to market, volatility of the stock and market, and so on. A put is precisely the opposite mechanism. The buyer has the option of selling the stock at a predetermined price for a predetermined time period. For the privilege, the seller again gets a premium dependent on the factors just outlined.

Options are normally listed on stock exchanges, and prices can be found daily in the financial newspapers; they are usually traded in the largest or most active stocks in price intervals of five dollars. Thus if a stock is trading at 45, there may be calls to buy it (and puts to sell it) at 40, 45, and 50. The more volatile the stock, the larger the number of option prices outstanding. Options on listed exchanges are traded for fixed periods up to nine months. Each contract has a definite expiration date—the last Friday in the second week of the month the option is due, for example.

Speculators love them because they greatly increase their leverage. If, for example, a chartist believes Avon is ready to make a major move in the next six months and it is currently trading around 45, he might buy the options instead of the stock. Suppose in this instance he decides to purchase calls on the Avon 45 options six months out. The call might cost $2.50 per share (more or less, depending on the current volatility of the stock). Each call represents one hundred shares; thus, if he decided twenty calls, or two thousand shares, would do the job, it would cost him only $5,000 (plus commissions), rather than the $90,000 he would have to put up for the stock.

If the stock ran beyond 47½, he would make money. At 50, he has doubled his investment. The stock itself moving from 45 to 50 rises only 11 percent. Thus, options provide leverage, dramatically increasing your bang for the buck. Every point move from the original price is a 2.2 percent move in the stock and 40 percent in the option. The action increases nearly twentyfold.

But of course you have to be right, and in a short period of time: if the stock stays where it is or goes down, your investment is wiped out.

Large numbers of investors use options as a massive crap shoot in an all-or-nothing manner. From the previous indications of market timing and stock selection, most often it is nothing.

However, conservative option strategies can be used in quite different ways. Some can help you to minimize your taxes. You can, for example, use an option to protect a short-term capital gain. Suppose you bought Honeywell (which has listed options traded) at 45, and you had a sudden sharp run-up to 76 in eight months. You might want to take profits but not the short-term gain because it would be treated like ordinary income. In this case, you would buy a put at 75, which would allow you to sell the stock at this price for a period long enough to give you a long-term capital gain. The put might cost $4 to $6 (depending again on the stock's volatility). If the stock goes up, you have an even larger capital gain; and it is long-term, with the option deductible as a short-term loss. If it goes down, $4 to $6 might prove cheap insurance.

Another possibility—one I've tried myself—is to use options in an attempt to reduce taxes if you have large short-term gains in any year. In 1977 I used them to try to offset some short-term gains that would have put me in a higher tax bracket than I was comfortable with. At the time, it seemed there were some excellent low P/E stocks with listed options in them. I bought calls "deep in the money" in Honeywell, Aetna, and Travelers. (A deep-in-the-money call is one where the stock is trading well above the option price. Honeywell trading at 48 with a 40 option outstanding would be such a case. Deep-in-the-money options normally trade at the smallest premiums of any contracts because of the larger downside risk.*) The calls were bought in August 1977, due to expire early in 1978. If they had gone up, the profits would be realized in 1978, making my 1977 tax bill more palatable. And if not, the loss could be deducted from the taxes on the short-term gains.

As it turned out, the market went down and the calls resulted in a loss. I sold them near year-end and switched ahead, keeping the position intact in options expiring later in 1978. Because of the

*If, in the Honeywell case, the stock had fallen to 42 at expiration date, I would have been out $6 and commissions.

short-term loss in these options, the 1977 taxes were reduced. And, in a falling market, premiums were lowered in buying the new options.

In the market rally of spring 1978, the options went up sharply, well above the original cost the year before. Once again, there was a choice of selling them and taking short-term profits (if the tax position allowed it) or converting them into long-term profits by exercising the option and then holding the stock for the required time period.*

A final example would be to use options as an adjunct to the low P/E approach when dollar cost averaging. Suppose you wish to put money into the market over time and have found attractive low P/E companies with listed puts on them. You might sell a put expiring six months ahead. (This is the opposite of the first strategy, where puts were bought.) If, for example, Aetna was at 40 and you wanted to dollar-cost-average, you might sell a 40 put, which would result in the stock being delivered to you if the stock dropped below the striking price. You would pocket the premium and get a somewhat cheaper price, trading into the position you wanted in any event. If the market went up, you would keep the premium and simply go out and buy the stock you intended to buy in any case,† following through on the principle of dollar cost averaging.

These are but several examples of the numerous option strategies that can be fitted into a conservative investment philosophy. The point to remember is that rather than using them as quick-kill vehicles, they can be tailored to assist your current investment objectives.

---

*A more common method of shifting gains from one year to the next is by employing option or commodity spreads in the following manner: the investor selects a volatile commodity or stock and then buys and sells offsetting contracts but for differing time periods (or in the case of options, for the same time period but at differing prices). Suppose, for example, HON is volatile, currently trades at 70 and has "deep-in-the-money" options outstanding, say 55s and 60s. The trader might sell the 60s and buy the 55s. For simplicity, let's eliminate premiums and assume the cost of 15 on the 55s and proceeds of 10 on the 60s. It doesn't matter which way the stock moves as long as the move is fairly significant. If HON rose to 80, the 60 call would be bought in at year-end, resulting in a $10 loss that year. To avoid market risk, the 55 call would be sold the first day of the following year, resulting in a $10 profit. If the stock fell to 60, the 55s would be sold at year-end at a $10 loss and the 60s bought in the first day of the following year at a $10 profit. While there are many variations on this strategy, in its simplest form it postpones short-term gains until the following year. But once again, as I've learned from my own earlier experience, you have to be careful with option and commodity spreads that you watch both the prices and the commissions beforehand, or you can wind up with heavy additional costs.

†If Aetna was still at a reasonable P/E to the market. If not, you could buy another stock. The risk in this strategy is if the market moves down sharply—more than the gain you received from the premium.

Good option strategies are sophisticated and often complex. For readers interested in more than this brief overview, I would recommend a number of publications of the Chicago Board of Trade (provided free) on understanding options. A couple of good books on the subject are Garry Gastineau's *The Stock Options Manual,* * and Max G. Anspacher's *The New Option Market.* †

Tax Shelters

These have most often proven to be fairly rewarding investments— for their promoters. And there are large numbers of salesmen, both inside and outside brokerage firms, pushing them. Many people who have dabbled in tax shelters have not fared well, and some have been badly burned, such as the herds of investors who purchased brokerage-house-sponsored cattle tax shelters in the early 1970s and saw their investments eaten to the bone. Overall, some estimates placed investor losses in cattle shelters in the twelve months ending October 1974 at $2 billion. However, brokerage houses fared somewhat better, receiving front-end fees of up to 18 percent.[6]

Tax shelters might be looked at from two points of view:

1. As investment write-offs designed simply to reduce your current tax, with little or no hope of recouping the investment—the saving in current taxes more than offsetting the costs of the shelter. But to do this you must be in a high tax bracket. An investor with $30,000 or more of income in a 65 percent bracket investing $10,000 in a shelter designed to give him an immediate $30,000 write-off will actually save $9,500 in taxes that year.

2. Primarily as an investment, but one that should shield you from some of your current tax load.

The former—now mainly in movies and records—is dangerous because the IRS is continually trying to plug the loopholes,‡ and many such schemes are marginal at best and may backfire on the investor, costing him both the money invested and the full tax rate.

Large numbers of tax shelters exist, some legitimate, others that

*2nd ed., New York: McGraw-Hill, 1979.
†New York: Walker, 1975.
‡Most were plugged by the Tax Reform Act of 1976.

skirt the boundaries of fraud. As an investor, you should remember two things: first, you will at times (as in some of the commodity schemes) be paying extremely high sales charges to participate. The people selling the most accessible of these packages are usually exceptionally smooth and well-heeled, often making six figures a year plus lavish expenses. Second, you should never consider a tax shelter unless you are in a very high tax bracket—60 percent or more.

There are naturally some very good shelters—in a wide range of investments from real estate to airplane and even railroad rolling-stock leasing—that shield income, provide comparatively high returns, and charge only a moderate load. But these are usually not available to average investors. Minimum participation can range to $100,000 or more, and benefits may extend only to people in very high tax brackets.

When you put half a million dollars into a tax shelter, you can afford a $10,000 examination by your own experts. When you are investing $5,000, you can afford a prayer.

Because the laws are extremely complicated, you must have a good understanding of the mechanics of the shelter and your income prospects or you may wind up with a form of tax alchemy that can turn your gold into lead. Dollars you shield at 45 or 50 percent one year may come back to haunt you at 65 or 70 percent tax rates a few years later.

Unless you are a very large investor, or have expert knowledge at your disposal, tax shelters constitute another area best to stay clear of. Finally, let's turn to some other schemes, all of which can definitely be of benefit to you.

Keough Plans and Individual Retirement Accounts (IRAs)

In 1974 Congress passed ERISA, the Employees Retirement Investment Security Act. Although it has proven almost mystical to money managers in interpreting the investments they can prudently make, the act has provided vastly improved safeguards for the pension rights of employees.

At the same time Congress established two other types of pension protection: Keough plans for people who are self-employed (doctors, dentists, lawyers, artists, accountants, etc.) and who are not covered by other pension plans; and Individual Retirement Accounts for people already employed but not participating in pension plans.

The Keough plans currently allow you to contribute up to 15 percent of your earnings each year to a maximum of $7,500. A $750 contribution is allowable regardless of the level of income. These contributions come off the upper level of your tax bracket. The IRA also allows a contribution of 15 percent of income each year, but the limit is set at $1,500.*

In both cases, no minimum requirement is necessary in any one year, and any amount up to the maximum may be invested. Contributions need not be made each year, but if they are omitted in any one year they cannot be made up in subsequent years.

Money in either plan must be invested with an authorized trustee. Investments can be made in a variety of alternatives ranging from savings bank certificates to life insurance plans to common stock mutual funds. Such plans can be tailored to the individual's personal investment needs.

The advantage of these plans is that all interest, dividends, and capital gains are tax-free throughout their lives. Thus, if you invest in common stocks in a Keough plan, have an income of $25,000 a year for a thirty-year period, and take the full 15 percent deduction (assuming the long-term rate of return on equities remains at the low 9.2 percent), you will have $579,425 at the end. Or if you have income high enough to take the full $7,500 deduction and do the same thing, you will show a mere $1,158,851 at the end of the thirty-year period. Not all that bad!

Now for the catches. The rules say you cannot begin to withdraw funds from these plans until you are fifty-nine-and-a-half, although you are not required to do so until you are seventy. Since most people retire by sixty or sixty-five, they should be paying taxes at significantly lower rates when they begin their withdrawals.

If money is taken out before the age of fifty-nine-and-a-half, there is a 10 percent penalty on withdrawal, and the entire amount including the 10 percent is taxed at your regular income rate. But because "top dollar" for some contributors can lie in the 60 percent tax bracket or above, and all interest and dividends in the interim are invested tax-free, the possible penalty does not turn out to be a particularly onerous burden. Chances are in any case that if money

*If you are married and your spouse has no pension plan, $1,750.

need be withdrawn, your income will be down fairly sharply that year. Thus, such plans are excellent tax shelters and should be used as investment vehicles for people who can qualify for them.

Money Market Funds

Money market funds normally pay higher rates of interest than day-to-day deposits in savings accounts. The usual minimum investment is a thousand dollars, but sometimes it is higher. In the last several years, these funds have become very hot items among investors, and had over $10 billion invested in them by December 1978. Currently, there are over fifty in operation. At present, the largest funds pay 10 to 11 percent, against 5.25 percent in the savings banks. Most funds allow you to write checks on them above $500, and you continue to get interest until the check clears.

Although the funds do not have government insurance (as do the savings banks), they normally invest in highly secure short-term debt instruments—treasury bills, certificates of deposit of commercial banks, commercial paper (usually short-term notes of large corporations with excellent credit ratings), and the like. There is no sales charge, only a management fee (calculated before, not after, the yield is stated).

However, if you buy a money market fund, yields can vary as much as 2 to 3 percent because of the differences in the average maturity of the portfolios. It is safest to stay in shorter maturities. Although somewhat longer maturities may provide higher yields, if interest rates rise, the investor can be caught. One glaring case was First MultiFund. Restructuring its portfolio into shorter maturities at the end of 1978 cost the fundholders 6 percent of their assets.[7]

Three of the largest are Merrill Lynch Ready Assets Trust, Dreyfus Liquid Assets, and Fidelity Daily Income. These all have toll-free numbers.*

One thing to remember is that money market funds are far more responsive to interest rate changes than are savings banks. If interest

*Merrill Lynch, 800-631-0749, extension 7976; Dreyfus, 800-223-5525; Fidelity Daily Income, 800-225-6190.

rates shift suddenly, the funds will immediately reflect this.* So you
will have to be fairly careful in watching the yields and moving out
of these funds as the occasion requires. Thus, for the investor who
has only several thousand dollars, the effort may not be worth the
few additional dollars gained in interest, unless he likes the game.

Next, let's turn to the role of the investment advisor. Is he likely
to be helpful to you in carrying out the strategies previously recommended?

---

*The portfolios are marked to market daily. Sometimes this will cause a peculiar blip in
yields. Some time back, one fund went from 6.65 to 4.81 in one day, and back to 6.75 the
following day. Thus thirty-day average yields normally provide the best tally of returns.

CHAPTER ELEVEN

The Problems of the Investment Advisor

If your broker is of limited help at best in guiding your investment decisions, is the investment advisor any better? Unlike a broker, the investment advisor, whether with a bank trust department, mutual fund, or independent investment advisory organization, is usually paid a flat fee for his services. He is thus under no pressure to trade your account or put you into the high-markup but dangerous games we have just seen. Quite the contrary, in fact: investment advisors like to point out that one of their chief functions is to make decisions solely in the client's best interest, an important result of which is to avoid precisely such pitfalls. Since their tenure depends on how well their accounts perform, their decisions must always be based on optimizing the client's results. At least this is how the matter is stated in theory.

However, from the statistics we saw earlier, investment advisors have also generally failed to provide clients with profit-making advice. Now we'll look at an important reason why. The professional investor often has a difficult psychological barrier to overcome, one that fortunately does not interfere with the judgment of the individual decision maker. The expert must cope with career pressures inside an organizational setting in addition to the cognitive biases each of us is subject to. Such pressures repeatedly result in groups of very bright people making poor decisions. In the investment setting, they normally lead many committees to follow the prevailing consensus and shun out-of-favor stocks.

Naturally, career pressures extend to decision making in many areas outside of the stock market. But in the investment scene, they are particularly striking because of the increasing dominance in the marketplace of the larger institutions. Because of this increasing domination, I believe the individual investor may very well maintain, if not increase, his "edge" over the institutions with time.

Further understanding of the forces that create institutional consensus should also prove helpful to investors who select and use investment advisors. Let's turn next to why these pressures exist and how strong they can be.

What Is Groupthink?

In *Victims of Groupthink,* Irving Janis, professor of psychology at Yale, analyzed the subtle pressures of career as they influenced the decision making of individuals in many areas, including the making of national policy. These pressures, according to Janis, caused people acting within committees to abandon time-tested standards and make extremely risky decisions, which often turned out badly.

In the committee situation, Janis indicates, the executive in charge may not intentionally try to influence the group; indeed, he may sincerely foster open discussion and encourage dissenting opinion. Too, its members are often anything but yes men; most firmly believe they can and should speak their minds. Still, members often do not fully assess the suggested course. Subtle restraints may prevent fully discussing all options or dwelling too long on dissenting views once most group members have made up their minds. By his stance, the leader may unintentionally reinforce the consensus. The subtle pressures of superiors and colleagues can make it easy for committees to follow what appear to outsiders at times to be inane courses of action.[1]

Janis defined groupthink as a "mode of thinking that people engage in when they are deeply involved in a cohesive in-group, when the members, striving for unanimity, override their motivation to realistically appraise alternative courses of action. . . . Groupthink refers to a deterioration of mental efficiency (and reality-testing) . . . that results from in-group pressures."[2]

The more cohesive the decision-making group and the more they respect and are attuned to each other's thinking, the greater the danger that independent assessment will be abandoned and will be replaced instead by concurrence-seeking tendencies. Poor decisions are frequently the result.

Victims of Groupthink describes in detail how such pressures affected some highly sophisticated groups: the Kennedy brain trust and the ill-fated Bay of Pigs invasion; the confidence of top advisors in the Truman administration that the Chinese would never enter the Korean War as MacArthur's troops fanned toward the Chinese border; the conviction of Admiral Husband E. Kimmel and his staff that the Japanese could not and would not launch an aerial attack on Pearl Harbor. In each case, a great deal of contradictory evidence was at hand but was ignored because of the pressures toward consensus.

Janis says that groups are not always affected by groupthink. However, when two conditions are present—an extremely cohesive group and consistently defective decision making—groupthink is often at work. In his words, "When the conditions specified by these two criteria are met, there is a better-than-chance likelihood that one of the causes of the defective decision-making was a strong concurrence-seeking tendency, which is the motivation that gives rise to all the symptoms of groupthink."[3]

Groupthink and Money Management

In the investment scene we have repeatedly seen the abandonment of past standards and the exceptional rate of error as a result. Career pressures subtle and not so subtle also serve to reinforce the prevailing consensus.*

Money managers in a bank trust department or an investment management firm are usually well qualified for their jobs. Clients turn money over to them because they believe the professionals are better equipped to deal with the problems of investing and because they are willing to delegate responsibility and pay for this expertise.

But what happens next hardly follows the script. Many clients second-guess the money manager when the decisions he makes run

*Chapters 5 through 9 of *Psychology and the Stock Market* provide considerably more detail of how this phenomenon affects institutional investors in the stock market.

counter to market fashions currently in vogue. If the manager holds firm, he may lose the account—a more than common occurrence. In 1973, for example, a money management firm, Capital Guardian, refused to play the soaring highfliers, favored by most, at P/E multiples of 40, 50, 60, and more. Instead, the firm invested primarily in low-multiple stocks faring poorly at the time. As a result, they lost a number of their clients. As one disgruntled client put it: "Capital Guardian was like an airline pilot in a power dive, hands frozen on the stick; the name of the game is to be where it's at."[4] Had the firm been "where it's at," the account would have been decimated in short order.

Money management is a business with a high break-even point, which, once passed, generates large and rapidly expanding profit margins. To be out of fashion for too long, even if the course eventually results in outstanding returns, may cause the firm to lose enough accounts in the meantime to force it to close shop or cut staff drastically. It is not surprising that few people have the conviction or resources to be proven "dead right" in this manner. Survival pressures in the committee, either with or without the decision makers' awareness, work in the direction of reinforcing the cognitive biases we've already seen. On the other hand, money management firms capturing trends early and staying with them can do remarkably well —some making incomes up to seven figures.

To complete the picture, it is not only the unsophisticated investor who puts pressure on the money manager. Executives representing billions of dollars of pension funds of many of the country's largest corporations do precisely the same thing!

Some estimates have indicated that a 1 percent improvement in the performance of corporate pension funds will result in a reduction of about 25 percent in the mandatory annual corporate contributions. Since pension fund contributions have been projected to be as large as 25 percent of corporate pretax profits, the urge to find money managers who will provide above-average performance is strong indeed.*[5]

Given such stakes, many corporations view pension funds as

*Since the passage of ERISA (the Employee Retirement Investment Security Act of 1974), pension fund contributions have skyrocketed. Peter Drucker, in a recent book, estimated that pension funds alone now account for over one third of all stock ownership on the New York Stock Exchange, and by 1980 they will account for 60 percent. Thus, huge and ever-increasing amounts of money are flowing into increasingly fewer large institutional hands.

independent profit centers and expect their managers to outperform the market and other money managers consistently. And because corporations divide their operations neatly into yearly, semiannual, and quarterly periods, money managers are often expected to turn in above-average performance smoothly—and on schedule. Good results should be almost as systematic as the flow of products down an assembly line.

Consequently, many financial officers, through their pension fund consultants, monitor in minute detail the performance of the professionals they have hired (as well as those of promising replacements). Usually, detailed review of the account takes place every three months. The manager whose moves are out of step, resulting in returns below par for even a relatively short time, is under mounting pressure. The "twelve/twenty-four rule," as it is called, is followed by not a few corporations—fire the manager whose performance is 12 percent below the S&P 500 for twenty-four months.[6] In short, money managers have increasingly found themselves in an impossible position—one that demands results far too quickly with its inevitable reliance on playing the popular trends.

Those who refuse can lose the account or a portion of it. One money manager, for example, was fired when his value-oriented philosophies did not work well. The corporate officer responsible for the dismissal justified it by saying: "I never asked him to change his approach, you know. . . . My attitude was 'fine, this is your philosophy, let's just wait and see what the figures show.' "[7] The figures, of course, were for a too brief time period. After the manager was dismissed, his philosophy proved to be dramatically correct in short order.

Similar pressures apply to institutional research firms specializing in in-depth research for the major money managers. With brokerage firms merging and going out of business on an accelerating basis, the job market for securities analysts has decreased sharply. Institutions demand the "best" research from the survivors. Since what is considered to be the "best" research is determined by the money managers through their allocation of commission dollars, the result is not surprising—"good" research usually means recommending the current fashions the institutions themselves are backed into.

A final source of pressure on the professional is ERISA (the Employee Retirement Investment Security Act of 1974), which mandates that pension fund managers be "prudent." Not to be so considered can result in crippling lawsuits against the money manager. At the present time, the definition of what is prudent is extremely "iffy," which results in advisors acting as most other investment advisors do. Those who don't—and prove wrong—may be staring at bankruptcy.

But market professionals are not alone, of course, in succumbing to career pressures. Indeed, the same forces apply to the "best and the brightest" in most areas of organizational decision making, and the push to conform can be found in Detroit or Georgetown as easily as on Wall or Broad streets. For us as investors, I think it is important to consider how pervasive and universal the problem actually is.

In *Bureaucratic Politics and Foreign Policy,* Morton Halperin, a former member of the staff of the National Security Council, speaks of exactly the same problems of the careerist in many branches of the federal government and the military. The desire for promotion forces a career officer to support the "shared images" of the day. Halperin writes: "Participants seem to believe that their influence and even their continuation in office depends on their endorsement or seeming endorsement of shared images. Even men who appear invulnerable to opposition zealously guard their reputation for accepting shared images."[8] When Dean Acheson, for example, accused Eisenhower of being soft on communism, the then-President vehemently denied it, reading from *Crusade in Europe* to defend himself. Even Eisenhower thought it essential to protect himself on this shared image.

"Wait a minute, you guys—I've decided to make it unanimous after all."

Drawing by Vietor; © 1978, The New Yorker Magazine, Inc.

Both Richard Neustadt, in *Alliance Politics,*[9] which discusses government policy making, and Adam Smith, writing about money managers in *The Money Game,*[10] speak of "players" in almost identical terms. Both sets of players are normally trying to accumulate as many career chips as they can. The career officer's major source of motivation is his desire for promotion; the foreign officer wants to reach ambassadorial rank; the military officer, flag or general rank; the money manager, a partnership. And each career officer believes that his promotion will further the national interest, just as the money manager or analyst feels his advancement will further the interests of the firm and its clients.

According to Halperin, bureaucratic players shape their arguments in terms of current shared images—because of their influence on others—even when they do not personally believe them: "If participants believe that taking a certain stand which they think wise will be interpreted as a deviation from shared images, they will take the opposite stand for fear of losing influence or indeed their position in government."[11]

Players quickly learn to avoid positions that mean abandoning shared images. Robert MacNamara did not view Russian missiles in Cuba as particularly dangerous. "A missile is a missile," he argued in the opening deliberations of the Cuban missile crisis of 1962, and advanced the case that no military action was necessary. He quickly dropped opposition when he saw that such was definitely not the view of the other important policy makers.

The problem in the foreign service is almost identical. In *Anatomy of the State Department,* Smith Simpson, a former career officer, writes of the tremendous stress on careerism in the department. "The desire for the top led to an overdeveloped sense of status, and minimized the sober business of policymaking, research, planning, management, and diplomacy itself. It developed self-promotion to a finished art, forcing officers to pay more attention to their personal security than to the nation's."[12]

According to Simpson, the problem has been exaggerated in recent years by the department's "up or out" rule—the officer either gets promoted or is forced to retire. "The yes man spirit, already developed to a fine art, has been enhanced by this practice; particularly vicious because the officer's prospects depend entirely on an efficiency report by a superior wherever he is located."[13] The report is reviewed many thousands of miles away in Washington by a board usually entirely unfamiliar with the officer. The assessment is the only evidence the board has to work from. The State Department panel reviewing the situation concluded the policy was a powerful detriment to officers expressing opinions at variance with those of their superiors—at best, a diplomatic understatement.

All of this is little different than the career pressures in the investment world. A recent article describing the pressures on a corporate officer administering his firm's pension fund revealed the parallels. Although the pension fund officer is responsible to his board of directors, he may be far more sophisticated in his investment understanding than its members. He thus often finds himself on a precarious perch, swinging between "professional conviction and career longevity. As an officer summed it up . . . 'you really don't have much choice . . . you either say what others wish to hear or the firm will hire someone else who will . . .' It is nonsense to blame someone in his thirties or forties with his corporate career ahead of him for judiciously ducking a confrontation with an opinionated director or senior officer who is perhaps fighting the equivalent of the Spanish-American War on the investment scene." Or, as Sam Rayburn put it, "To get along, go along."

In the market the threat of outright dismissal or the downgrading of the Wall Streeter's role is always present if he does not go along. In the words of one manager of corporate pension funds: "If the committee doesn't approve of my recommendations, it's like a vote of No Confidence, and, like a Prime Minister of England, I'd have to think about resigning."[14] Pressure enough to share the investment image of the moment.

With the increasing job scarcity of recent years, deteriorating institutional performance, and the crumbling of the brokerage industry, survival pressures have gotten worse. In 1977, for example, 25 percent of all money managers lost one or more accounts. The money managers in turn have been dealing with fewer and fewer research firms. One major New York City bank cut its list of brokers from 105 to 30 that same year. An out-of-towner observing the institutional research scene in New York City commented: "It's absurd, impossible to talk to any analyst. You can't get on with business . . . because these guys are worried about their jobs."

While it's impossible to say with any finality whether career pressures on Wall Street professionals are worse than elsewhere, it's obvious that they are not light and that they push many a player toward consensus opinion.

But of course there are still individuals who see through the prevailing images when they are wrong, and some of them adamantly refuse to be swept along, even by the influential organizations to which they belong.

Unfortunately, as any careerist knows, the ending is all too often the same. A long literature exists in psychology on deviancy—people who refuse to accept the opinion of the group. One experiment showed that dissenters were always chosen to perform unpleasant tasks. Another required a group to select someone from among them to receive electric shocks. Naturally, it always chose the deviant.[15]

And in sophisticated committees, the proceedings, while more subtle, are really little different. Historian James Thomson, Jr., a member of McGeorge Bundy's White House staff, illustrated the dangers for careerists who stand against current policy in what he called the "effectiveness trap": "The effectiveness trap [is] the trap that keeps men from speaking out as clearly or as often as they might in Government. . . . The most important asset that a man brings to bureaucratic life is his 'effectiveness,' a mysterious combination of training, style, and connections. The most ominous complaint that can be whispered about a bureaucrat is 'I'm afraid Charlie's beginning to lose his effectiveness.' "[16] The enigmatic quality of effectiveness is just as vital in the investment scene as it is in government.

David Halberstam captured the committee spirit well in *The Best and the Brightest* when he wrote of the "Harvard Business School approach played with loaded dice": speak out and present the situation and alternatives realistically; points are given for examining contrary arguments. But don't overstay, don't present opposing views too forcefully or you may wind up on the outside.[17]

The same game, of course, with the same loaded dice is an essential part of the current investment environment. Portfolio managers can speak out, but they had better take note of which way the wind is blowing. A lawyer from Boston once told me of a suit he was filing for a bank money manager who spoke out against the dangers of investing in the highfliers in 1972. He saved his clients large sums of money and found himself unemployed in the process. And a highly successful manager of a bank trust department in Denver was fired because the board of directors thought his investment strategies were out of line with those of the big city banks (all of which were doing poorly at the time). Effectiveness in career, then, is a compelling inducement to follow the prevailing images.

The Use of an Investment Advisor

The combination of the powerful individual cognitive biases that are reinforced by organizational consensus pressures provides a good explanation, I think, of why professional performance has been mediocre through the years. The problem is one not of the quality of people but of basic flaws in the individual's ability to make some types of decisions and in the institutional structures themselves. The group-decision problem can occur in many a sophisticated committee or organization.

Yes, there are numbers of talented advisors who can avoid the hurdles, but unless you search carefully, your odds of finding one are not great. If you try, it's important to discover how successful and independent a decision maker your investment advisor actually is, and, of course, to carefully measure his record over a significant period of time.*

It seems best to avoid committee decision making wherever possible. Naturally, there will be outstanding leaders heading first-rate committees, but usually the makeup changes with time, and you will probably end up having your money managed by a hardworking group that has the problems indicated in this chapter.

If you are lucky enough to find a money manager, whether in an organization or independent, who has a long-standing record of success, remember the problems just outlined. Don't second-guess him. Give him enough time for his philosophy to work. I know I've said it before, but time is one of the crucial elements in investment success and also the single commodity in shortest supply.

But for most investors, judging from the professional record, it seems better to go it alone. It's obviously not the popular route, and very often you are going to be considered misguided for investing in out-of-favor stocks. But if the goal is market success, it certainly appears the best bet, for the methods eliminate most of the problems we have seen.

The institution's problems become the individual's edge. At

*Ideally, three to five years.

least until the causes of consensus opinion in committee decisions are better understood, and "prudent" investments are more liberally defined by the regulators or the courts, the individual possesses an advantage that looks much like the elusive Holy Grail of the technical analyst: a system for beating the market that can't be universally adapted. And, as was indicated earlier, he is left in the out-of-favor ball park with fewer and fewer players as ever larger amounts of money are concentrated in institutional hands. All he needs to make the method work, it would appear, are faith in the efficacy of the low P/E method and the conviction to follow it up.

The last topic in this book, and one as important as any we have discussed thus far, is why common stocks represent good value in today's inflationary environment, where inflation may increase at much faster rates than through much of the postwar period.

CHAPTER TWELVE

Are Common Stocks a Good Inflation Hedge?

The persistent inflation the Western world has experienced since the advent of the Keynesian revolution has no precedent in history.* And, in the radically changed world economic environment of the 1970s, the rate of inflation has been accelerating. The roots of the new phenomenon often seem as baffling to the expert as to the average investor. Nevertheless, reasonable assumptions about future inflation are crucial to a successful investment strategy.

Inflation is a problem of enormous economic complexity, involving not only many controversial monetary and fiscal inputs but also a web of political and sociological factors. In recent years, new forces appear to be at work which are far less susceptible, if at times seemingly immune, to the fiscal and monetary remedies that have been traditionally applied. We'll now look at current inflation and some of the reasons why it may persist at levels higher—perhaps substantially higher—than any prior to this decade.

As investors, we have been accustomed to assume that rising inflation is bad for equity investments. But is this necessarily so? The evidence of the recent past indicates that corporations can survive and even flourish during periods of rapid price escalation. While the

---

*With the exception of a few isolated cases, such as Germany's Weimar Republic in 1920–22.

Figure 15.
A seven-hundred-year consumer price index.

SOURCE: Reprinted by permission of *Forbes* Magazine from the November 15, 1976, issue.

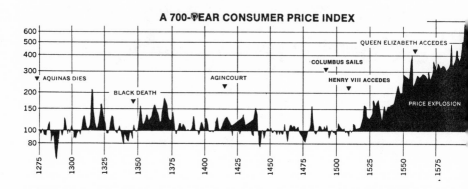

discussion that follows is intended to be anything but definitive, I believe it focuses on some of the major contributors to accelerating rates of inflation. If the analysis makes sense, it should prove useful to investors as they decide how to structure their portfolios and what role common stocks should play within them.

The New Inflationary Environment

Figure 15 shows the rate of inflation over a time span of seven hundred years.* As can be seen from the chart, prices exploded in the century following 1528, fueled by the plundered gold and silver of the Inca and Aztec empires. This was the classic type of inflation economists understand so well—too much money chasing too few goods. The primitive production capacity of the time could not keep up with the vast increase in money supply, and wild inflation resulted, first in Spain and not long thereafter in England. Price levels

---

*The *Forbes* figures come from a variety of sources. English economist E.H. Phelps Brown carefully checked both the salaries of carpenters (three pennies a day in 1275) and what this "market basket" should buy (food, fuel, and clothing) to 1660. From 1661 on, *Forbes* used more sophisticated indices, which they indicated "nevertheless conformed neatly to those of the Professor."

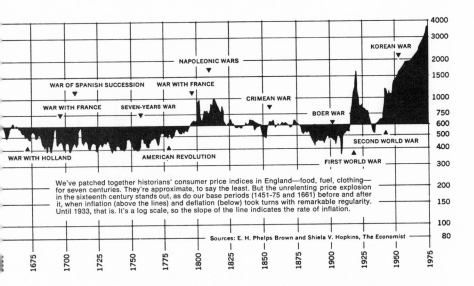

We've patched together historians' consumer price indices in England—food, fuel, clothing—for seven centuries. They're approximate, to say the least. But the unrelenting price explosion in the sixteenth century stands out, as do our base periods (1451-75 and 1661) before and after it, when inflation (above the lines) and deflation (below) took turns with remarkable regularity. Until 1933, that is. It's a log scale, so the slope of the line indicates the rate of inflation.

Sources: E. H. Phelps Brown and Shiela V. Hopkins, *The Economist*

then remained stationary for almost three hundred years and were actually higher in 1650 than they were in 1932.

So, with the exception of odd and quickly corrected price surges (at least when looked at over the long historical time span), the world enjoyed relative price stability. For example, prices rose 75 percent between 1350 and 1370, but by 1380 they were lower than they had been in 1350. Similar price surges and corrections accompanied most major wars. In Victorian England, price levels were so stable that government bonds for the most part returned 2.5 percent, as we saw earlier.

If you examine the chart, you will see that there have been only two periods of sustained inflation—the one lasting a hundred years, beginning in the sixteenth century, and the one we are currently undergoing. The chart makes clear that the current inflationary period is by far the worst of the two. By the end of 1974, prices had appreciated over 480 percent in twenty-eight years, and by the end of 1977, 620 percent!

More alarming, however, is that the inflation rate has been accelerating in recent years, as figure 16 indicates. Further, while other periods, even the 1500s, show sharp deflationary dips, the current inflation has moved continuously higher with virtually no respite.

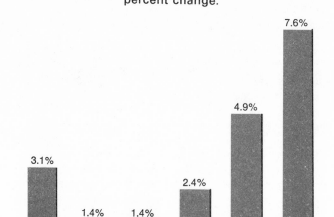

Figure 16.
Thirty years of U.S. price history: average annual percent change.

SOURCE: Department of Labor, Bureau of Labor Statistics, Consumer Price Index.

Recent statistics are even worse. In 1978 the consumer price index rose at a 9 percent annual rate, and in January 1979 wholesale prices were up almost 16 percent. In February 1979 government officials projected a minimum 9 percent increase in the consumer price index for the year, an estimate which, in April at least, appeared conservative in view of the 13 percent rise in this index on an annual basis in the first quarter.

What does one make of such figures? As chairman of the Federal Reserve Board, Arthur Burns warned repeatedly that inflation might mean the end of Western civilization, and Burns's own precipitous monetary policy, a major factor in two sharp recessions—one the worst of the postwar period—almost made him a self-fulfilling prophet.

However, before drawing any doomsday conclusions either for the economy or for the investor, we should look carefully at some of the fundamentals of the new inflation and see why they appear so different from those we have traditionally viewed. What are the forces at work that move prices higher without relapse, a pattern unknown to any previous period in economic history? And why do the fine-tuned methods of contemporary economic theory seem unable to cope effectively with the phenomenon? A good place to start is the Phillips curve, one of the mainstays of current inflation theory.

The Phillips Curve

In 1958 Professor A.W. Phillips, a British economist, formulated an important hypothesis on inflation, one still at the forefront of a good part of economic planning. According to Phillips, there is a definite correlation between the rate of inflation and the level of unemployment. Higher levels of unemployment produce less pressure for wage increases, and dampened wages in turn keep down price increases* and result in lower levels of inflation. With higher levels of employment the reasoning is reversed.

The Phillips curve quickly became a chief support of Keynesian economics. If the government could hold the rate of wage gains equal to the level of productivity increases, profits would not be squeezed, and prices would not have to be increased—the business cycle would finally be tamed.

You can see why the Phillips curve appeals to government policy makers. For by using monetary and fiscal policy properly, the rate of inflation or unemployment could be precisely calibrated (or so it was thought) as surely as altering the rate of production on a complex assembly line by turning a number of knobs and dials. Figure 17 on page 224 shows a simple Phillips curve. If policy makers chose a low rate of unemployment *(OB),* it would come at the cost of a higher rate of inflation *(OA).* On the other hand, they may accept an Arthur Burns crusade against inflation and demand zero inflation, in which case unemployment would rise sharply *(OC).* Or if they chose even more drastic measures and opted for deflation, unemployment would expand *(OD)*—perhaps a not entirely inappropriate pairing of letters.

As I said, an appealing hypothesis, and one that leaves the policy makers with an exciting sense of control over inflation and unemployment. And it's a game that has been played avidly by one

---

*Productivity also increases with recessionary conditions, as business tightens up and eliminates marginal jobs, resulting in less need for rising prices, and perhaps even in falling ones.

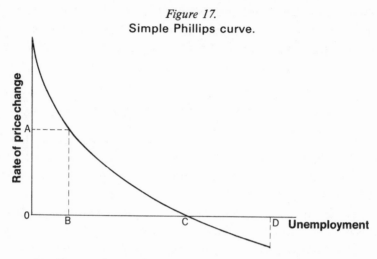

Figure 17.
Simple Phillips curve.

group of policy makers after another, beginning with the Kennedy administration.

But again, we come to one of the problems of economic theory —its ofttimes stubborn refusal to explain or reflect conditions in the real world. For in this form, the Phillips curve does not work and never has worked.

If we look at the five recessions in the postwar period,* we see that prices during these periods have actually increased. The average rate of inflation measured by the GNP deflator was 4.5 percent compared with 2.9 percent for periods of expansion and 4.4 percent in the latter stages of expansion,† when price increases are theoretically skyrocketing, supposedly because of increasing wage demands, shortages, and capacity bottlenecks.[1] Figure 18 shows other corroborating evidence. According to contemporary theory, low capacity utilization (indicating low material and labor demand) should be accompanied by a moderation in price rises at the very least. But the figure paints a very different picture. Capacity utilization falls to abnormally low levels, yet is accompanied by continuing price increases.

Adequate plant and labor exists to produce significantly more goods and services without pushing up prices in the traditional manner. This phenomenon, first noted in the recession of 1953–54 and

*1953–54, 1957–58, 1960–61, 1969–70, 1974–75.
†The four quarters prior to the cyclical peak.

Figure 18.
Inflation and capacity utilization.

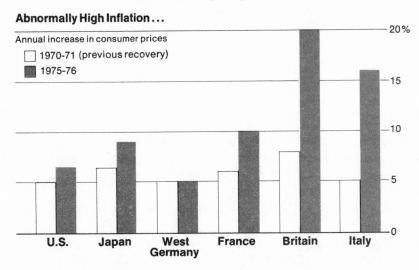

Abnormally High Inflation...

Annual increase in consumer prices
☐ 1970-71 (previous recovery)
■ 1975-76

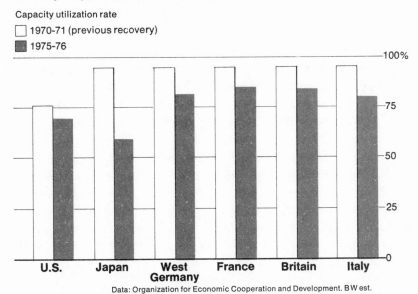

And Capacity Utilization is Abnormally Low

Capacity utilization rate
☐ 1970-71 (previous recovery)
■ 1975-76

Data: Organization for Economic Cooperation and Development. BW est.

again in 1969–70, was far more dramatic in 1974–75. In the words of Lord Nicholas Kaldor, then president of Britain's Royal Economic Society, the situation was "totally unpredecented."[2]

Thus, we have gone through the "stagflation" of a decade ago (a stagnating economy with inflation) and the "slumpflation" of the recent past.

Some New Causes

Let's turn to some of the new developments that may be responsible for the "totally unprecedented" situation. First, a look at a wild card —the rise in prices in the 1970s of commodities in general and of oil in particular.

The moderate rise in inflation in the 1950s and 1960s was much more wage- than commodity-induced (food and industrial commodity prices increased at barely 1 percent annually from 1953 to 1970). But this was also a time of major social and economic change. Rapid industrial expansion in Japan, Germany, France, and other Western and Third World countries, together with the desire for rising standards of living, progressively expanded the demand for commodities, while rising pay scales often increased the cost base. Both the demand and the supply curves were shifting sharply—the new equilibrium would be at much higher prices. As figure 19 indicates, beginning in 1971, industrial commodity prices took off. By 1976, the price of thirteen key raw industrial commodities had doubled, and by the end of 1978, they were up almost another 25 percent. All this before food and oil.

Back in 1973 it seemed the price of oil at least would be held in check, probably not increasing much faster than the rate of inflation. True, world demand was growing quickly, and the major exporters were taking control of some of their own production. But OPEC, the Organization of Petroleum Exporting Countries, a cartel formed over a decade earlier with the sole purpose of getting higher oil prices, had up to that time improved its bargaining leverage precious little against the industrial countries.

The Arab embargo after the Yom Kippur war changed the path of economic history. Although a political act, it produced staggering economic consequences beyond the expectations of even the most optimistic OPEC policy maker. The embargo was initiated at a

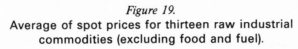

Figure 19.
Average of spot prices for thirteen raw industrial
commodities (excluding food and fuel).

Data: Bureau of Economic Analysis.

time when an altered political structure meant that Western military power could not be used to procure the most vital of industrial commodities. Frantic nations with limited reserves of oil were willing to pay almost any price to keep their economies from grinding to a halt. At the height of the embargo, oil was auctioned off at six to seven times the price of only weeks before. Oil prices rose fourfold between late 1973 and the end of 1974, and were boosted further in both 1975 and 1977. By the end of 1977 they had almost quintupled.

However, even this substantial price rise did not satisfy many producing nations. Under the guise that oil was a nonreplaceable natural resource, various partners demanded an acceleration of the increases—in spite of soft world demand for the twenty-four months prior to the fall of 1978. (OPEC's production was actually down 5.4 percent in October 1978 from a year earlier.) In December of 1978 prices were hiked again by 14.5 percent, to take place in stages through 1979.

Taking advantage of the shock waves and production shutdown during Khomeini's struggle for power in Iran, eight members, including such conservatives as Abu Dhabi, Qatar, and Kuwait, put large surcharges on their posted prices. Spot prices for some grades rose from $13.50 to $20.00 a barrel by February and to $40.00 by June.

On March 27 the official OPEC price was raised by the full 14½ percent, effective April 1. At the same time, the cartel also sanctioned sweeping surcharges by individual members to take advantage of temporary supply shortages. And by late June 1979, OPEC prices were pushed up again, this time to anywhere from $18.00 to $23.50 a barrel. Since January the price of U.S. imported oil had risen 50 percent, resulting in an additional drain of $30 billion annually on our balance of payments. OPEC ministers indicated that further increases might be forthcoming, perhaps in 1979.

The West had hoped for the moderating influence of Saudi Arabia. With large trade surpluses ($13 billion in 1977), the Saudis are generating funds far faster than they can be put to work, and in the past have been a major restraint on even more rapid price increases because they have the reserves to produce enough oil to flood international markets.* Recently, however, they have shown that they are becoming more and more reluctant to increase their own output significantly to check rising prices. To keep prices up, production is held near 8.5 million barrels a day (against estimated capacity of 11 to 12 billion). Plans to increase capacity to 16 million barrels a day by the mid-1980s have been quietly shelved. Thus, barring massive new discoveries outside of OPEC that will somehow quickly find their way to market and break the cartel, prices are likely to keep pace with rising inflation at the very least and will most likely outrun it, particularly given any new conditions that disrupt normal supply.

The surge in oil prices has played a significant role in the acceleration of the rate of inflation around the world. Because in the United States there are complicated pricing formulas to determine the price of "old" or "new" oil or gas (according to when it was discovered), the effects of the inflationary increases of oil and gas have not been fully felt here even today.†

All the same, as table 29 indicates, the price of fuel in the United States has been skyrocketing. In the period between 1972 and 1978, fuel costs increased at a 11.6 percent compound rate, while food prices rose at 9.4 percent—both well above the general rise in the

---

*Saudi Arabia has already demonstrated the capacity (in 1977) to negate the price increases of other OPEC members.

†President Carter has recently announced his intention to decontrol oil.

consumer price index. In the first quarter of 1979 the two increased at annualized rates of 13.6 percent and 18.4 percent respectively. By the end of April fuel costs were 20 percent higher than the level twelve months earlier. Some estimates have put oil-related inputs as high as 20 percent of agricultural costs, which may make oil one of the major contributing factors to rapidly rising food prices. Oil pricing, then, is a wild card that filters into our domestic inflation rate —one that we can do very little to control by conventional fiscal and monetary mechanisms.*

Aside from OPEC itself, there have been numerous attempts to set up "little OPECs" for a variety of products ranging from copper to coffee by nations facing large trade deficits created by higher oil costs. Some have been successful. The fledgling uranium cartel (the Uranium Institute), organized in 1974, is made up of the producers,

Table 29
RECENT DOMESTIC INCREASES IN FUEL AND FOOD PRICES

YEAR	FUEL	FUEL PERCENTAGE INCREASE OVER PRECEDING YEAR	FOOD	FOOD PERCENTAGE INCREASE OVER PRECEDING YEAR
1972	114.3	8.0%	123.5	14.5%
1973	123.5	8.0	141.4	14.3
1974	159.7	29.3	161.7	8.4
1975	176.6	10.6	175.4	7.2
1976	189.3	17.2	180.8	3.1
1977	207.3	9.5	192.2	6.0
1978	220.4	6.3	211.4	10.0
Average 1972–78	170.2	11.6%	169.5	9.4%

INDEX: 1967 = 100.
SOURCE: Bureau of Labor Statistics, National Energy Index. Components: gasoline, fuel oil and coal, motor oil, gas, and electricity.

*The Carter energy proposals introduced as this book went to press would appear, if anything, to intensify the inflationary problems relating to rising energy prices, if adapted. The cost of developing synfuels in large quantities is at present indeterminable, although some informed estimates believe it must be substantially more than the current price of oil—possibly two or three times as much. Further, the time required to develop the massive multibillion dollar projects on a commercial basis seems even more a matter of conjecture. Finally, the shift to energy conservation by American industry must necessarily result in higher costs because of both the installation of more expensive energy-saving equipment and the use of more costly products and materials. As an example, General Motors recently estimated it would cost some $80 billion industry-wide by 1985 alone—more than the combined profits of all U.S. corporations in 1975—to redesign "downsize" every car and truck model made.

and at times government agencies, in France, South Africa, Australia, Great Britain, and Canada. Together they produce some 60 percent of the non-communist world's uranium (40 percent comes from the United States). Since 1974 the price of uranium has quadrupled and is expected to continue to rise rapidly as increasing numbers of nuclear power plants come on stream worldwide.

The new policy toward oligopolistic pricing appears to be taking hold wherever the opportunity allows. In the spring of 1978 wild speculation took place in diamond prices, and DeBeers, by far the largest international producer, tacked on a 60 percent surcharge.[3] It was cut later in the year, but diamond prices at the retail level have continued to move sharply higher into 1979. Similar patterns can be found in a number of other commodities.

We have moved from a period of low commodities price increase into one where both industrial and agricultural prices have risen rapidly and oil has gone through the roof. The cost of basic commodities, then, is an important contributor to worldwide inflation.

The problem that we face with traditional fiscal and monetary cures is that they are most effective on inflationary pressures within our domestic control, and indeed for decades such internal forces were the prime influences upon rising prices. High interest rates and tighter money along with reduced government spending and higher taxes, for example, can certainly cut back production and demand, cooling off price pressures that stem from an overheated economy. However, when price increases are transmitted to our economy from abroad, through skyrocketing oil, diamond, bauxite, and other industrial and agricultural commodity costs, traditional fiscal and monetary policies become far less effective as a counter to inflation experienced domestically. Because the United States plays only a part in the supply and demand schedules of many of these major commodities, it naturally finds itself having a less than definitive role in setting prices, which are determined in the world market. In effect, many commodity prices are shielded from our domestic inflation-fighting techniques. A falling dollar simply serves to worsen inflationary pressures imported from abroad.

Perhaps OPEC, and even the diamond and uranium cartels, could be broken by actions taken solely by the United States. But the cost would be prohibitive. To succeed, actions of this sort would require massive cutbacks in our industrial output, employment, and demand, through the use of extreme fiscal and monetary measures. A depression would probably result, and a depression accompanied by 1930s-style unemployment is politically and socially unacceptable to practical policy makers today.

But it is by no means commodity pricing alone that is responsible for the new inflation. Next, let's see how it interacts with wage demands and business expectations.

Another Wild Card

After World War II a crucial new socioeconomic variable was introduced to the inflation picture in the United States—a variable that has become increasingly important ever since. In traditional microeconomic theory, labor is treated as a commodity, and its cost, like those of all other commodities, might rise or fall according to changing market conditions. In 1946 Congress passed the Full Employment Act, making labor something quite different. In the parlance of some economists labor is an administered market—or a market in which the flexibility of price movement is significantly restrained on the part of the buyer or the seller.[4]

In the labor market, as we all know, wages are expected to be renegotiated upward regardless of prosperity or recession—and to move up in real terms. This means faster than the current rate of inflation. Moreover, the rigidity of the labor price structure is strengthened by high unemployment benefits, welfare, and the increasing number of women who work. So unions can afford long walkouts to achieve their goals. If strike funds run out, a wife or another member of the family working or welfare payments could ease the strain.

By 1977 the U.S. labor market had been an administered one for thirty years. During that time average weekly earnings increased from $45.58 to $189.53, or at almost a 5 percent annual rate. During the same period the cost of living increased at only a 3.2 percent annual rate. By 1974 the median wage income had risen more than 70 percent in terms of real purchasing power. The improvement came both through increased productivity and at the cost of rising inflation. Thus, once again, we have a commodity whose cost is for the most part fixed and outside the reach of traditional economic remedies.

The Stress on Income Growth in Real Terms

How does the political principle of increasing real wage income, predominant in all Western and Third World nations, relate to the secular change in commodity pricing? Unless the principle changes drastically, it means that wages must now be increased not only to cover the rapidly rising cost of food, fuel, service, housing, and consumer goods, but usually at a rate high enough to provide increased "real buying power" as well. By and large, wages have more than kept pace with inflation in the United States. Wage rates increased 2.0 percent per year from 1962 to 1967, 4.6 percent annually from 1967 to 1972, and 7.7 percent per year from 1972 to 1977. As figure 20 shows, with the exception of the inflationary explosion in 1973–74, wage rates have outpaced one of the most rapid inflationary spirals in history, thus providing today's wage earner with slightly increased purchasing power in real terms.

It is important to note the growing use of cost-of-living adjust-

Figure 20.
Wage rates versus inflation.

Source: Department of Labor, Bureau of Labor Statistics.

ment contracts (COLAs). Such contracts provide adjustments to offset inflation, along with the basic wage increase, which, as noted, labor almost invariably receives even during a recession. Unions have been in the forefront of negotiating such cost-of-living adjustment contracts, but it is likely their use will become increasingly more widespread among nonunionized workers.

The Carter administration has attempted to attack the wage-price spiral by urging professionals and unions to decrease their wage demands voluntarily.* This has proven to be impossible since World War II, and with increasing inflationary expectations, it should become even more difficult in the future.

Nevertheless, the director of wage and price stability, Barry Bosworth, and President Carter's chief inflation counselor, Alfred E. Kahn, have tried very hard to effect Carter's plan. In Bosworth's words (quoted in May 1978, regarding the teamsters, rubber workers, electrical unions, and auto workers): "If next year's labor contracts again approach 30 percent [for the following three years, as the 1976 contracts did] we might as well forget about talking about decelerating inflation any time in the near future. I think it is absolutely crucial that large union wage settlements show significant deceleration."[5]

Mr. Bosworth's statements seem a fair illustration of the understanding of the workings of the real world often displayed among economists, particularly those who are in positions of responsibility. Only a month before he made the statement, the coal miners settled a strike that had lasted over three months at an average wage increase estimated at nearly 15 percent annually over a three-year period. And the increases continued. In mid-December 1978, the conference board panel on the labor outlook projected wage hikes of about 11 percent in 1979 after estimating the teamsters settlement would result in wage boosts of 12 percent or more annually.

No evidence exists in the postwar period that workers, or lawyers, or doctors, or anyone else will voluntarily curtail their earnings power. Put in its simplest form, each economic group says: "Why me?" It appears, then, that increases in wage rates, the major push behind previous inflation, will continue to accelerate and contribute to the very inflation they attempt to overcome. It might be called a rat race, or the American Dream, or perhaps both.

*President Carter, on May 4, 1978, admonished lawyers for increasing their fees "even faster than oil prices."

A Final Part of the Equation

The expectations of businessmen constitute a third factor behind current inflation. Unlike many of our friends in the economics profession, a significant number of corporate leaders do not nurture the belief that costs will drop off. Accordingly, they have projected recent rates of labor, material, and other cost increases into their selling prices in an attempt to maintain profit margins. Some economists have labeled this phenomenon "anticipatory price hedging."

Such conditions explain the combination of both excess capacity and rising prices we saw earlier. Thus, even under recessionary conditions, once inflationary expectations have been built into the system, as they obviously have through the decade, businessmen will often attempt to increase prices, knowing the cost squeeze they face if they don't.

In summary, then, I believe there are at least three major inputs to contemporary inflation, all interacting, none of which were nearly as persistent in the past:

1a. The ability of OPEC and of increasing numbers of junior international commodity cartels to hike prices sharply in line with or often ahead of the rate of world inflation.

1b. Strong upward pressure on other important agricultural and industrial commodity prices beginning in the early 1970s and in line with expanding world consumption after almost two decades of minimal commodity inflation.

Because prices are frequently set to a significant extent in world, not U.S., markets, domestic policies have far less influence and effect upon them.

2. The sociopolitical belief that real income of the workingman must increase (or at the very least hold constant), and the effective economic power to back it up—regardless of the implications to the general rate of inflation. Commodity inflation, then, serves to accelerate the rate of wage hikes.

3. The rising inflationary expectations of larger numbers of corporations, resulting in a policy of pushing up prices to maintain profit margins even during times of far less than optimal levels of production.

As noted, a rise in one of these forces triggers a rise in the other two. For example, an increase in the price of oil affects hundreds of manufactured products—from tires, synthetic fibers, and clothing, to plastics*—as well as gasoline and fuel oil. The manufacturer passes on not only the increased price of oil but also an additional percentage of the increase in order to maintain his profit margins on sales (see table 30, page 242). The same markup is applied to increases in the dozens or even hundreds of items that make up his cost schedule.

Finding higher prices for clothing, tires, gasoline, and numerous other petroleum-based products, along with price rises in other goods and services, the consumer naturally escalates his wage demands. These wage hikes in turn are likely to touch off another round of commodity boosts. The spiral moves merrily along.

To me, this combination of factors could sustain rates of inflation well above those we considered tolerable in the past. No offsetting domestic action short of depression-creating fiscal and monetary policies can really cope with the puissant forces.†

"Too much gold chasing too few goods," while applying perfectly to the Spanish and English economies of the sixteenth century, does not appear to fit what we are seeing now.

Investing Under Conditions of Accelerating Inflation

Assuming there will be no depression, what investment guidelines should one follow to withstand the inflation of our times?

Obviously, housing will make an excellent investment, as will revenue-producing real estate bought on reasonable terms.‡ But the investor must be knowledgeable in the area and avoid speculative binges. As I noted earlier, just such a binge took place in raw farmland, primarily in Illinois. One wag, figuring the price paid for the

---

*The 4 percent monthly increase (48 percent annualized) in plastics in April 1979 was partially attributed by industry spokesman to the higher cost of oil.

†Policy makers seem to be moving toward similar conclusions. Commerce Secretary Juanita Kreps was quoted in mid-January 1979 in part: "The inflation problem isn't one of shortages or bottlenecks . . . it is due primarily to a spiral of wages and prices."[6] And a *Wall Street Journal* article on February 23, 1979, quoted Federal Reserve Board Chairman G. William Miller as saying he didn't expect price increases to slow down markedly from 1978's 9 percent rate. Miller blamed higher food prices, higher oil, the impact of the dollar's recent depreciation and labor's desire to make up for the last year's inflation, and higher Social Security taxes as the reasons.[7] Even the redoubtable Barry Bosworth seems to be shifting his view. "The United States," he was quoted as saying in the April 1, 1979 *New York Times,* "is at the mercy of other countries determining our economic policy."[8]

‡See Appendix II for just how important housing can be under these circumstances.

land against the income received from the crops after taxes, calculated the going rate at fifty times earnings, fully as expensive as the
price exuberant investors paid for the top tier just before its dramatic
collapse of 1973–74.

The case for bonds is more troublesome. We have already seen
that at an 8 percent rate of inflation, an investor in a 50 percent tax
bracket buying a 9 percent ten-year bond finds himself losing 34
percent of his capital (after including interest) in real purchasing
power at maturity. If inflation went up to 10 percent, he would lose
45 percent of his purchasing power, again after including both interest and principal.

It is possible that bond rates could rise to 10 or 12 percent, but
even so, the increase is not large enough to offset the rate of inflation
after deducting taxes. And there are, of course, strong institutional
and political pressures in the United States against such high interest
rates—home building, for example, a major industry, would be
stifled. Thus, if our inflationary premise is correct, better a borrower
than a lender be.

A case can be made to place a portion of your savings in gold,
precious stones, and good artwork. But once again, you must be very
careful.

1. Do not pay ridiculous prices. In buying gold, for example, the
unwary investor can sometimes pay 50 percent or more above the
going market. There are also all sorts of other ways for the investor
to get bagged (chapter 10 only skimmed the surface). When people
began collecting coins in droves in 1973–74, some Westchester dealers came up with the idea of selling coins with some silver content
in sixty-pound bags on margin.[9] But naturally, there was a catch: the
buyers were not allowed to open the bags. Since the silver content
of different coinage varies enormously, it's not hard to figure who the
count favored in this case. Still, there were many takers.

And beware of the valuable "first edition" sets of gold and silver
commemorative coins put out by a number of sophisticated market-
ers at three or four times the value of the specie. Parke Bernet
absolutely refuses to handle the merchandise, which, in the words of
its first vice-president, Canton Kabe, is "limited edition trash."[10]

Curious about the value of one "limited edition set of 25 unique
sterling silver gambling coins, one from each of the world's most
glamorous casinos," Andrew Tobias, author of the very readable *The*

Only Investment Guide You'll Ever Need, phoned the Franklin Mint to check the silver content. As Tobias relates: "After a little hesitation—the collector service representative knew everything about the offer but this—I was told that the entire set of coins would weigh about 16 troy ounces, $86 worth at current prices. Yours for only $875 plus tax."[11]

Supposed inflation hedges have also taken investors in many other ingenious ways. Money manager John Train wrote in *Forbes* about how Scottish whisky brokers canvas gullible U.S. residents with direct mail advertisements that proclaim that 20 to 25 percent annual gains can be made by owning aging Scottish whisky.[12] The investor buys certificates presumably indicating the whisky is stored in bonded warehouses. In fact, the price of aged whisky has dropped very steeply over the last two decades. Moreover, the customers are sold the whisky at several times the going rate and often do not get the grades they've contracted for or sometimes even real title. Some inflation hedge!

· **2.** Do not enter near the top of a period of excessive speculation (see chapter 4 for the symptoms).

3. Have some expertise if you are going into out-of-the-ordinary ventures. This is absolutely crucial in any form of collecting, from antiques to art. In art, for example, be wary of high prices of many contemporary artists—some have been known to rig their markets by bogus transactions very much like stock rigging by unscrupulous dealers. Further, what is considered "outstanding" at the moment can be almost valueless a decade later. The gallery also tacks on a 40 percent markup to the price the artist receives, so you need a bit of appreciation to break even, even if you are proven right on the particular piece of artwork.

One final illustration indicating the hazards of collecting art: two fine figurines of the T'ang dynasty, a camel and a horse, were put up for auction at the same time. One was sold for $92,000 and the other fetched $7,000. The reason, according to the auctioneer, was, "The rich love horses, but they have no romance with camels."[13]

Collecting, then, seems a game best left up to the experts.

Since this book is primarily concerned with investing in common stocks, how might they perform under the inflationary conditions anticipated?

For the thirteen years prior to 1979, stocks were most assuredly not a hedge. After all, the market in mid-1979 was some 18 percent below where it had been in 1966, and in constant dollars was lower than it had been in 1951, or for that matter, at the end of 1929. The anything-but-sterling record of equities in recent years has been accompanied by a forceful argument accepted by a good part of informed opinion that corporate earnings are significantly overstated in periods of rapidly rising prices. The rate of return, so the reasoning goes, was near 12 percent through most of the postwar period. But when capital assets had to be replaced, they would cost much more in "real dollars," thanks to inflation; therefore, the rate of return in constant dollars must necessarily have been dropping.

Take the example of a company that has been earning 12 percent, or $120,000, on its assets of $1 million. Assume when the assets have to be replaced, their cost has doubled to $2 million because of inflation. The company's rate of return on the new assets, adjusting for rising replacement costs, drops to 6 percent—if it continues to earn the same $120,000. The question, then, is raised, quite legitimately, about the quality of a company's earnings. Does rapid inflation mean that replacement costs are understated, thereby resulting in an overstatement of a company's income?

Some new work makes the answer appear to be no. Burton Malkiel, the head of the economics department at Princeton, points out that the return on corporate assets was fairly stationary, even with rising inflation. In other words, the companies earned these returns on the replacement value, not on the original cost, of the assets, thus offsetting inflationary penalties.[14] Malkiel cited a study made by Martin Feldstein and Lawrence Summers of the Brookings Institution showing that there was no long-term decline in corporate profitability after correcting for inflation.[15]

Feldstein and Summers presented statistics to indicate that the major squeeze on corporate profits in recent years has been low rates of capacity utilization. In figure 21 (based on their numbers), Malkiel shows what the return on capital *at replacement value* would have been with full employment (defined as 5 percent unemployment) and

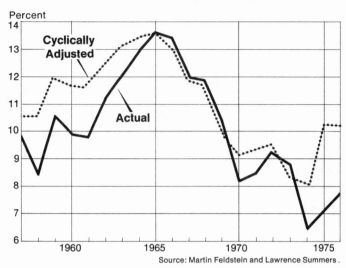

Figure 21.
Returns on total corporate capital.

Source: Martin Feldstein and Lawrence Summers.

an optimum utilization rate of capacity of 86 percent.* As the figure shows, the cyclically adjusted rate of return of just over 10 percent in 1976 (after the abnormal 1971–74 period of price controls and the quintupling of oil prices) was not far from the more normal level of profitability of the late 1950s.

Too, return on equity of the Dow-Jones Industrial Average has not varied substantially over the past thirty years. In the 1945–55 period, it was 12.8 percent; in the 1955–65 period, 10.1 percent; and in the 1965–75 period, 10.9 percent. Thus, even using these calculations, we see that profitability held up over a thirty-year period, although inflation supposedly ate into plant and equipment at a rate of better than 3 percent annually (or, for the twenty years between 1945 and 1965, 2.97).

Further, as Warren Buffett recently noted in *Forbes,* this argument would not be applicable to a large segment of the market— banks, insurance and finance companies, publishing houses, service companies, and the like—where buildings, plant, and equipment are a relatively small percentage of earning assets.[16] It would appear,

*Return on capital was calculated by adding corporate profits (excluding inventory gains) along with interest payments, and dividing the sum by the replacement value of the assets.

then, if earnings of such companies were increasing at a rate faster than inflation, and in many cases they are (Aetna's, for example, grew at a cyclical but nevertheless 20 percent annual rate over the last decade), these stocks would continue to provide good value.

A recent paper by Franco Modigliani, a past president of the American Economic Association, also produced evidence against the widely accepted belief that corporate profits decline sharply during periods of high inflation. Modigliani, along with Richard Cohn, concluded that the poor performance of equity markets in recent years could be largely attributed to the inability of both institutional investors and brokerage houses to understand the effect of inflation on corporate profits.[17]

According to Modigliani and Cohn, investors repeat two mistakes in valuing common stocks during inflationary periods. First, they place too low a valuation on stock earnings relative to the interest rates on high-grade bonds. There is a relationship between the rate of return earned on common stocks and that on long-term bonds. Since stocks are riskier, they traditionally return somewhat more. This return on common stocks, called the earnings yield, is simply the earnings per share divided by the market price. Thus, if a stock earns $1 and the market price is $10, it would have an earnings yield of 10 percent.*

An error investors make during inflationary times is to calculate bond interest at nominal rates (the rate presently in effect, i.e., about 9 percent today) rather than at the real rate (the present rate minus the current rate of inflation). If the nominal rate is 9 percent and inflation is running at 7 percent, the real rate of interest is 2 percent. However, because investors ignore the real rate of interest and focus solely on the nominal rate, they consistently demand returns from stocks that are far too high.

As an example, take the Dow-Jones Industrial Average today. The average is presently trading at a P/E ratio of about 7, or provides an "earnings yield" of 14.2 percent. With inflation running at 9 percent or more, the "real interest rate" for bonds is zero at best. We are, then, comparing a return of 14.2 percent on the Dow with a "real interest rate" on bonds of zero. Thus, while stocks may have traditionally provided returns 3, 4, or 5 percentage points higher in terms

---

*To get the earnings yield from a P/E ratio, simply apply the numerator 1 over the P/E ratio. If the P/E ratio is 8, the earnings yield is ⅛, or 12.5 percent.

of earnings yield than those of real interest rates, today, because of this investor misunderstanding, the spread between earnings yield and "real interest rates" is substantially higher (about triple the upper end of the previous range). By this measurement, then, equities appear dirt cheap!

The second Modigliani-Cohn argument is that although investment professionals continually adjust earnings downward to take account of "swollen inventory profits" and "inadequate depreciation of buildings, plant, and equipment," at the same time they ignore the fact that a good part of corporate assets are provided from borrowings, which in inflationary times will be repaid in much cheaper dollars. The assets purchased with borrowed funds will appreciate relative to the shrinking dollars required to repay the debt. The burden of the "real debt" relative to the cost of the assets, then, continually diminishes. The greater the rate of inflation, the more "real debt" is reduced. The two sets of accounting adjustments—the overstating of inventory profits along with the understatement of depreciation reserves, and the appreciation of assets purchased with borrowed dollars—will about offset one another. However, investors concentrate only on the first adjustment, which reduces profitability, and ignore the second, which improves it. The result is to consistently undervalue the earnings of stocks.

Modigliani and Cohn conclude: "Rationally valued, the level of the S&P 500 at the end of 1977 should have been 200. Its actual value at the time was 100. Because of inflation-induced errors, investors have systematically undervalued the stock market by 50 percent."

Inflation and Corporate Earnings and Dividends

If the above arguments are valid, and they appear well supported, we should consider one final important question: how able are corporations to pass on costs of wages, materials, and services in inflationary times? If corporations can maintain their profit margins on sales (the rate of sales before taxes in this case) and prices increase in line with inflation rates, as they have to date, then earnings should at the very least keep pace with higher inflation rates. Table 30, using the S&P 400 Industrials (where plant and equipment are weighted relatively heavier than in the S&P 500), shows how profit margins have fared.

In the 1967–77 period they were 14.91 percent of sales, compared with 15.4 percent for the 1957–67 span and 14.9 percent for the previous ten years. Thus, profit margins in the last decade held up exceptionally well through accelerating inflation, two credit crunches, the wage-price freeze, and two sharp recessions. And, as the table shows, with the increasing rate of price rise, annual earnings growth has moved up above the previous two decades.

Table 30
PROFIT MARGINS, EARNINGS GROWTH, AND RETURN ON EQUITY OF THE S&P 400 INDUSTRIALS, 1947–77

	AVERAGE ANNUAL PROFIT MARGIN	AVERAGE ANNUAL EARNINGS PER-SHARE GROWTH	AVERAGE ANNUAL RETURN ON BOOK VALUE
1947–57	14.93	6.25	13.70
1957–67	15.40	4.72	11.10
1967–77	14.91	7.40	12.54
1977–78	n.a.	14.0	14.7

But indeed, the growth of the S&P 400 and 500 earnings has been increasing somewhat faster than the rate of inflation in the last decade, as table 31 indicates. Even more impressive is that in the last six years of accelerating inflation ending in 1978, corporate earnings far outdistanced the rise in prices. Earnings of the S&P 400 and 500 were up 11.5 percent annually through this period, versus 7.7 percent for inflation. Corporate earnings, then, rather than being crippled, have fared remarkably well through some particularly heavy sailing. If the previous arguments stand, common stocks have provided not just a relative but an absolute hedge in terms of real purchasing power, despite what many market doomsayers have said.

As important to the investor is that dividends of the S&P 500 in the 1972–78 period have been increasing faster than the rise in prices. (For the ten-year period, however, dividends lagged inflation somewhat.) And for the two years ending in 1978, dividends of the S&P 500 were up 13.4 percent annually, some 60 percent more than the rate of price increase. Hardly an argument that common stock earnings and dividends are crippled under conditions of rapidly rising prices! Common stocks, then, by the most crucial yardsticks of worth—earnings and dividends—have proved to be a very good inflation hedge indeed. By comparison, the bondholder, as we have seen, would have had his capital severely reduced.

Table 31

S&P ANNUAL EARNINGS AND DIVIDEND GROWTH RELATIVE TO INFLATION

| | AVERAGE ANNUAL EARNINGS AND DIVIDEND GROWTH | | | |
| | EARNINGS | | DIVIDENDS | |
	S&P 400	S&P 500	S&P 400	S&P 500
1968–78	7.6%	8.0%	5.4%	5.1%
1972–78	11.5	11.5	8.8	8.2

Rise in Consumer Price Index
1968–78	6.8%
1972–78	7.7

NOTE: The S&P 500, apart from the 400 Industrials, includes twenty transportation, forty utilities, and forty financial stocks.

Just how much the return between stocks and bonds differs, even using some dour premises on inflation, is shown in table 32 (page 244). The table gives the market doomsayers their due and assumes corporate earnings are mauled by inflation. Price/earnings ratios are down and surely ought to be. But if our more pessimistic friends do not see the end of our economic system—at least for another decade or so—the results for the interim are interesting.

Five- and ten-year total returns are presented for both stocks and bonds. In the three cases $1,000 is invested, in the first in equities and in the next two in taxable and nontaxable bonds. In each case, the investor is assumed to be in a 40 percent tax bracket.

Stocks, meanwhile, are assumed to remain at the currently depressed P/E ratio of about 8 (the equivalent of an earnings yield of 12.5 percent). We also assume that 40 percent of earnings will be paid out in dividends (about the dividend payout ratio of both the S&P 400 and the 500 over a fairly long period of time), and that dividends, after deducting income taxes, will be reinvested by investors each year. Finally, corporate price hikes are assumed to offset rising costs, as they have over the years. In the case of bonds, the interest is also reinvested after taxes.

Turning first to stocks, the top row of the table shows the total returns earned (price appreciation and reinvested dividends) if earnings increase at a 7 percent rate—below the average annual gain of both the S&P 400 and the 500 in the most recent ten-year period. Capital invested in stocks increases 74 percent in five years and 139 percent in ten years using this earnings growth rate, as compared

Table 32

*AFTERTAX RETURNS, INVESTING IN COMMON STOCKS VERSUS
BONDS*

ANNUAL EARNINGS GROWTH RATE	5-YEAR TOTAL STOCK RETURN	10-YEAR TOTAL STOCK RETURN
7%	73.9%	139.2%
8	82.1	167.8
9	90.8	193.5
10	100.0	221.0
11	108.9	252.0

	5-YEAR TOTAL BOND RETURN	10-YEAR TOTAL BOND RETURN
6½% tax-exempt bond	40.0%	93.8%
9% taxable bond	30.7	79.4

Assumptions: 1. 40 percent dividend payout ratio, and shareholders rein-
vest dividends each year after taxes.
2. Investor is in a 40 percent tax bracket in both the stock and
the bond cases.
3. P/E ratios remain at current depressed level of 8.
4. All bond interest is reinvested.

to 31 percent and 79 percent respectively for taxable bonds.

Using a 9 percent earnings growth rate, stocks provide more than double the return over tax-exempt bonds for both the five- and the ten-year periods. Finally, how would the comparisons fare if earnings increased at 11 percent annually, about the growth rate of both S&P averages for the 1970–78 period? For both five and ten years, equity returns would be more than triple those of taxable bonds and over two and one half times those of tax-exempts.

The table shows us, then, no matter which assumptions on earnings growth rates are used, *equities provide better returns than bonds in every case.*

Remember that the table assumes a very pessimistic outlook for stocks, based on the current consensus. But it is possible that investor consensus may be wrong—something we've seen happen on occasion throughout the work. Suppose, in fact, institutional investors begin to accept arguments such as those we've just viewed, and evaluate stocks upwards. If earnings yields go back to their more traditional levels, stock prices could more than double from current levels. If P/E ratios increase 50 percent to 12, stocks would still provide more than twice the earnings return relative to "real interest rates" on bonds than they have in the past. Thus whatever assumptions are used, including the "worst case" ones of table 32, the argument in favor of equities today is one not easy to dismiss.

Other valuation yardsticks also indicate that the market appears very cheap. The Dow-Jones Industrial Average is currently trading below book value (the value of all assets less all liabilities). Even in 1932, the year the market reached an all-time low in the Great Depression, the Dow did not trade below book value for more than a few months. In other words, the Dow presents better value by this widely followed measurement than it has for any prolonged period in the past.

The present situation has resulted in a rash of takeovers by foreign and domestic companies alike. (It is much cheaper to buy a company with a going business than to invest anew.) While the premiums vary, some analysts have estimated they average about 50 percent above book value.*

Although the market multiple is near the bottom of its postwar range, there are still exceptional opportunities available for the low P/E investor. Today, large companies such as Ford, Aetna, General Tire and Rubber, and Travelers are trading at only three or four times earnings (about half of the market multiple) and yield 5 or 6 percent or more. When a company trades at three times earnings, you are buying it in effect at a 33 percent aftertax return and about a 66 percent pretax return. Not many investments—other than the odd lucky hit at the gaming tables—even remotely provide rewards like these.

To me, the stock market, then, appears cheap by nearly every historical standard. Since the 1930s, with the exception of the bottom of the 1974 market, stocks have never been as totally washed out as they are today. Though higher rates of inflation are a phenomenon I am convinced investors will have to live with from here on in, they are not devastating.† Companies have proven they can not only survive but prosper in this environment. The psychology of markets being what it is, it is probable that when this awareness becomes widespread, it will be anything but gradual.

*Another argument that the best-case assumptions are closer to the facts than those of the worst case.

†In the 1975–78 period of higher inflation, GNP growth averaged 4.8 percent in constant terms.

Our economic system does face new, increasingly difficult problems: energy shortages and the oil cartel, excessive (and in the short term, sometimes prohibitive) ecological costs, government policies that tax business profits and capital gains too heavily,* and the virulent antibusiness climate in the country.

I remain an optimist for the reasons I hope I have made clear to you. Industrial economies in the recent past have survived and even increased their productivity under far more severe conditions of economic disequilibrium than those we are now experiencing. We need only go back to 1941 to recall how the entire Russian industrial base was shifted east beyond the Urals in a matter of six weeks in order to avoid being captured by the swiftly moving Nazi Panzers; or how German industrial production was higher in 1944 than in 1941, in spite of the millions of tons of bombs dropped with precision on the most crucial segments of their industry—railroads, ball-bearing plants, and oil refineries.

As to destroying the profit system itself by government regulation, if ownership of stock is made valueless, it is not probable that other major classes of property will be unaffected. Real estate, bonds, and numerous other assets can maintain their value only within a flourishing economic system. Many investors lose sight of the fact that values are usually interrelated. If corporations falter, it is hardly likely that many other assets will be left untouched.

When I was a student reading the newspapers of the 1930s, 1940s, and 1950s, I was amazed by the value so abundant in the stock markets of those days and felt a little cheated because I thought the great days of investment coups all lay in the past.

Today, nothing seems further from the truth. Institutional concentration, conformity pressures on professionals, and overreactions to the current economic problems seem to me to present the investor with some of the greatest stock market opportunities in decades.

*Although new pending legislation may change this.

APPENDICES

The Performance of the Favorite Stocks of Groups of Professional Investors

Surveys: Industrial Favorites

NAME OF SURVEY	NUMBER CONDUCTED	YEARS(S)	NUMBER OF PARTICIPANTS	FAVORITE STOCK OR INDUSTRY	PERFORMANCE IN NEXT 12 MONTHS	S&P 500 PERFORMANCE IN NEXT 12 MONTHS
Trusts and Estates[a]	21	1953–56	75–175			
California Business	5	1967	100–150	Litton Industries	− 15.3	+ 20.0
		1968	100+	Occidental Petrol.	+ 51.0	+ 7.7
		1969	100+	Collins Food	− 50.0	− 11.5
		1970	100+	GRT	− 78.6	0.0
		1971	100+	Diagnostic Data	+103.8	+ 10.8
Callan Associates[b]	2					
Business Week[c]	2	9/15/73	1	(ten favorite stocks)	− 48.6	− 37.6
Institutional Investor	3	Feb. 1972	2000+	National Student Marketing	− 26.0	− 36.7
		Mar. 1972	1,500+	Airlines	− 93.0	+ 12.8
		Mar. 1972	1,500+	Pan American	− 50.00	+ 4.0
				and IBM	− 10.0	+ 4.0

NAME OF SURVEY	NUMBER CONDUCTED	YEARS(S)	NUMBER OF PARTICIPANTS	FAVORITE STOCK OR INDUSTRY	PERFORMANCE IN NEXT 12 MONTHS	S&P 500 PERFORMANCE IN NEXT 12 MONTHS
Edson Gould Market Forecastᵈ	1		75	Market Direction	− 35.0	−27.0
Total number of surveys conducted	34					
Percentage under-performing market	71					

ªSee table 6, page 99.
ᵇSee table 8, page 100.
ᶜSurvey of the ten favorite stocks for capital appreciation of two of the most prominent institutional brokerage research houses.
ᵈAs reported in the *Wall Street Letter*, December 17, 1973. The survey consisted of seventy-five portfolio managers representing "well over 100 billion dollars." The manager predicted the market as represented by the Dow-Jones Industrial Average, then at 840, would rise to between 900 and 1,000 by the end of the next year. In fact, it declined to 616.

Favorites, Five Stocks or More

NAME OF SURVEY	NUMBER CONDUCTED	YEAR(S)	NUMBER OF PARTICIPANTS	SIZE OF PORTFOLIO	PERFORMANCE IN NEXT 12 MONTHS	S&P 500 PERFORMANCE IN NEXT 12 MONTHS
Cowles	1	1927–32	16a	469		
Cowles	1	1928–31	20b	—		
Cowles	1	Jan. 1928–June 1932	29c	113.7		
Institutional Investor	4	Jan. 1972	150	10	+ 1.3	+15.6
		1972	150	50	− 4.7	+15.6
		Jan. 1973	160	10	−40.4	−17.4
		1973	160	27	−25.6	−17.4
California Business	2	Jan. 1971	134	10	− 9.7	+12.4
		Aug. 1976	125	25	− 1.6	− 6.3
Edson Gould *Seminar*	1	1974	75	8	−35.0	−28.1
Callan Associates	2	12/31/74	36	6d		
Diefenbach		11/17/66–				
Buy & Sell	1	5/23/69	30e	42		
Mueller	4	Jan. 1974	275	9	−31.7	−28.1
		Jan. 1975	304f	7	+58.0	+29.4
		Jan. 1976	312g	13	− 4.6	+17.7
		Jan. 1977	264h	10	−10.2	− 2.9

NAME OF SURVEY	NUMBER CONDUCTED	YEAR(S)	NUMBER OF PARTICIPANTS	SIZE OF PORTFOLIO	PERFORMANCE IN NEXT 12 MONTHS	S&P 500 PERFORMANCE IN NEXT 12 MONTHS
Total number of surveys conducted	17					

NOTE: 88.3 percent underperformed market. All participants are from different investment firms.

aCowles measured the results of sixteen leading financial services firms. Overall, 7,500 recommendations were made; on average, they lagged the market by 1.43 percent annually.

bThe actual purchases and sales of twenty leading fire insurance companies were compared with the market in the 1928–31 time period.

cAll recommendations of twenty-four leading financial services publications, including four financial weeklies, one bank letter, and one investment advisory letter. On average they lagged the market by 4.0 percent annually.

dSee table 8, page 100.

eDiefenbach survey of twenty-four brokerage firms that in total made 1,209 buy recommendations between November 17, 1966, and May 23, 1969. The number per firm varied from 8 to 288, and averaged 50. He also measured the results of forty-six sell decisions by eight firms. The results were compared against the S&P 425. Of all recommendations, 53.2 percent subsequently underperformed this average.

fRepresenting assets of $86 billion.

gRepresenting assets of $102.9 billion.

hRepresenting assets of $98 billion.

Steps in Your Financial Planning

If you are something less than a seasoned investor, you may want to look at a number of important steps that should be considered in financial planning, along with some of the more common investment vehicles other than equities available.

The Starting Point: Liquid Assets and Insurance

Savings Banks

Everyone needs some liquid reserves, either for emergencies or to take advantage of unforeseen opportunities. The amount might vary anywhere from a few month's living expenses to a full year's, depending on both your personal temperament and how secure you believe your regular income is. Three months of living expenses kept in a savings account might allow some of you to sleep comfortably, while it may give others nightmares.

The investor can choose a number of places to place liquid reserves. He might put the funds into a savings bank, converting them to a checking account as funds are required. The current yield on savings accounts is 5.47 percent annually. It's foolish to keep money in a non-interest-bearing checking account without good reason.*

Money market funds (discussed on pages 205–206) are another alternative for these funds. Yields are normally higher, but they will change more frequently than savings bank rates.

Savings Certificates

You can invest a portion of your liquid assets in savings certificates (from one to eight years). The rates are higher than in the day-to-day savings deposit and withdrawal accounts.† (At the present time, a yield ranges from 6.81 percent for a one-year certificate up to 8.17 percent for a six- or seven-year note, and 8.45 for an eight-year note.)

Naturally, there is a catch. If you cash these certificates in before they mature, as their commercials advertise, the banks penalize you some of the interest. (The ads make it sound as though they are woeful about being forced to do this by law, although undoubtedly it was their lobbying skill that pushed the legislation through in the first place.) Such penalties may not be inconsequential. Should you withdraw early, you will receive the same amount of interest as you would have on the regular day-to-day rate and forfeit three months of interest. Thus, if you purchased a $5,000 seven-year note and cashed it several months before it was due, you would lose over $1,000 in interest. Before putting money in longer savings certificates, you should look at the additional choices available in bonds, unless the amounts are small or you are absolutely sure you will not cash them prematurely.

Treasury Notes

Another alternative to savings bank certificates for cash reserves likely to be held for a year or two is U.S. government notes. The minimum denomination is $1,000. Treasury notes react much more quickly to changes in monetary policy than do savings bank certificates. So when interest rates are moving up, you may be able to enhance your yield by investing in them. However, once

*Recently, some commercial banks have instituted free check writing on savings accounts, but minimum balances are normally high—$2,500 to $3,000—or monthly fees are instituted.

†However, the minimum investment varies between $500 and $1,000.

again, if the amounts involved are small, it may not be worth the effort.

Accident and Health Insurance

For years, many pundits have considered the American Medical Association one of the best-run unions in the country. There were about the same number of doctors in the country per capita in 1970 as in 1880.* Naturally, the union says this ratio has improved the quality of the graduates. An obviously unanticipated result of such quality control is a major shortage of doctors and skyrocketing medical costs, which have been rising at about twice the rate of inflation for the past decade. Other medical expenses have risen almost as sharply.

It seems absolutely essential, then, to have adequate medical coverage. We've all heard stories of how unexpected serious illnesses have wiped out the savings of fairly affluent families. If you are employed by a corporation, you can probably get good low-cost group insurance, which you should take advantage of. If you are self-employed, it is well worth the cost to have Blue Cross, Blue Shield, and Major Medical.

A few years back, I ran into the tower of a chair lift on a ski slope, had to have a cartilage operation, and was hospitalized for six days. The hospital bill, tests, and drugs alone came to $2,800, all of which Blue Cross, Blue Shield paid. The surgeon and anesthesiologist's fees were another $1,200, half of which was paid by my Major Medical. This minor operation, then, cost $4,000, of which I paid only $600, thanks to my insurance.

Without medical coverage, there is simply no way of establishing what an adequate cash reserve is for you. A serious operation and recuperation might dock you two or three years' income or more. Such coverage is thus an essential aspect of proper investment planning.

Life Insurance

There are two kinds of insurance you can buy: whole (or ordinary) life, and term. But, as an investor, there is only one kind to consider—term.

*163 per 100,000 in 1880; 166 per 100,000 in 1970.

Term provides you with no frills. It is bare-bones life coverage that can be bought on a renewable basis for twenty years or more. A decreasing renewable policy (decreasing coverage in later years when your family has matured and your needs probably diminish) will allow you to renew over a number of fixed periods, usually every five years, normally to age sixty-five, when it terminates.* Renewal can be made without having to take a new physical, which is important if your health begins to deteriorate.

The cheapest term insurance offered is usually through a group plan where you are employed. In some states, insurance almost as cheap can also be purchased through savings banks. However, SBLI (Savings Bank Life Insurance) does have maximums on the amounts an individual can purchase.†

Whole, or ordinary, life, rather than providing just life insurance, has a myriad of other benefits, such as policyholder dividends, borrowing features, and cash payments upon maturity. But this is no free lunch. You pay far more for these perks than you would if you bought each feature on an item-by-item basis.

Whole life and endowment is by far the most profitable line of business for the insurance company and the salesman. In fact, one of the standard operating ratios in measuring an insurance company's success is the amount of premium per thousand dollars of insurance the company gets. The premium on term, as table 33 shows, is often a very small fraction of what it is on whole life. For example, a male at age forty-five pays almost five times as much for the highest-priced whole-life policy as he would for SBLI insurance.

Whole life is actually so lucrative to the companies that about half of the first year's premium and a smaller but not inconsequential portion of the premiums for the next several years go directly into the salesman's pockets. By contrast, term yields very little in commissions. These policies are probably buried deep in the salesman's briefcase, not to be brought out until he knows there is no hope of selling anything else.

The whole-life policyholder is affected by more than just the initial commission. Insurance companies usually have very high administrative charges on the money they invest for you, far higher than for stock or bond mutual funds. So you are better advised to

*Each renewal is at a somewhat higher price.
†At present, it can be bought only in New York, Connecticut, California, and Massachusetts, and the maximum amount is around $30,000.

Table 33
LIFE INSURANCE SHOPPING: COMPARATIVE RATES

	COST PER $10,000	
TERM: FIVE-YEAR RENEWABLE	MALE, AGE 35	AGE 45
Best special policy	48.8	114.0
Best generally available policy	63.6	131.6
Median policy	73.2	111.6
Worst policy	87.2	181.6
Savings bank life insurance (SBLI)	34.62	62.96
WHOLE LIFE: NON-PARTICIPATORY POLICIES		
Best special policy	150.0	231.60
Best generally available policy	150.0	231.60
Median policy	166.0	261.80
Worst policy	194.0	294.42

NOTE: All policies are $25,000, with the exception of SBLI, which is for $30,000. Cost figures make assumptions for dividends received.

SOURCES: Consumers Union Report on Life Insurance, 1977 (which surveyed 125 companies), and New York SBLI rates.

do your investing yourself. The difference saved in a ten- or twenty-year period will prove substantial.

As I've indicated, there are hundreds of ordinary- and whole-life plans available, each with its own unique characteristics and salient marketing features. The important point to remember is that the basics are the same.

The table gave you some idea of just how much life insurance premiums per thousand dollars of coverage can vary. It will pay you to shop around if you need additional coverage, and *specify term, demanding no frills.* For guidance, you might look at the Consumers Union survey on life insurance, which is updated periodically and lists numbers of companies providing low-cost term coverage.*

Investing in Your Own Home

In chapter 12, I indicated why I believe inflation should persist at fairly high rates—probably at 6 or 7 percent a year, perhaps more —rather than at the 2½ percent of previous decades. Costs of con-

*The cost is currently $2.95 through Consumers Union, Orangeburg, New York 10962.

struction and land should rise somewhat faster. If I am right, we should see continued rapid increases in the value of homes—the average new house rose at an 11.3 percent rate for the five years ending in 1977.

Given these circumstances, a house should be one of the initial considerations in your investment portfolio: first, because it is a leveraged hedge against inflation (since you are putting down only 25 to 35 percent of the total, sometimes less, but will get the appreciation on the entire property value); and second, because it is an effective and safe method of sheltering your income from taxes. The higher your tax bracket, the more beneficial the shelter proves.

Take the following example: suppose a couple finds a $100,000 house that they like very much. However, they think it is a cut above what they can currently afford, something they might put off buying for four or five years. Given our assumptions about inflation, the couple should buy all the house today that they can comfortably handle and then some, even if it means liquidating a portion of their investment portfolio (above liquid reserves). Table 34 projects a 7 percent rate of inflation and makes some assumptions on the cost of maintaining the house. It also assumes that the couple is currently spending $7,500 to $8,000 a year (which is $625 to $665 a month) renting a home.

The $13,500 in interest and expenses is considerably above the $7,500 to $8,000 the couple is currently paying in rent, to be sure. But rent is not tax-deductible, and mortgage interest and taxes are.

Table 34
PURCHASE ASSUMPTIONS: $100,000 HOUSE

1. A $30,000 down payment on a $100,000 house, which the couple meets by reducing their securities portfolio.
2. A thirty-year mortgage at 10 percent.
3. A rate of inflation in housing of 7 percent.
4. An effective tax rate of 45 percent for the homeowners.
5. Home costs:

	Taxes	$ 2,000
	Insurance	700
	Maintenance	2,300
	Sundry	1,500
	Mortgage interest	7,000[a]
	Total annual costs	$13,500

[a]Excluding principal repayment.

The couple will thus deduct the following from their taxes:

Real estate tax	$2,000
Mortgage interest	$7,000
Reduction in investment income	$2,400*

At a 45 percent tax bracket, the couple will save $5,130 in taxes, which results in total costs declining from $13,500 to $8,370.

Thus, if the couple has enough surplus income to undertake the somewhat higher ownership costs (including the small initial repayment of principal and the reduction of $1,500 or so in aftertax investment income), it would be to their advantage to do so.

Now, using our assumptions, let's look ahead ten years and see why. With a 7 percent rate of inflation in housing (well below that of the last five years), the $100,000 house is now worth $196,214. Obviously, the upkeep costs have risen (the nondeductible items are now $735 a month instead of $375). But rent will probably rise as fast. Thus, if they had been paying $750 or $800 a month, they will now be paying almost double this amount.

The combination of inflation and tax deductions make it an overwhelming advantage to own rather than rent in most cases.† Buying under the conditions outlined would have resulted in a $30,000 equity increasing to $126,714, or over fourfold. This works out to 15 percent annually—all in a decade! With the tax advantages stacked in favor of the buyer and against the renter, this is a "must" investment wherever circumstances make it possible. Further, the annual cash outlay at the end of the period will be less for the owner than the renter.

Nowhere else does it appear that the investor can make such a high and secure return while enjoying his investment at the same time. The case, then, for home ownership is a compelling one for today's investor.

---

*This assumes that the $30,000 down payment was taken out of their portfolio and had been yielding 8 percent.

†I am excluding the height of speculative real estate booms, such as the one which seems to be peaking in southern California today, which I described in chapter 1. But the same telltale pennants of speculative manias (seen in chapter 4)—crowd obsession, continuous talk of rising prices, major play by the media—are all apparent, and buying during such periods should be postponed.

Stockholders are the owners of the corporation and participate in its fortunes, either good or bad. The price of the stock and the company's dividends will vary with the corporation's success or failure. By contrast, in buying a bond, you are merely one of the company's creditors. You do not share in its rewards (and theoretically at least, in its risks). A bond, whether corporate, federal, state, or municipal, is simply an obligation to repay a loan at a specific time, promising a contractual rate of interest. It is, then, a far safer investment from the viewpoint of financial risk than a common stock. (Bondholders and other creditors must be paid in full before the common gets anything.) Nevertheless, bonds, too, have distinct risks.

An investor who is fairly certain he will not have to cash his savings certificates might ask why he should bother at all with government bonds, which yield in the vicinity of 8½ to 9 percent, when he can get over 8 percent in the certificates (federally insured up to $40,000 individually and $80,000 for a joint account).

For one thing, the maximum savings certificate length is normally eight years. After this time, if interest rates go down, your 8 percent may become 6 percent or even 5 percent—although the latter seems pretty unlikely. The bond, on the other hand, can have a very long maturity (time outstanding before it is due)—twenty and twenty-five years or more are quite common. Thus, you may be assured of your income for a much longer period (but see "Call Features" on page 266).

Then, too, there are many excellent corporate bonds available that provide not only very long life spans but also higher rates of interest than you can get on savings certificates (9¼ percent or more, versus 8.45 percent on an eight-year time deposit). Finally, some types of bonds provide distinct tax advantages to high-income investors that are not available in savings banks.

Tax-Exempt Bonds

If you buy a government or corporate bond, full tax rates apply. But bonds issued by state and municipal governments (and various state and local authorities, such as port authorities, toll roads, and so forth) are exempt from federal taxes. Too, if you buy a state or municipal bond where you reside, you are exempt from state and municipal taxes. New York City residents buying Big Mac bonds would be exempt from all taxes—federal, state, and city. However, if they bought Dallas bonds, they would only be exempt from federal taxes.

Naturally, tax-exempt bonds trade at lower yields than other bonds (a twenty-year AA-rated state bond would yield 6½ percent against about 9.40 percent for a corporate bond with the same credit rating and maturity). So they are not useful to everybody, as table 35 indicates.

The person in the 30 percent tax bracket is still better off in corporate bonds at current rates. However, at the 40 percent level and above, he progressively loses ground by not buying tax-exempts.* If, for example, the bond buyer decided to invest $50,000 in long-term bonds and was in the 50 percent tax bracket, he would save $900 a year through the purchase of tax-exempts. Thus, under conditions of accelerating inflation and higher interest rates, tax-exempts are increasingly valuable investment vehicles for high-tax-bracket investors who desire fixed-income securities.

The spread between tax-exempts and fully taxable bonds will change periodically according to conditions of supply and demand and risk assessment in the corporate and municipal sectors. The potential for default, for example, of New York City bonds in late 1976 drove many tax-exempts down fairly sharply for a time.

State and local guaranteed bonds usually provide somewhat better yields although less marketability than the issues of the state

Table 35
CORPORATE VERSUS TAX-EXEMPT BONDS

TAX BRACKET	6.5 TAX-EXEMPT BOND[a]	9.4 AA CORPORATE	AFTERTAX YIELD ON CORPORATE
30 percent	6.5	9.4	6.58
40 percent	6.5	9.4	5.64
50 percent	6.5	9.4	4.70
60 percent	6.5	9.4	3.80

NOTE: All bonds have AA rating and mature in twenty-five years.
[a] Assuming no state or local taxes in each case.

*If he is buying out-of-state tax-exempts, the state and local taxes will reduce the disparity to some extent.

or municipality themselves. So these may be worth shopping for if liquidity is not a prime consideration.

Discount Bonds

If you are in a high tax bracket, you might also consider discount bonds. These are bonds that were issued years ago when interest rates were considerably lower. As interest rates have risen, these bonds have dropped in price to provide yields more attuned to other bonds of similar credit ratings and maturities. For example, suppose the government 2⅞ of 1987 currently trades at 63½. The investor not only gets a 4.5 percent current yield, but on maturity in 1987 will be paid a premium of 36½ over the current price. This premium is treated as a capital gain and will be taxed at a lower rate than regular income.

The discount bond, then, provides less ordinary income, important to taxpayers in higher tax brackets, because of its lower coupon, and a capital gain at maturity. Normally, these advantages cause some yield differential, but it can be worth it in a higher tax bracket.

Two Don'ts

1. Avoid U.S. savings bonds. These yield far less than you can get in either treasury bonds or savings bank certificates. This form of investing is only a step more sophisticated than stuffing money in a mattress.

2. There are also savings certificates (not government guaranteed) that are sold in some rural parts of the country by fast-talking salesmen, usually with the aid of large stocks of booze in the trunks of their cars. These certificates give you returns of about 60 to 70 percent of going interest rates. And as you can guess, commissions on these certificates are not exactly low. If one of these fellows calls on you, drink his booze if you're in the mood, but avoid his wares.

Risk Features

FINANCIAL RISK.   Before you buy a corporate, state, or municipal bond, a number of their features should be scrutinized closely.

Financial risk is the risk that the principal and interest will not be paid when due. Fortunately, since the Great Depression, default has been relatively rare. If you are not a credit analyst, there are two major credit-rating services that provide good information on the safety of individual bond issues: Standard & Poor's, and Moody's.

Table 36 gives the rating categories of the two services. Usually the ratings by the two organizations are identical for most major corporate, state, and municipal bonds. If not, they normally don't vary more than one rank.

As the table shows, the very highest credit rating is AAA for Standard & Poor's and Aaa for Moody's; the lowest is D for S&P, C for Moody's. The higher the credit rating, naturally, the lower the interest. There are only about a dozen AAA-rated corporations in the country: Ma Bell, DuPont, General Motors, and the like. In the AA's one would find excellent companies such as Xerox, Mobil Oil, and Monsanto, and in the A's Honeywell, Tenneco, and Philip Morris.

My own feeling is that even for very conservative investors, a rating of BBB or A is high enough. The yields are significantly better and defaults are extremely rare. It seems that if we suddenly started to get large-scale defaults in these categories, a chain reaction would begin that would make everything else kaput anyway.

Bonds of the same credit rating may trade at slightly different

Table 36
BOND-RATING CATEGORIES

STANDARD & POOR'S	RATING	MOODY'S	RATING
AAA	Highest quality	Aaa	Highest quality
AA	Very high	Aa	Very high
A	High	A	High
BBB	Adequate	Baa	Medium
BB	Low degree of speculation	Ba	Speculative element
B	Higher degree of speculation	B	Speculative
CCC	Still higher degree of speculation	Caa	Poor standing
CC	Highest degree of speculation	Ca	Highly speculative
C	Income bonds on which no interest is being paid		
D	In default	C	Lowest rating

yields. The industry may be somewhat out of favor at the time, or there may be an overabundance of financing in one industry that results in lower yields (institutional investors like well-diversified portfolios, and too many bonds issued by one industry may require extra "sweeteners" to sell). This is something the bargain hunter can take advantage of, as is the fact that new issues normally provide slightly higher returns than those currently outstanding in order to make them sell smoothly.

CALL FEATURES.   A second important factor in assessing bond risk is known as the call feature—the length of time an issue must remain outstanding before it can be recalled. Suppose you chose an A-rated industrial bond that is paying you 9 percent and is due in twenty-five years, but it has a five-year refunding call (it can be called away from you in five-years time if interest rates are lower, and the company can issue new bonds at the cheaper rates). You then have the chance of losing your investment in five years. Before selecting a long-term bond, you should therefore make sure it has a call feature of fairly extensive duration—aim for ten years or more. Most new issues have such call provisions. Your broker or investment advisor can readily provide you with the information on individual issues.

CHANGING INTEREST RATES.   This is a third risk in bonds. All bond prices fluctuate with changes in market interest rates. Thus, if you do not hold your bonds to maturity, you have the chance of gain or loss depending on current interest rates. The longer the maturity, the more the movement of interest rates will affect the price. Table 37 shows you the effect of changes in the interest rate on the price of bonds with varying maturities from one to twenty-five years. For simplicity, it is assumed that all bonds have 8 percent coupons and cannot be called before maturity.

If interest rates drop to 6 percent, a twenty-five-year bondholder would be the greatest beneficiary, with his bond appreciating 25.7 percent versus 1.9 percent for the one-year issue. But this is a two-way street, and if yields went to 10 percent, his bond would drop to 81.7, while the one-year bond would decline only to 98.1.

As we have seen, then, the longer the maturity, the greater the market risk. Thus, before buying long-term bonds, you must decide how much market risk you can afford. If you intend to hold the issues for a fairly long time, you can probably place a portion of your bond portfolio in such issues, but look at table 37 to estimate your risk if

Table 37

THE EFFECT OF INTEREST-RATE CHANGES ON BOND PRICES

TERM OF BOND[a]	6 PERCENT[b]	7 PERCENT	8 PERCENT	9 PERCENT	10 PERCENT
1 year	101.9	101.0	100	99.1	98.1
5 years	108.5	104.2	100	96.0	92.3
10 years	114.8	107.1	100	93.5	87.5
15 years	119.5	109.2	100	91.9	84.6
20 years	123.1	110.7	100	90.8	82.8
25 years	125.7	111.7	100	90.1	81.7

[a]For simplicity, it is assumed that all bonds have 8 percent coupons and cannot be called before maturity.
[b]The yield to maturity was calculated in all cases. This is the most accurate way of calculating yield, since it takes into account the principal to be received as well as the interest.

you are forced to liquidate sooner than you had intended.

In a credit crunch there is also the chance to reap excellent gains if you have liquid funds available. The classic case is probably the AA-rated Public Service Electric and Gas of New Jersey. In the credit squeeze of 1970 it issued a long-term bond at an astounding 12 percent rate, and with good call protection. Not too long afterward the issue traded at a large premium over par.

INFLATION. A fourth risk, and as I've previously indicated the most serious one for the investor today, is inflation. In the past, bonds with little financial risk have tended to yield 2½ percent or so above the rate of inflation. However, with inflation currently running at 9 percent or higher, this is no longer the case. As table 1 (page 6) showed quite clearly, investors, whether in bonds or savings banks, were losing a portion of their capital each year in terms of real purchasing power. Inflation, then, is a factor to pay particularly close attention to in portfolio composition. At its current rates inflation destroys much of the traditional conservativism inherent in buying bonds or putting your money in the bank.

Convertible Debentures

Convertible debentures can be turned in for a fixed number of shares in a company. You thus have a part of both worlds: the lesser financial risk of debt, with the appreciation potential of equity if the company prospers. Sometimes the gains can be spectacular. Investment columnist Vartanig G. Vartan wrote about a Wainoco convertible issued at $100 in September 1977 which traded at 187½ less than eight months later as the stock moved sharply higher.*

However, as Vartan indicated, there is naturally a price to pay. Such debentures normally give you less interest because of the conversion privilege, and the conversion price is usually fixed 10 to 12 percent or more above the current market price of the stock. Convertible debentures are often overpriced in relation to the features offered in a bull market. In a bear market, or periods of tight money, the situation is frequently quite different. In this case, the conversion privilege is offered at a very limited premium, and the interest rates may not be too far off going rates for the particular credit rating.

Bond Funds

Selected by experts, these provide wide diversification. Many types are available, some specializing in tax-exempts, some in diversified funds, and others in lower- or medium-grade corporations. Some charge buying commissions and all charge management fees, usually between one-half and one percent a year, which is a good slice of your income.

The funds provide greater diversification, but that's about all. If you can select a number of bonds with good credit ratings, it is questionable whether the extra costs are worthwhile. (The extra diversification necessary with junk bonds would be an exception.)

Preferred Shares

These are a hybrid. Like a bond, they pay a fixed return,† which is almost invariably cumulative, which means that if it is omitted for any reason, it must be paid in the future. However, although preferred shares are considered to be stock, the holder has no participation in the fortunes of the business.‡ Preferred shareholders' rights to dividends and principal are subordinated to those of bondholders and other creditors, who must be paid in full before the preferred gets a penny.

---

*New York Times, June 4, 1978.

†But it is called dividend rather than interest. Preferreds have no maturity date (although usually the company has the right to recall them on prestated terms).

‡Unless the preferred is a convertible, when it would be in most ways very similar to a convertible debenture.

When you buy a preferred, the most important thing to note is the credit worthiness of the issue, because of its lesser protection. However, once again, the rating agencies provide you with this information, and there are many excellent preferreds providing good yields with strong credit ratings.

References

Chapter One

1. James Grant, "Don't Be a Gambler," *Barron's,* June 11, 1978.
2. Dr. Martin Zweig, *Investor Expectations* (New York: Martin Zweig, not dated).
3. Technometrics, a financial consulting firm, for example, measured the results of 261 major insurance companies, investment advisors, and mutual funds, as well as 37 of their large European counterparts. The results: at almost the exact 1974 market bottom, the cash positions of these institutions climbed to 19 percent from 13.7 percent a year earlier—an inordinately high figure on its own.
4. *Pensions and Investments,* August 18, 1976.
5. A. F. Ehrbar, "Index Funds—An Idea Whose Time Is Coming," *Fortune,* June 1976, pp. 144–148.
6. Charles J. Elia, "Heard on the Street," *Wall Street Journal,* March 26, 1979.

Chapter Two

1. Robert D. Edwards and John Magee, *Technical Analysis of Stock Trends,* 7th ed. (Springfield, Mass.: J. Magee, 1967).
2. Joseph Granville, *Granville's New Strategy of Daily Stock Market Timing for Maximum Profit* (Englewood Cliffs, N.J.: Prentice-Hall, 1976), p. 5.
3. Nikolai Kondratieff, "The Long Cycles," *Review of Economic Statistics* (November 1935).
4. R. N. Elliot, *The Bank Credit Analyst* (Toronto: Boulton, Trombley Report).
5. Granville, *Granville's New Strategy,* p. 103.
6. Paul H. Cootner, ed., *The Random Character of Stock Market Prices* (Cambridge, Mass.: MIT Press, 1964), pp. 17–78. A translation by A. James Boness

from Louis Bachelier, *Theorie de la Speculation* (Paris: Gauthier-Villars, 1900).

7. Harry V. Roberts, "Stock Market Patterns and Financial Analysis: Methodological Suggestions," *Journal of Finance* 14 (March 1959): 1–10.

8. M.F.M. Osborne, "Brownian Motion in the Stock Market," *Operations Research* 7 (March–April 1959): 145–173.

9. Arnold B. Moore, "Some Characteristics of Changes in Common Stock Prices," *The Random Character of Stock Market Prices,* pp. 139–161.

10. Clive W. J. Granger and Oskar Morgenstern, "Spectral Analysis of New York Stock Market Prices," *Kyklos* 16 (1963): 1–27.

11. Eugene F. Fama, "The Behavior of Stock Market Prices," *Journal of Business* 38 (January 1965): 34–105.

12. Eugene F. Fama and Marshall E. Blume, "Filter Rules and Stock Market Trading," *Journal of Business—Security Prices: A Supplement* 39 (No. 1, January 1966): 226–241.

13. Eugene F. Fama, "Efficient Capital Markets: A Review of the Theory and Empirical Work," *Journal of Finance* 25 (May 1970): 383–423.

14. Burton Malkiel, *A Random Walk Down Wall Street* (New York: Norton, 1973), p. 127.

Chapter Three

1. John Burr Williams, *The Theory of Investment Value* (Cambridge, Mass.: Harvard University Press, 1938).

2. J. Peter Williamson, *Investments: New Analytic Techniques* (New York: Praeger, 1974), pp. 152ff.

3. Benjamin Graham, David Dodd, Sidney Cottle, and Charles Tatham, *Security Analysis,* 4th ed. (New York: McGraw-Hill, 1962).

4. Irving Kahn and Robert D. Milne, *Benjamin Graham—The Father of Financial Analysis,* Occasional Paper No. 5, Financial Analysts Research Foundation, 1977.

5. Benjamin Graham, *The Intelligent Investor,* 2nd ed. (New York: Harper & Row, 1955).

6. Williamson, *Investments: New Analytic Techniques.*

7. *Financial World,* May 1, 1977, p. 27.

8. Robert Cirino, "Timing: Can Money Managers Deliver on Their Promises?" *Institutional Investor* 11 (March 1976): 277–279.

9. Ibid.

10. William F. Sharpe, "Likely Gains from Market Timing," *Financial Analysts Journal* 31 (March–April 1975): 60–69.

11. Michael C. Jensen, "The Performance of Mutual Funds in the Period 1945–1964," *Journal of Finance* 23 (May 1968): 389–416.

12. Irwin Friend, Marshall Blume, and Jean Crockett, *Mutual Funds and Other Institutional Investors: A New Perspective,* Twentieth Century Fund Study (New York: McGraw-Hill, 1970).

13. James Lorie and Richard Brealey, *Modern Developments in Investment Management* (New York: Praeger, 1972).

14. Charles H. Dow, *Wall Street Journal,* July 20, 1901.

15. William Peter Hamilton, *Wall Street Journal,* October 4, 1921.

16. Eugene F. Fama, Lawrence Fisher, Michael Jensen, and Richard Roll, "The Adjustment of Stock Prices to New Information," *International Economic Review* 10 (February 1969): 1–21; James H. Lorie and Mary T. Hamilton, *The Stock Market: Theories and Evidence* (Homewood, Ill.: Dow Jones–Irwin, 1973), pp. 171ff.

17. Roy Ball and Phillip Brown, "An Empirical Evaluation of Accounting Income Numbers," *Journal of Accounting Research* 6 (Fall 1968): 159–178.

18. James H. Lorie and Victor Niederhoffer, "Predictive and Statistical Properties of Insider Trading," *Journal of Law and Economics* 11 (April 1968): 35–53.

19. Eugene F. Fama, "Efficient Capital Markets: A Review of the Theory and Empirical Work," *Journal of Finance* 25 (No. 2, May 1970): 383–417.

GENERAL REFERENCES, CHAPTER THREE

Cohen, Jerome B., Edward D. Zenbar, and Arthur Zeikel, *Investment Analysis and Portfolio Management,* rev. ed. (Homewood, Ill.: Richard Irwin, 1973).

Crane, Burton, *The Sophisticated Investor,* 9th ed. (New York: Simon & Schuster, 1963).

Crowell, Richard, *Stock Market Strategy* (New York: McGraw-Hill, 1977).

Dougall, Herbert, *Investments,* 9th ed. (Englewood Cliffs, N.J.: Prentice-Hall, 1973).

Ellis, John, *Self-Reliant Investing* (Chicago: H. Regnery, 1971).

Engel, Louis, and Peter Wyckoff, *How to Buy Stocks,* 6th ed. rev. (Boston: Little, Brown, 1976).

Hazard, John W., *Choosing Tomorrow's Growth Stocks Today* (New York: Doubleday, 1968).

Knowlton, Winthrop, and John Furth, *Shaking the Money Tree* (New York: Harper & Row, 1965).

Levine, Sumner L., ed., *Financial Analysts Handbook* (Homewood, Ill.: Dow Jones–Irwin, 1975).

Loeb, Gerald M., *The Battle for Investment Survival* (New York: Simon & Schuster, 1957).

Loeb, Gerald M., *The Battle for Stock Market Profits* (New York: Simon & Schuster, 1971).

McWilliams, James D., "The Benefits and Costs of Timing Equity Investments," *Journal of Bank Research* 7 (Spring 1976): 22–29.

Phelon, Richard, "Time to Shun Stocks?" *New York Times,* August 20, 1977.

Chapter Four

1. Charles Mackay, *Extraordinary Popular Delusions and the Madness of Crowds* (New York: Noonday Press, 1974), p. 421. Originally published in London in 1841 by Richard Bently.

2. Gustave LeBon, *The Crowd* (New York: Viking, 1960), pp. 23–24.

3. Ibid., pp. 41, 61.

4. Ibid., p. 70.

5. John Kenneth Galbraith, *The Great Crash* (Boston: Houghton Mifflin, 1961), p. 9.
6. LeBon, *The Crowd,* p. 62.
7. Carl Sandburg, *Abraham Lincoln: Volume 2, 1861–1864* (New York: Dell, 1970), p. 410.
8. Leon Festinger, "A Theory of Social Comparison Processes," *Human Relations* 7 (1954): 117–140.
9. S. Schacter and J. E. Singer, "Cognitive, Social, and Psychological Determinants of Emotional States," *Psychological Review* 69 (1962): 379–399.
10. J. C. Flugel, *The Psychology of Clothes* (New York: Universities Press, 1969).
11. "Over the Counter: Frantic, Frenetic, Frazzled," *Dun's Review* 92 (August 1968): 32–37.
12. Robert Sobel, *The Big Board* (New York: Free Press, 1965).
13. M. Sherif and C. W. Sherif, *Social Psychology* (New York: Harper & Row, 1969), pp. 208–209.
14. William Samuels, *Contemporary Social Psychology* (Englewood Cliffs, N.J.: Prentice-Hall, 1973), p. 10.
15. Gilbert Kaplan and Chris Welles, *The Money Managers* (New York: Random House, 1969).
16. "Performance in Reverse?" *Forbes,* March 15, 1969.
17. *Forbes,* October 15, 1968.
18. GiGi Mahon, "Landing on Boardwalk," *Barron's,* November 20, 1978.
19. Charles Elia, "Here's a Short Story of a Short Gamble That Didn't Pay Off," *Wall Street Journal,* October 4, 1978, p. 1.
20. Virginia Cowles, *South Sea: The Great Swindle* (London: Crowley Feature, 1960).
21. *Dun's Review,* August 1968, p. 36.

GENERAL REFERENCES, CHAPTER FOUR

Allport, Gordon W., and Leo Postman, *The Psychology of Rumor* (New York: Russell & Russell, 1965).

Asch, S. E., *Social Psychology* (Englewood Cliffs, N.J.: Prentice-Hall, 1952).

Brooks, John, *The Go-Go Years* (New York: Weybright and Talley, 1973).

Brooks, John, *Seven Fat Years* (New York: Harper & Row, 1958).

Clough, Shepard B., *European Economic History: The Economic Development of Western Civilization,* 2nd ed. (New York: McGraw-Hill, 1968).

Durant, Will, and Ariel Durant, *The Age of Voltaire* (New York: Simon & Schuster, 1965).

Freedman, J. L., J. M. Carlsmith, and D. O. Sears, *Social Psychology* (Englewood Cliffs, N.J.: Prentice-Hall, 1970).

Gerard, H. B., and J. M. Rabbie, "Fear and Social Comparison," *Journal of Abnormal and Social Psychology* 62 (1961): 586–592.

Gerard, H. B., R. A. Wilhelmy, and Edward S. Conolley, "Conformity and Group Size," *Journal of Personality and Social Psychology* 8 (1968): 79–82.

Hollander, E. P., "Confidence and Conformity in the Acceptance of Influence," *Journal of Abnormal and Social Psychology* 61 (1960): 365–369.

Kaplan, Gilbert, and Chris Welles, *The Money Managers* (New York: Random House, 1969).

Katona, George, *Psychological Economics* (New York: American Elsevier, 1976).

Kiesler, C. A., and S. B. Kiesler, *Conformity* (Reading, Mass.: Addison-Wesley, 1969).

Melville, Louis, *The South Sea Bubble* (London: Burt Franklin, 1968).

Posthumus, N. W., "The Tulipmania in Holland in 1636 and 1637," in *The Sixteenth and Seventeenth Centuries,* ed. Warren C. Scoville, J. Claybouch, and T. LaForce (Lexington, Mass.: D.C. Heath, 1969).

Regan, Donald T., *A View from the Street* (New York: New American Library, 1972).

Robbins, Paul R., "Immediate and Delayed Effects of Social Influence upon Individual Opinion," *Journal of Social Psychology* 53 (1961): 159–169.

Smith, Adam, *The Money Game* (New York: Dell, 1969).

Smith, Adam, *Supermoney* (New York: Popular Library, 1973).

The Wall Street Reader (New York: World Publishing, 1972).

Zimbardo, P. G., "Involvement in Communication Discrepancies as Determinants of Opinion Conformity," *Journal of Abnormal and Social Psychology* 61 (1960): 86–94.

Chapter Five

1. Warren Buffett, partnership letter, January 1966.
2. Herbert Simon, "Theories of Decision Making in Economics and Behavioral Sciences," *American Economic Review* 69 (No. 2, June 1959): 273.
3. Ibid.
4. Herbert Simon, *Models of Man: Social and Rational* (New York: Wiley, 1970).
5. P. E. Meehl, *Clinical Versus Statistical Predictions: A Theoretical Analysis and Review of the Literature* (Minneapolis: University of Minnesota Press, 1954); Robyn M. Dawes and Bernard Corrigan, "Linear Models in Decision Making," *Psychological Bulletin* 81 (No. 2, 1974): 95–106.
6. Stewart Oskamp, "Overconfidence in Case Study Judgments," *Journal of Consulting Psychology* 29 (1965): 261, 265.
7. L. H. Garland, "The Problem of Observer Error," *Bulletin of the New York Academy of Medicine* 36 (1960); Hans Elias, "Three-Dimensional Structure Identified from Single Sections," *Science* 174 (December 1971): 993–1000.
8. Harry Bakwin, "Pseudodoxia Pediatricia," *New England Journal of Medicine* 232 (1945): 691–697.
9. P. J. Hoffman, P. Slovic, and L. G. Rorer, "An Analysis of Variance Models for the Assessment of Configural Cue Utilization in Clinical Judgment," *Psychological Bulletin* 69 (1968): 338–349.
10. L. G. Rorer, P. J. Hoffman, B. D. Dickman, and P. Slovic, "Configural Judgments Revealed," *Proceedings of the 75th Annual Convention of the American Psychological Association* 2 (Washington, D.C.: American Psychological Association, 1967): 195–196.
11. Lewis R. Goldberg, "Simple Models or Simple Processes? Some Research on Clinical Judgments," *American Psychologist* 23 (1968): 483–496.

12. Paul Slovic, "Analyzing the Expert Judge: A Descriptive Study of a Stockbroker's Decision Processes," *Journal of Applied Psychology* 53 (No. 4, August 1969): 225–263; P. Slovic, D. Fleissner, and W. S. Bauman, "Analyzing the Use of Information in Investment Decision Making: A Methodological Proposal," *Journal of Business* 45 (No. 2, 1972): 283–301.
13. Goldberg, "Simple Models."
14. Paul Slovic, "Behavioral Problems of Adhering to a Decision Policy," IGRF speech, May 1973.
15. Reba F. White, "The Dangers of Falling in Love with a Company," *Institutional Investor,* November 1975.
16. *Wall Street Transcript,* September 23, 1974.
17. Garfield A. Drew, *New Methods of Profit in the Stock Market* (Boston: Metcalf Press, 1941).
18. L. Chapman and J. P. Chapman, "Genesis of Popular but Erroneous Psychodiagnostic Observations," *Journal of Abnormal Psychology* (1967): 193–204; Chapman and Chapman, "Illusory Correlations As an Obstacle to the Use of Valid Psychodiagnostic Signs," *Journal of Abnormal Psychology* (1974): 271–280.
19. Alfred Cowles III, "Can Stock Market Forecasters Forecast?" *Econometria* 1 (1933): 309–324.
20. "What's in the Cards for 1972?" *Institutional Investor* 6 (January 1972): 25–36.
21. The favorites are listed in *Institutional Investor,* January 1973.

GENERAL REFERENCES, CHAPTER FIVE

Anderson, N. H., "Looking for Configurality in Clinical Judgments," *Psychological Bulletin* 78 (1972): 93–102.
Dawes, R. M., "The Mind, the Model, and the Task," in *Cognitive Theory,* vol. 1, ed. F. Restle, R. M. Shiffron, N. J. Castellan, H. R. Lindman, and D. B. Pisone (Hillsdale, N.J.: Lawrence Erlbaum Associates, 1975).
Dawes, R. M., and B. Corrigan, "Linear Models in Decision Making," *Psychological Bulletin* 81 (No. 2, 1974): 95–106.
Goldberg, L. R., "Five Models of Clinical Judgment: An Empirical Comparison Between Linear and Nonlinear Representations of the Human Inference Process," *Organizational Behavior and Human Performance* 6 (1971): 458–479.
Goldberg, L. R., "Man Versus Model of Man: Just How Conflicting Is that Evidence?" *Organizational Behavior and Human Performance* 16 (1976): 13–22.
March, James G., and Herbert A. Simon, *Organizations* (New York: Wiley, 1967).
Simon, Herbert A., *Administrative Behavior* (New York: Free Press, 1976).

Chapter Six

1. Amos Tversky and Daniel Kahneman, "Judgments Under Uncertainty: Heuristics and Biases," *Science* 185 (September 27, 1974): 1124–1131; Paul Slovic, Baruch Fischhoff, and Sarah Lichtenstein, "Cognitive Processes and Societal Risk Taking," in *Cognition and Social Behavior,* ed. J. W. Payne and J. S. Carroll (Hillsdale, N.J.: Lawrence Erlbaum Associates, 1976).

2. Amos Tversky and Daniel Kahneman, "Belief in the Law of Small Numbers," *Psychological Bulletin* 76 (No. 2, 1971): 105–110.

3. Tversky and Kahneman, "Judgments Under Uncertainty: Heuristics and Biases"; Tversky and Kahneman, "Intuitive Predictions: Biases and Corrective Procedures," *Management Science,* in press.

4. Amos Tversky and Daniel Kahneman, "Causal Schemata in Judgments Under Uncertainty," in *Progress in Social Psychology,* ed. M. Fishbein (Hillsdale, N.J.: Lawrence Erlbaum Associates, 1973); Daniel Kahneman and Amos Tversky, "On the Psychology of Prediction," *Psychological Review* 80 (1973): 237–251.

5. Tversky and Kahneman, "Judgments Under Uncertainty: Heuristics and Biases"; Tversky and Kahneman, "Intuitive Predictions: Biases and Corrective Procedures."

6. Roger G. Ibbotson and Rex A. Sinquefield, *Stocks, Bonds, Bills, and Inflation: The Past (1926–1976) and the Future (1977–2000)* (Charlottesville, Va.: Financial Analysts Research Foundation, 1977).

7. Tversky and Kahneman, "Intuitive Predictions: Biases and Corrective Procedures."

8. Kahneman and Tversky, "On the Psychology of Prediction."

9. Benjamin Graham, David Dodd, Sidney Cottle, and Charles Tatham, *Security Analysis,* 4th ed. (New York: McGraw-Hill, 1962), p. 424.

10. Amos Tversky and Daniel Kahneman, "Availability: A Heuristic for Judging Frequency and Probability," *Cognitive Psychology* 5 (1973): 207–232.

11. Tversky and Kahneman, "Intuitive Predictions: Biases and Corrective Procedures"; Tversky and Kahneman, "Causal Schemata in Judgments Under Uncertainty"; Don Lyon and Paul Slovic, "Dominance of Accuracy Information and Neglect of Base Rates in Probability Estimation," *Acta Psychologica* 40 (No. 4, August 1976): 287–298.

12. R. W. Kates, *Hazard and Choice Perception in Flood Plain Management,* Research Paper No. 78, University of Chicago Department of Geology, 1962.

13. S. C. Lichtenstein and Paul Slovic, "Reversals of Preference Between Bids and Choices in Gambling Decisions," *Journal of Experimental Psychology* 89 (1971): 46–55; S. C. Lichtenstein, B. Fischhoff, and L. Phillips, "Calibration of Probabilities: The State of the Art," in *Decision Making and Change in Human Affairs,* ed. H. Jungermann and G. de Zeeuw (Amsterdam: D. Reidel, 1977).

14. Baruch Fischhoff, "Hindsight Does Not Equal Foresight: The Effect of Outcome Knowledge on Judgment Under Uncertainty," *Journal of Experimental Psychology: Human Perception and Performance* 1 (August 1975): 288–299; Fischhoff, "Hindsight: Thinking Backward?" *Psychology Today,* April 1975, p. 8; Fischhoff, "Perceived Informativeness of Facts," *Journal of Experimental Psychology: Human Perception and Performance* 3 (1977): 349–358; Baruch Fischhoff and Ruth Beyth, "I Knew It Would Happen: Remembered Probabilities of Once-Future Things," *Organizational Behavior and Human Performance* 13 (No. 1, 1975): 1–16; Paul Slovic and Baruch Fischhoff, "On the Psychology of Experimental Surprises," *Journal of Experimental Psychology: Human Perception and Performance* 3 (1977): 544–551.

15. Paul Slovic, Baruch Fischhoff, and Sarah Lichtenstein, "Behavioral Decision Theory," *Annual Review of Psychology* 28 (1977): 1–39.

GENERAL REFERENCES, CHAPTER SIX

Bar-Hillel, M., "The Base Rate Fallacy in Probability Judgments," *Acta Psychologica,* in press.

Dawes, Robyn M., and Bernard Corrigan, "Linear Models in Decision Making," *Psychological Bulletin* 81 (No. 2, 1974): 95–106.

Fischhoff, Baruch, Paul Slovic, and Sarah Lichtenstein, "Knowing with Certainty: The Appropriateness of Extreme Confidence," *Journal of Experimental Psychology: Human Perception and Performance* 3 (1977): 552–564.

Kahneman, Daniel, and Amos Tversky, "Subjective Probability: A Judgment of Representativeness," *Cognitive Psychology* 3 (No. 3, July 1972): 430–454.

Payne, J. W., "Alternative Approaches to Decision Making Under Risk: Moments Versus Risk Dimensions," *Psychological Bulletin* 80 (1973): 439–453.

Shaklee, Harriet, "Limited Minds and Multiple Causes: Discounting in Multicausal Attribution," Doctoral dissertation, University of Oregon.

Slovic, Paul, "Choice Between Equally Valued Alternatives," *Journal of Experimental Psychology: Human Perception and Performance* 1 (No. 3, 1975): 280–287.

Slovic, Paul, "Psychological Study of Human Judgment: Implications for Investment Decision Making," *Journal of Finance* 27 (September 1972): 779–799. I think this is a particularly interesting article and one easily understood by the lay financial reader.

Slovic, Paul, "From Shakespeare to Simon: Speculations—and Some Evidence—About Man's Ability to Process Information," Oregon Research Institute Research Monograph 12 (No. 2, April 1972).

Slovic, Paul, and Baruch Fischhoff, "On the Psychology of Experimental Surprises," *Journal of Experimental Psychology: Human Perception and Performance* 3 (1977): 544–551.

Slovic, Paul, Baruch Fischhoff, and Sarah Lichtenstein, "Behavioral Decision Theory," *Annual Review of Psychology* 28 (1977): 1–39. A thorough review of the literature in the field.

Slovic, Paul, Baruch Fischhoff, Sarah Lichtenstein, Bernard Corrigan, and Barbara Combs, "Preference for Insuring Against Probable Small Losses: Implications for the Theory and Practice of Insurance," *Journal of Risk and Insurance* 44 (No. 2, June 1977): 237–258.

Slovic, Paul, Howard Kunreuther, and Gilbert F. White, "Decision Processes, Rationality, and Adjustment to Natural Hazards," in *Natural Hazards, Local, National and Global,* ed. Gilbert F. White (New York: Oxford University Press, 1974).

Tversky, Amos, and Daniel Kahneman, "Availability: A Heuristic for Judging Frequency and Probability," *Cognitive Psychology* 5 (1973): 207–232.

Tversky, Amos, and Daniel Kahneman, "On the Psychology of Prediction," *Psychological Review* 8 (No. 4, 1973): 237–251.

von Holstein, C. S., "Probabilistic Forecasting in Experiments Relating to the Stock Market," *Organizational Behavior and Human Performance* 8 (1972): 139–158.

Chapter Seven

1. Most analysts arrive at prices by estimating future earnings. For example, see Ralph A. Bing, "Survey of Practitioner's Stock Evaluation Methods," *Financial Analysts Journal* 27 (May–June 1971): 55–60.
2. Paul F. Miller, Jr., Drexel Harriman and Ripley, Inc., Report, October 1966.
3. Francis Nicholson, "Price/Earnings Ratios," *Financial Analysts Journal* 16 (July–August 1960): 43–45.
4. James D. McWilliams, "Price-Earnings and P/E Ratios," *Financial Analysts Journal* 22 (May–June 1966): 137–142.
5. William Breen, "Low Price/Earnings Ratios and Industry Relatives," *Financial Analysts Journal* 24 (July–August 1968): 125–127.
6. Sanjoy Basu, "The Information Content of Price/Earnings Ratios," *Financial Management* 4 (No. 2, Summer 1975): 53–60; Sanjoy Basu, "Investment Performance of Common Stocks in Relation to Their Price/Earnings Ratios: A Test of the Efficient Market Hypothesis," *Journal of Finance* 32 (No. 3, June 1977): 663–682.

Chapter Eight

1. Victor Niederhoffer and Patrick J. Regan, "Earnings Changes, Analysts' Forecasts, and Stock Prices," *Financial Analysts Journal* 28 (May–June 1972): 65–71.
2. "Analysts Find Ways to Improve Forecasts of Economy's Course," *Wall Street Journal,* December 30, 1977, p. 1.
3. "Here Comes 1970," *Wall Street Journal,* September 30, 1969, p. 1.
4. James Ramsey, "Economic Forecasts—Models or Markets?" Hobart Paper No. 74 (London: The Institute of Economic Affairs, 1978).
5. Lester Thurow, "Economics 1977," *Daedalus* 2 (October 1977): 79–94.
6. Ronald M. Copeland and Robert J. Marioni, "Executives' Forecasts of Earnings per Share Versus Forecasts of Naive Models," *Journal of Business* 45 (October 1972): 497–512.
7. David Green, Jr., and Joel Segall, "The Predictive Power of First Quarter Earnings Reports," *Journal of Business* 40 (January 1967): 44–55.
8. Bart A. Basi, Kenneth J. Carey, and Richard D. Twark, "Comparison of the Accuracy of Corporate and Security Analysts' Forecasts of Earnings," *Accounting Review* 51 (1976): 244–254.
9. R. Malcolm Richards and Donald R. Frazer, "Further Evidence on the Accuracy of Analysts' Earnings Forecasts: A Comparison Among Analysts," *Journal of Economics and Business* 29 (No. 3, Spring–Summer 1977): 193–197.
10. R. Malcolm Richards, James J. Benjamin, and Robert W. Strawser, "An Examination of the Accuracy of Earnings Forecasts," *Financial Management* (Fall 1977).
11. J. G. Cragg and Burton Malkiel, "The Consensus and Accuracy of Some Predictions of the Growth of Corporate Earnings," *Journal of Finance* 23 (March 1968): 67–84.

12. Ibid.
13. Edwin J. Elton and Martin J. Gruber, "Earnings Estimates and the Accuracy of Expectational Data," *Management Science* 18 (April 1972): 409–424.
14. I.M.D. Little, "Higgledly Piggledly Growth," *Bulletin of the Oxford University Institute of Economics and Statistics* (November 1962).
15. I.M.D. Little and A. C. Rayner, *Higgledly Piggledly Growth Again* (Oxford, Eng.: Basil Blackwell, 1966).
16. See, for example, Joseph E. Murphy, Jr., "Relative Growth in Earnings per Share—Past and Future," *Financial Analysts Journal* 22 (November–December 1966): 73–76.
17. Richard A. Brealey, *An Introduction to Risk and Return from Common Stocks* (Cambridge, Mass.: MIT Press, 1968).
18. J. E. Murphy and H. W. Stevenson, "P/E Ratios and Future Growth of Earnings and Dividends," *Financial Analysts Journal* 23 (No. 6, November–December 1967): 111–114.
19. Ibid., p. 112.
20. Aharon Ofer, "Investors' Expectations of Earnings Growth, Their Accuracy and Effect on the Structure of Realized Rates of Return," *Journal of Finance* 3 (No. 2, May 1975): 509–523.
21. Benjamin Graham, David Dodd, Sidney Cottle, and Charles Tatham, *Security Analysis,* 4th ed. (New York: McGraw-Hill, 1962), p. 179.

GENERAL REFERENCES, CHAPTER EIGHT

Hammel, J. E., and D. A. Hodes, "Factors Influencing Price-Earnings Multiples," *Financial Analysts Journal* 23 (No. 1, January–February 1967): 90–93.

Chapter Nine

1. "How to Read a Financial Report," Merrill, Lynch, Pierce, Fenner & Smith, 1975.
2. David N. Dreman, "What Is the 'Best' Investment Strategy?" Rauscher Pierce Securities Corporation Research Report, April 1976.

Chapter Ten

1. "Up and Down Wall Street," *Barron's,* September 4, 1978.
2. "Speculative Bonds," *Barron's,* October 10, 1977, p. 5.
3. Jerry Edgerton, "Junk Bonds: Wall Street Lays a Golden Egg," *Money,* May 1978.
4. Newton Lamson, "A New Way to Ride the Commodity Roller Coaster," *Money,* September 1975, p. 39.
5. "Let the Buyer Beware," *Barron's,* November 7, 1977.
6. Dana L. Thomas, "Gimme Shelter," *Barron's,* October 21, 1974, p. 3.
7. "Up and Down Wall Street," *Barron's,* January 15, 1979.

GENERAL REFERENCES, CHAPTER TEN

Hershman, Arlene, "Born-Again Tax Shelters," *Dun's Review* 109 (April 1977): 55–66.

The Only Investment Guide You'll Ever Need, by Andrew Tobias (New York: Harcourt Brace Jovanovich, 1978), covers a lot of the material that has been outlined in this chapter in an amusing, clever, and far more detailed manner than here.

White, Shelby, "Reaping the Rewards of Junk Bonds," *Institutional Investor,* March 1976, pp. 51–52.

Readers interested in up-to-date articles on many of the subjects discussed in this chapter will often find them in such periodicals as *Barron's, Business Week, Dun's Review, Esquire, Forbes, Financial World, Money, New York,* and the *New York Times.*

Chapter Eleven

1. Irving L. Janis, *Victims of Groupthink* (Boston: Houghton Mifflin, 1972).
2. Ibid., p. 9.
3. Ibid., pp. 11, 13.
4. Nancy Belliveau, "Why Pension Funds Are Firing Their Money Managers," *Institutional Investor,* February 1974.
5. Edward Malca, *Proceedings, Hearings by the Benson Committee on S 2787 and S 2842,* Subcommittee on Financial Markets, U.S. Senate Committee on Finance, 93 Cong., 2 sess., 1976; Peter F. Drucker, "American Business' New Owners," *Wall Street Journal,* May 27, 1976.
6. John Quirt, "Confessions of an Underperformer," *Institutional Investor,* July 1973.
7. Robert J. Cirino, "The Pension Fund Officer Versus the Board," *Institutional Investor,* July 1973.
8. Morton H. Halperin, *Bureaucratic Politics and Foreign Policy* (Washington, D.C.: Brookings Institution, 1974), p. 152.
9. Richard Neustadt, *Alliance Politics* (New York: Columbia University Press, 1970).
10. Adam Smith, *The Money Game* (New York: Dell, 1969).
11. Halperin, *Bureaucratic Politics and Foreign Policy,* p. 155.
12. Smith Simpson, *The Anatomy of the State Department* (Boston: Houghton Mifflin, 1967), p. 28.
13. Ibid., p. 17.
14. Cirino, "The Pension Fund Officer Versus the Board."
15. J. L. Freedman, J. M. Carlsmith, and D. O. Sears, *Social Psychology* (Englewood Cliffs, N.J.: Prentice-Hall, 1970), p. 122.
16. James Thomson, Jr., "How Could Vietnam Happen?" in *Who We Are: Chronicle of the United States and Vietnam,* ed. Manning and Janeway (Boston: Little, Brown, 1965).
17. David Halberstam, *The Best and the Brightest* (Greenwich, Conn.: Fawcett Publications, 1973).

GENERAL REFERENCES, CHAPTER ELEVEN

Bower, Joseph L., "The Role of Conflict in Economic Decision-Making Groups: Some Empirical Results," *Quarterly Journal of Economics* 79 (May 1965): 263–277.

Dudar, Helen, "The Price of Blowing the Whistle," *New York Times Magazine,* October 30, 1977.

Green, D., and E. Conolley, "Groupthink and Watergate," Paper presented at the annual meeting of the American Psychological Association, 1974.

Janis, Irving, *Decision Making* (New York: Free Press, 1977).

Katona, George, *Psychological Economics* (New York: Elsevier Publishing, 1976).

Katz, Daniel, and Robert L. Kahn, *The Social Psychology of Organizations* (New York: Wiley, 1967).

Kiesler, C. A., and S. A. Kiesler, *Conformity* (Reading, Mass.: Addison-Wesley, 1969).

Lindblom, Charles E., *The Intelligence of Democracy* (New York: Free Press, 1965).

McGarvey, Patrick J., *CIA: The Myth and the Madness* (New York: Penguin, 1973).

Mills, C. Wright, *White Collar* (Oxford, Eng.: Oxford University Press, 1951).

Stagner, Ross, "Corporate Decision Making: An Empirical Study," *Journal of Applied Psychology* 3 (February 1969): 1–13.

Chapter Twelve

1. Harold L. Shapiro, "Inflation in the United States," in *World Inflation,* ed. L. Krause and W. Salant (Washington, D.C.: Brookings Institution, 1977).
2. *Business Week,* March 21, 1977.
3. "A Diamond Is Forever . . . Rising in Price," *Forbes,* April 17, 1978.
4. William D. Nordhaus, "The Flexibility of Wages and Prices," *Inflation Theory and Policy, American Economic Review* 66 (May 1976): 59–64.
5. *Wall Street Journal,* May 5, 1978.
6. *Wall Street Journal,* January 19, 1979.
7. *Wall Street Journal,* February 23, 1979.
8. *New York Times,* April 1, 1979.
9. "Inflation: You Are Losing Your Assets," *Forbes,* April 1, 1974.
10. Ibid.
11. *Esquire,* November 21, 1978.
12. *Forbes,* May 29, 1978.
13. "Inflation: You Are Losing Your Assets."
14. Burton Malkiel, "Reports of the Death of Common Stocks Are Greatly Exaggerated," *Fortune,* November 1977.
15. Martin Feldstein and Lawrence Summers, *Brookings Paper on Economic Activity, 1977–I* (Washington, D.C.: Brookings Institution, 1977).
16. Warren Buffett, *Forbes,* August 6, 1979, pp. 25–26.
17. Franco Modigliani and Richard Cohn, "Inflation and the Stock Market," *Financial Analysts Journal* 35 (March–April 1979): 24–44.

GENERAL REFERENCES, CHAPTER TWELVE

Beaman, Louis, "Capacity: The New Questions About the American Economy," *Fortune,* May 1974.

Brinner, Roger, "The Death of the Phillips Curve Reconsidered," *Quarterly Journal of Economics* 91 (August 1977): 389–407.

Brunner, Karl, and Allan H. Meltzer, "The Explanations of Inflation: Some International Evidence," *American Economic Review* 67 (February 1977): 148–154.

Foster, John, and Mary Gregory, "Inflation Expectations: The Use of Qualitative Survey Data," *University of Glasgow Applied Economics* 9 (1977): 19–29.

Friedman, Milton, "Nobel Lecture: Inflation and Unemployment," *Journal of Political Economy* 85 (No. 3, 1977): 451–471.

Kravis, Irving B., and Robert E. Lipsey, "Export Prices and the Transmission of Inflation," *American Economic Review* 67 (February 1977): 155–163.

Laidler, David, "The 1974 Report of the President's Council of Economic Advisors: The Control of Inflation and the Future of the International Monetary System," *American Economic Review* 64 (No. 4, September 1974).

Nadler, Paul S., "Inflation, Unemployment, Why Both at Once?" *Banker's Monthly,* November 15, 1977.

Nordhaus, William D., "The 1974 Report of the President's Council of Economic Advisors: Energy in the Economic Report," *American Economic Review* 64 (No. 4, September 1974).

Rose, Sanford, "Far-Reaching Consequences of Higher-Priced Oil," *Fortune,* March 1974.

Shepard, David, "Unemployment and the Current Inflation," *The Banker,* January 1978, p. 41.

"South Land Values Rise 60 Percent in Three Years," *Los Angeles Times,* November 14, 1976.

Wachter, Michael, "Some Problems in Wage Stabilization," *American Economic Review* 66 (May 1976): 65–71.

INDEX

About the Author

DAVID DREMAN is president of Dreman Associates, a New York–based investment management firm. He was formerly a consultant to Rauscher, Pierce, Refsnes, a national brokerage house; a senior investment officer for J.&W. Seligman, an investment advisory and mutual fund organization; and a senior editor/analyst for the *Value Line Investment Survey.* Author of the critically accalimed *Psychology and the Stock Market,* Dreman lectures before groups of professional and individual investors.